S0-AAD-789

Arthur I. Belkin
Vice President
SBC Government Securities Inc.
Box 395, Church Street Station
New York, NY 10008
(212) 574-6851

2/92

Kate

Seasons Greetings
from Swiss Bank

Arth

Direct from the
North Pole:
Seasons Greetings
Carl

AN INSTITUTIONAL INVESTOR PUBLICATION

SWISS BANK
CORPORATION

DICTIONARY
of
FINANCIAL
RISK
MANAGEMENT

GARY L. GASTINEAU

PROBUS PUBLISHING COMPANY
Chicago, Illinois
Cambridge, England

© 1992 Swiss Bank Corporation

ALL RIGHTS RESERVED. No part of this publication may be reproduced, stored in a retrieval system, or transmitted, in any form or by any means, electronic, mechanical, photocopying, recording, or otherwise, without the prior written permission of the publisher and the copyright holder.

This publication is designed to provide accurate and authoritative information in regard to the subject matter covered. It is sold with the understanding that the publisher is not engaged in rendering legal, accounting, or other professional service.

Authorization to photocopy items for internal or personal use, or the internal or personal use of specific clients, is granted by PROBUS PUBLISHING COMPANY, provided that the U.S. $7.00 per page fee is paid directly to Copyright Clearance Center, 27 Congress Street, Salem, MA 01970, USA. For those organizations that have been granted a photocopy license by CCC, a separate system of payment has been arranged. The fee code for users of the Transactional Reporting Service is 1-55738-443-6/92/$00.00 + $7.00.

The dictionary has been prepared and is being distributed by Swiss Bank Corporation, New York Branch, and is being made available for sale to the public.

ISBN 1-55738-443-6

Printed in the United States of America

BB

2   3   4   5   6   7   8   9   0

TABLE OF CONTENTS

PREFACE

In 1990, Swiss Bank Corporation, one of the world's largest banks and one of the few banks rated AAA by most rating agencies, formed a strategic alliance with O'Connor, a world leader in financial risk management technology. The objective of this strategic alliance is to capitalize on the strengths of both partners — the balance sheet and worldwide presence of Swiss Bank Corporation and the risk management and technology strengths of O'Connor.

Apart from the business implications of this alliance, it has created an unusual pool of talent and a reservoir of knowledge. This dictionary is an attempt to tap one part of that knowledge. In compiling the vocabulary of financial risk management, I have had extensive help and support from many of my colleagues. Major assistance from Perry Beaumont, David Dubendorfer, Arash Farmanfarmaian, Gerald Herman, Phillip Nehro, David Purcell, Glenn Satty, Sebastian Steib, Joseph Troccolo, and Eric Weinstein was essential in preparing this volume. Their willingness to suggest additions and clarifications has added materially to any usefulness this volume will have to risk management professionals. Albert Gerra and Masatsugu Takahashi made important contributions to the preparation of the graphs.

Suggestions and criticisms from Charles Baubonis, Rolf Böni, Edward Chambliss, Thomas Curran, Steven Depp, Jeffrey Diehl, Keith Fishe, Michael Gorham, Thomas Hickey, Gordon Holterman, Claire Leaman, Suzanne Martin-Reay, Satish Nandapurkar, Michael Reveley, Barry Seeman, Sam Serisier, Jim Singh, Christophe Trefalt, and David Weiner on specific topics or issues is also gratefully acknowledged. Their individual contributions were varied and useful.

Special recognition is due to Elizabeth Thompson who prepared and edited the text and the graphs from a combination of barely audible mumblings and illegible scribblings.

Gary L. Gastineau

THE ESSENTIALS OF
FINANCIAL RISK MANAGEMENT

"New financial instruments are not created simply because someone on Wall Street believes that it would be 'fun' to introduce an instrument with more 'bells and whistles' than existing instruments. The demand for new instruments is driven by the needs of borrowers and investors based on their asset/liability management situation, regulatory constraints (if any), financial accounting considerations, and tax considerations."[1]

Introduction

In a recent speech, the chairman of the Federal Reserve Bank of New York suggested that developments in international banking, particularly in swaps and other derivative risk management markets, were cause for regulatory concern.

"The growth and complexity of off-balance sheet activities and the nature of the credit, price and settlement risk they entail should give us all cause for concern . . ."[2]

---

[1] Frank J. Fabozzi and Franco Modigliani, *Capital Markets—Institutions and Instruments,* (Englewood Cliffs, New Jersey: Prentice Hall, 1992), p. xxi.

[2] E. Gerald Corrigan, "Remarks Before the 64th Annual Mid-Winter Meeting of the New York State Bankers Association," (Waldorf Astoria, New York, January 30, 1992).

Similar comments from the Bank for International Settlements, from two SEC commissioners, and in the financial press have hinted at large and ill-defined risks taken by major financial intermediaries. The implicit or explicit warning is of danger to the world financial structure.

We agree with Mr. Corrigan that there are unnecessary risks in the system. In this introductory chapter, we attempt to distinguish among various kinds of risk and discuss how they affect the soundness of the financial system.

We also explain how financial intermediaries provide financial risk management products and services to a variety of institutional investors, corporations, and governments around the world—without necessarily taking on the risks themselves. This risk transfer process is far simpler than much recent commentary suggests. The market risks which financial intermediaries exchange with and among their clients can be broken into basic components which are readily understandable and manageable. On the other hand, some non-market risks are more difficult to manage. The latter are an appropriate topic for public policy debate and political or regulatory resolution. The policy issues are clear and, given appropriate political will, can be resolved—with an attendant improvement in public confidence in financial markets and institutions.

Shifting Price or Rate Risk—The Primary Focus of Risk Management

The market risks which financial intermediaries reallocate are price, interest rate, and currency exchange rate risks. Price and rate risks come in a variety of flavors, but all markets share two features:

1. Any movement in a price or rate will be undesirable to some market participants. The popular name for exposure to an undesirable market movement is **market risk.**

2. One person's risk is usually someone else's potential reward. By exchanging packages of risks and rewards, *both parties to a risk management transaction can be better off.*

To draw an illustration from a prototypical price risk environment, consider a new issue of common stock from the viewpoints of three key market participants:

- The corporate **issuer** who sells the new stock into the marketplace.
- The asset manager or **investor** who buys the stock on the initial offering or in the secondary market.
- The **market maker** who trades the stock in the secondary market as the needs of asset managers and investors change over time.

The figure below illustrates each market participant's notion of risk. The common feature of their respective notions of risk is exposure to financial loss — accounting loss or opportunity loss — but each views the possibility of loss from a different perspective.

Market Risk from the Viewpoints of Three Participants

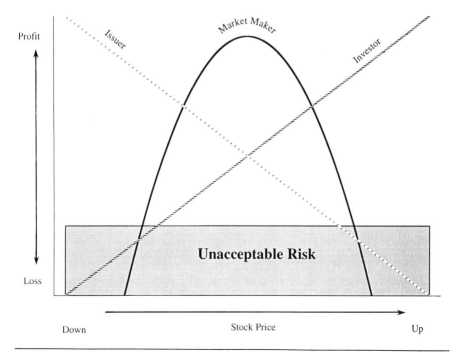

Starting our examination of risk with the market maker, we find a classic risk position. His risk is exposure to any large price change. Nothing could make him happier than a regular alternation of buyers who take his offer, and sellers who hit his bid. However, by posting a continuous bid and offer, the market maker exposes himself to potential loss if the stock price moves very far in either direction. If the market falls, the market maker will be called upon to buy more stock, and his inventory will decline in value. If the price of the stock rises, the market maker will be called upon to deplete his inventory of stock. With a reduced inventory, the market maker's participation in the rally will be limited. He might even sell stock short to meet market demand. As a short seller, the market maker will face out-of-pocket losses in a market advance. The market maker's position is disadvantageous — risky — if prices fall or rise sharply.

The stock's issuer and the investors who hold the stock in portfolios view risk from very different perspectives. Each views risk from only one side of the market. The issuing corporation views risk as exposure to a rising market. If the corporation had waited to issue the stock until after the market rise, it could have obtained the same amount of cash for fewer shares. For the issuer, risk is a stock price that rises after he sells stock. If the stock price falls tomorrow, the issuer's sale of the stock today will appear fortuitous.

The asset manager or investor who buys stock as a portfolio investment sees risk as the possibility of a stock price decline. If prices drop tomorrow, the investor will wish she had waited to buy. Of course, a stock price that rises after purchase is a favorable development for the investor.

In this simplified picture of the stock market, participants have no obvious way to trade some of their return potential for a reduction in risk. In the real world, risk management products and services provided by options and futures exchanges and by financial intermediaries are a response to demands for help in reducing risks.

Many market participants are willing to trade some of their opportunity to profit from favorable price behavior for protection against an adverse price move. The essential role of options and futures markets and financial intermediaries is to help asset and liability managers — investors and issuers — modify risks and rewards so that some or all of the effects of price movements are transferred to others. Actual or opportunity losses often cause more pain than an equivalent profit causes pleasure. Consequently, many market participants are willing to give up sizable profit opportunities in exchange for protection from risk. This normal human risk aversion creates the market for financial risk management products and services.

In the stock market or in virtually any other price or rate risk situation, combinations of swaps, options, forward or futures contracts, and traditional financial instruments can reallocate participation in price or rate movements in a variety of ways. When a single market or market sector is integrated with financial instruments and markets around the world, the opportunities for risk and return reallocation become extremely complex. However, the basic principle behind all financial risk management is the exchange of one set of risks and rewards for another set that fits a market participant's utility preferences more closely.

The Price or Rate Risk Management Process

The most complicated risk management structure can be broken down into components that any high school graduate should be able to understand thoroughly. Ph.D.'s with various specialties — the "rocket scientists" described in the press — play an important role in financial risk management. But a Ph.D. is not necessary to understand any single aspect of financial risk or to evaluate the overall effectiveness of risk control.

In the simplified stock market example, options can help the issuer trade some of the possible opportunity gain from a falling stock price for protection from the opportunity loss associated with a rising stock price. Correspondingly, the investor can use options to exchange some of her upside potential for downside protection. Convertible bonds and some recent equity offerings have risk-reallocating option provisions embedded in the security itself. The market maker can buy options for protection from large price movements in either direction.

If price or rate risk were the only kind of risk, there would be no controversy over the market in risk management agreements of any kind. After all, consenting adults are simply exchanging cash flows, and they expect these exchanges to improve or protect their financial well-being.

When customized risk management contracts transfer financial risk from one party to another, the process often leads to the mistaken view that these instruments are used exclusively to reduce some specific risk element—and that the financial intermediary who creates the product or facilitates the risk exchange is acting as reservoir for risk absorption. Actually, the creator of the product is primarily a provider of liquidity. The financial intermediary typically disaggregates, repackages, and redistributes risks and their corresponding rewards to other market participants. As a simple example of risk transfer, one contract may insulate a pension or profit-sharing plan from a downside stock market move. Another contract may transfer equivalent stock market exposure to an investor who expects substantial cash inflows in the near future and who wants immediate participation in stock prices. The intermediary who handles the transfer is not taking *any* increased stock price risk.

The financial intermediary who sells risk management products is the ultimate risk manager—but not the ultimate risk taker. In addition to managing risk-balanced "books" in one or a variety of markets, the financial intermediary is sharply attuned to the credit of counterparties (in cases where credit is a significant issue). Cash securities markets and exchange-traded option and futures contracts are used extensively by the providers of liquidity to manage the risks of their customer positions. The financial intermediary—by linking specific customer needs through cash markets and exchange-traded and OTC derivatives—provides liquidity to international capital markets.

Liquidity Risks

Our stock market example assumed that the market maker was prepared to make a market, and our discussion of risk management has implicitly assumed that the appropriate financial instruments can be traded. In reality, not all packages of risks and rewards are freely or actively traded. Many financial markets are characterized by extreme illiquidity. Examples of illiquid markets include real estate, small capitalization stocks, and a variety of debt contracts between financial institutions and consumers (accounts receivable, credit card debt, auto loans, etc.). Financial market innovations have sharply reduced many liquidity risks in recent years. Real estate investment trusts, publicly traded limited partnerships, and several other vehicles have made modest steps toward improving liquidity in real estate markets. Smaller capitalization stocks have some way to go before acceptable liquidity is achieved, but exchange-traded contracts like the S&P mid-cap options and futures are a small step in the right direction.

Probably the greatest achievement in improving the liquidity of financial instruments has come in the area of securitization. Credit card debt, automobile paper, and consumer loans have joined mortgages as prime candidates for securitization. A bank or other loan originator is no longer committed to holding these instruments for the life of the loan. They can be traded in securitized form as easily as any traditional security. Government affiliates like Ginnie Mae, Fannie Mae, and Freddy Mac have played essential roles in mortgage securitization, but most of the steps taken to improve liquidity have occurred at the initiation of private market practitioners searching for liquidity or trying to earn a profit by providing it. Fortunately, many market structures and regulations have been sufficiently flexible to permit the introduction of new securitized instruments. The phenomenon of securitization illustrates what market forces can accomplish in an environment that permits innovation. However, innovation has not yet eliminated market price discontinuities, a particularly severe liquidity problem.

The Risk of Market Price Discontinuities

The classic market of economic theory is a call auction market where all market participants meet in one place at one time to arrive at a market clearing price through open outcry of bids and offers. In agricultural societies, these markets were often held annually at harvest time, but the development of futures contracts has spread commodities trading over the year. Financial markets have traditionally been open each business day. As volume in many markets has grown, efficient continuous markets — some operating on a 24-hour basis — have become the norm in currencies and in a few widely held securities. Implicit in many naive risk management calculations is the doubtful assumption that most markets are continuous from one trade to the next with only gradual price changes. The October 1987 stock market break was a dramatic challenge to the assumption of market continuity.

In general, market forces have dealt effectively with the reallocation of price and rate risk and have provided liquidity through securitization and the allocation of capital to market making. Market forces have not yet dealt adequately with the risk of market discontinuities. Ironically, the mechanism for dealing with this problem is in place: the option market. Anyone willing to accept downside discontinuity risk can sell a put option. Unfortunately, regulation of securities option position limits restricts the number of exchange-traded option contracts any market participant can buy or sell. As a result, large investors who want to buy or sell protection against market discontinuities are denied meaningful access to the exchange-traded option markets. Listed option markets often lack depth due to the virtual absence of large investors. The thinness of the option market denies all investors opportunities to use options to build automatic risk adjustments into their portfolios at a reasonable cost.

Financial intermediaries have provided some help in bringing the providers of this specialized form of liquidity to buyers who value it highly, but an intermediary's role is limited if both sides of the discontinuity risk exchange are not accessible. Financial intermediaries are not in the business of betting their companies on the proposition that October '87 will never happen again. So-called dynamic hedging or replication of option risk and return patterns with futures and cash market trades may occur on the margin, but major financial intermediaries serve by redistributing financial risk, not by absorbing it. Until position limits and other restrictions on widespread use of option markets are eliminated, market discontinuities will be an unnecessarily large risk to the financial system.

Credit or Counterparty Risk

Some of the concern which regulators and the financial press have expressed over the state of the market in risk management products has centered on the issue of credit or counterparty risk. Credit evaluation will never be an exact science. However, appropriate price or rate discounts and premiums that reflect differences in credit quality can adjust for reasonable differences in credit risk exposure. Financial intermediaries closely scrutinize the credit risk element in a risk management agreement because most intermediaries have experienced sizable credit losses in recent years. The credit exposure of a risk management agreement depends on the type of contract and on the underlying markets as well as on the credit status of the counterparty. In most instances, credit issues are manageable if both parties are imaginative and the incentive for undertaking the risk management agreement is strong enough.

To encourage financial and non-financial parties to enter risk transfer agreements that improve market liquidity, public policy often helps counterparties reduce unnecessary credit risks. Netting arrangements and collateralization agreements made in good faith are often protected in the event of a counterparty's subsequent financial distress. One justification for this policy is that an appropriate risk transfer agreement can often alleviate or even prevent distress.

Some regulations applied to hybrid derivatives contracts and some bankruptcy policies *create* credit and counterparty problems where none need exist. Clearing up confusion and eliminating inappropriate regulation will require an internationally coordinated effort toward policy change. As an example of movement in the right direction, U.S. bankruptcy law reform has sharply reduced many credit and counterparty risks when U.S. law applies. The U.S. example and competition from the U.S. has pushed the U.K. government in a similar direction.

Legal and Regulatory Risk

Legal and regulatory risk is one of the greatest obstacles to effective functioning of the market in risk management agreements. In the notorious case of *Hazell v. The Council of the London Borough of Hammersmith and Fulham and Others,* the House of Lords held that, as a matter of public law, entering into swap transactions was beyond the legal capacity of the counterparty. This case is the kind of financial land mine that reduces the efficiency of the market in risk management products and endangers the financial structure. The solution is to clarify the legal and regulatory framework so that parties to risk management agreements need not fear similar events in the future. Such events impose a "tax" on the financial system which is reflected in wider trading spreads and in a reluctance to trade with some parties who need to transfer risks. Financial intermediaries can manage market risks, but they cannot protect themselves from legal and regulatory risks except by declining to trade.

Another extremely important legal and regulatory "tax" is the cost of keeping the financial system afloat. Major financial firms rarely create public distress when they fail. Their problem positions are transferred to a stronger competitor or divided among several firms. The cost of their break-up and absorption is spread among former competitors and major creditors. Often, customers outside the financial industry are protected at the expense of the financial industry's survivors.

The recent demise of much of the savings and loan industry in the United States is an example of a problem too large to be absorbed by the remaining companies in the financial industry. The S&L crisis was essentially caused by a regulatory and incentive structure that created a moral hazard — the system rewarded management handsomely if it took huge risks that paid off and protected depositors from loss if management's high risk business strategies failed. Depositors had no incentive to limit management's risk taking. Some simple changes in the regulatory structure could have prevented a large part of this fiasco. Unfortunately, the legal and regulatory framework within which financial industry failures occur changes slowly.

Partly in response to the savings and loan example and partly in response to widely expressed concerns, risk management transactions have become a popular subject for study. Among others, the General Accounting Office (GAO) and the Group of 30 (G30) are planning to study the markets in swaps and other derivatives. A sound financial intermediary should not be reluctant to meet with these groups or face any other open-minded inquiry. Broad and deep knowledge of these markets is the world financial structure's best protection from groups which articulate their conclusions before they ask questions.

Tax Risk

The S&L situation is not the only recent case where risk reduction and/or effective risk management have been discouraged by government policy. In the Arkansas Best case, the U.S. Supreme Court affirmed an Internal Revenue Service position that certain losses on risk-reducing (hedging) positions were capital losses and, thus, could not be offset against ordinary income. This ruling will generate very little incremental tax revenue, but it encourages corporations to retain risks they would layoff in a tax-neutral environment.

Recently, the Internal Revenue Service removed a tax obstacle to financial risk reduction. Uncertainty over application of the Unrelated Business Income Tax (UBIT) has kept many tax-exempt investors out of swaps markets. Now, an IRS ruling has eliminated UBIT concern for swaps and other notional principal contracts such as caps, collars, and floors.

Accounting Risk

The Securities and Exchange Commission's opposition to matching risk management gains and losses for accounting purposes creates uncertainty over the financial reporting impact of risk management solutions that make economic sense. In the United States, and, to a lesser extent in other countries, sensible risk management policies are often in conflict with results reported on a corporation's tax return, income statement, or balance sheet. No simple or imminent solution to this problem is in sight.

Reducing Risk in the System—Improving Settlements

The comments from the Chairman of the Federal Reserve Bank of New York cited in the Introduction reflect intelligent concern for some important risks in the system. His greatest concern seems to be the risks associated with slow and uncoordinated settlement of international financial transactions. Two articles in a recent issue of the St. Louis Federal Reserve Bank's *Review* discuss weaknesses in foreign exchange transaction settlements and global security market settlements. Clearly, the Federal Reserve System is attuned to the settlement risk problem.[3]

While financial intermediaries can take some steps to protect themselves and, consequently, the structure of the system, many improvements require the powers of a regulator or even a legislature. When cross-border and cross-currency payment systems are involved, regulators in each country are critical participants in the process. The Lamfalussy Report on foreign exchange settlements issued through the Bank for International

---

[3] R. Alton Gilbert, "Implications of Netting Arrangements for Bank Risk in Foreign Exchange Transactions," pp. 3–16; and Jodi G. Scarlata, "Institutional Developments in the Globalization of Securities and Futures Markets," pp. 17–31, in *The Federal Reserve Bank of St. Louis Review,* January/February 1992.

Settlements and the Group of Thirty proposal for coordination of world-wide security market clearing and settlement are important steps in improving cross-border payment procedures — and central bankers seem to have the will to implement necessary reforms.

Summary and Conclusion

The central bankers' efforts on settlements — and the progress on payment netting cited earlier — must extend to securities regulation, accounting rules, and tax policy. The SEC, the IRS, and their counterparts in other countries often send conflicting signals. The SEC recently has shown some interest in shortening the stock settlement period from a week to three business days, but its accounting pronouncements and option policies are far from progressive. The IRS ruling that excludes swaps and other notional principal contracts used by tax-exempt institutions from the Unrelated Business Income Tax removed an important obstacle to effective financial risk management by pension funds and endowments. On the other hand, the Arkansas Best decision creates an obstacle to risk management by corporations.

It is unfair and unnecessary to assign blame for weaknesses in the global financial structure to the regulatory agencies, the legislature, or the executive branch of any government. It *is* both fair and reasonable to expect their help in making improvements. The world's central bankers are moving toward system risk reduction with settlement procedure improvements that risk managers and financial intermediaries cannot achieve on their own initiative. The central bankers' example is a model for others.

It is common to address concerns for the stability of the financial system by emphasizing strict capital requirements and by increasing capital charges for certain banking and securities transactions. Capital adequacy is certainly important, but no amount of capital can substitute for intelligent management of a firm's business risks in a legal and regulatory framework that is free of unnecessary hazards. Even the best capital rules create inappropriate behavioral incentives as they oversimplify risk analysis to standardize capital charges. Capital rules are no substitute for a thorough understanding — by both managements and regulators — of the risk characteristics of diverse transactions.

The only viable legal and regulatory framework for financial markets is a system that rewards intelligent decisions with profit, encourages constructive innovation, and discourages risk taking for its own sake. Capital requirements play a role in ensuring the integrity of the market, but rigid proscriptions stifle innovation. Improving the clarity and rationality of commercial, bankruptcy, and tax codes to give the parties to financial contracts a clear picture of their non-market risks will do more than stricter capital rules to remove unnecessary risks from the global financial structure.

Using the Dictionary

The Swiss Bank Corporation *Dictionary of Financial Risk Management* is intended primarily as a reference manual for finance professionals. Virtually everyone involved in financial risk management has heard a colleague or a client mention the name of a financial product and wondered what the product was and how it worked. Many of us have suspected someone's use of a term was not quite right, yet we have been reluctant to suggest that the word meant something slightly different. Open disagreements about the provisions of a specialized contract or the meaning of unfamiliar risk management terminology are common. The number of hybrid creations and financial product names in circulation suggests that a dictionary is needed to codify the financial risk management lexicon.

We have no illusions that this dictionary will answer every question or resolve every dispute. During its preparation, we encountered a number of modifications of traditional product structures and a few entirely unfamiliar products. Regular additions to the list of instruments available to risk managers will make periodic updates of this listing necessary. We encourage anyone who finds this compilation useful to tell us about any disagreements he or she might have with a definition and to make suggestions for additional listings.

Risk management markets are global markets. Consequently, we have included pertinent vocabulary from most market centers. Many firms make up their own "proprietary" labels for relatively standard products. Rather than repeat definitions under each such label, we refer the reader to one or two of the more common names for each product or structure for a comprehensive definition of the generic instrument. If some definitions seem too brief, they should at least provide the reader with general information on the product or structure described. Consulting one of the standard texts in each submarket usually will provide additional information. We have not hesitated to use the basic language of financial risk management itself in defining specific products, because redefining each basic term each time it is used would have been too cumbersome.

We have not tried to include all the terminology of the cash and derivatives markets which underlie risk management transactions. We have, however, felt it necessary to include some terminology from equity, bond, and currency cash markets as well as more comprehensive vocabulary from the major derivative markets. Certain statistical concepts that play a major role in the analysis of risk are listed along with terminology used primarily by lawyers, regulators, accountants, and other professionals active in some aspect of risk management. The tests for inclusion in each case were (1) the applicability of a term to financial risk management activities and (2) the likelihood that someone using this book might want to know what it means. If one term has more than one meaning, the common usages are listed in approximate order of usage frequency or importance.

Many words have been omitted. The basic language of the cash markets themselves, such as types of orders and operating procedures, is not covered. Exchange-listed products and the exchanges themselves are not listed because up-to-date listings are published frequently in industry trade publications. We have not provided a separate listing of the incredible number of acronyms used in risk management activities. A reader confronted with an acronym should scan the alphabetical listings under the first letter in the acronym. Common acronyms are in bold type in parentheses after each term. The listings are alphabetized in a word-by-word style, and hyphenated words are treated as two distinct words.

Dictionary Listings

A

A/B Structure: A two tranche senior–(A) subordinated–(B) securitized loan portfolio.

Abandonment: (1) In Switzerland, the act of withdrawal from a cancellable forward contract to purchase securities. *See Premium Business.* (2) Also used infrequently in other markets as a reference to letting an option expire unexercised.

Absolute Rate: An interest rate provision of a swap expressed as a percentage return rather than as a premium or discount to a reference rate such as LIBOR.

Absolute Swap Yield: The fixed rate in an interest rate swap expressed as a percentage rate. *See also Absolute Rate.*

Acceleration Covenant: A provision of a debt or swap agreement requiring early payment and termination in the event of default or credit downgrade.

Accounting Standards Board (ASB): The organization with primary responsibility for accounting standards in the United Kingdom.

Accredited Investor: An individual or institutional investor who meets the eligibility requirements of the Securities Act of 1933 for purchase of securities in a private placement.

Accreting Principal Swap: In contrast to a traditional swap where the notional principal amount is fixed for the life of the swap and an amortizing swap where the notional principal declines as a mortgage or other loan is repaid, an accreting swap has a *growing* notional principal amount. Applications might include a situation in which a fixed rate payer had growing working capital requirements. *Also called Accumulation Swap, Construction Loan Swap, Drawdown Swap, Staged Drawdown Swap, or Step-Up Swap. See also Swap.*

Accretion Directed (AD) Bond: A collateralized mortgage obligation that pays principal from specified accretions of accrual bonds. An AD may, in addition, receive principal from the collateral paydowns.

Accrued Interest: The current value of the next coupon payment due on a bond or note.

Accumulated Benefit Obligation (ABO): An actuarial estimate of the aggregate amount to be paid to retirees and present employees assuming immediate termination of a pension plan. *See also Projected Benefit Obligation.*

Accumulation Swap: *See Accreting Principal Swap.*

Active Manager: A reference to an asset or, less frequently, a liability manager who takes an active role in security selection and risk management in an attempt to improve a portfolio's risk-adjusted return or reduce an issuer's cost of capital. *Contrast with Passive Manager.*

Actuals: Physical commodities, typically those which underlie commodity futures contracts. The comparable expression and concept in financial markets would be the underlying cash market or instrument.

Actuarial Rate: The rate of return assumed by a pension plan actuary in calculating liability coverage and coverage gaps.

Adjustable Long-term Puttable Securities (ALPS): *See Dual Currency Bond.*

Adjustable Rate Convertible Debt: (1) A convertible bond with no conversion premium and a coupon equivalent to or tied to the dividend on the underlying common stock. This structure was designed to make dividend equivalents deductible by the issuer. Frustrating this effort, the Internal Revenue Service has held that the coupon on such instruments is paid from after-tax income. (2) A convertible bond or note with a variable (floating rate) coupon set by reference to a standard index rate (e.g., LIBOR).

Adjustable Rate Instruments: Any of a wide variety of fixed principal obligations whose periodic payout is set relative to a reference index rate (such as LIBOR) to create a longer-term fixed principal obligation with a floating rate interim cost. *See, for example, Floating Rate Note, Adjustable Rate Preferred Stock.*

Adjustable Rate Mortgage (ARM): A mortgage agreement with interest costs tied to a short- or intermediate-term interest rate index such as the rates on United States Treasury bills or notes. Rate adjustments are made at intervals and the premium over the index rate may vary over the term of the mortgage.

Adjustable Rate Note: *See Floating Rate Note.*

Adjustable Rate Preferred Stock: Floating rate preferred stock with a dividend rate reset based, for example, on the maximum of a series of short- and long-term rates plus or minus a designated spread. Designed to permit corporate investors to take advantage of the 70 percent intercorporate dividend exclusion. *See also Auction Rate Preferred Stock (ARPS), Remarketed Preferred Stock.*

Adjustable Tender Securities: *See Puttable Bonds.*

Adjusted Duration: *See Modified Duration. See also Option-adjusted Duration.*

Adjusted Strike Price or Adjusted Exercise Price: (1) When any capital change affects the shares subject to a stock option, the strike price and the number of shares subject to option are adjusted to reflect the change. For example, if a stock is split 3 for 2 and the original strike price of an option is $60, the adjusted strike price is $40, and the option becomes an option on 150 shares of the split stock. (2) Strike price adjustments are uncommon in interest rate and currency option markets, but the exercise price of Government National Mortgage Association (GNMA) options, for example, is adjusted to reflect the coupon rates on mortgages in the settlement pool.

Adjustment Swap: *See Off-Market Coupon Swap.*

Advance Corporation Tax (ACT): A tax paid by United Kingdom companies on the dividends they pay. The ACT is subject to recapture by certain shareholders. It complicates the withholding tax picture in the United Kingdom and provides a modest additional incentive for some cross-border traders in United Kingdom securities and indexes to use derivatives.

Advance Guarantee: A call option.

Advance Pricing Agreement: A private tax ruling from two countries' tax agencies on how the earnings from a financial transaction or series of transactions will be allocated between the countries for tax purposes.

Agency Relationship: In securities markets, a broker may act as agent and charge a commission for finding a trading counterparty for her customer. In contrast to dealer or principal relationships, an agent does not trade with a customer for the agent's own account.

Aggregate Exercise Price: The exercise or strike price of an option contract multiplied by the number of units of the underlying security or instrument covered by the option contract. For example, a bond option with a strike price of 101 ($1,010 per bond) covering 1,000 bonds would have an aggregate exercise price of 1,010 times 1,000 or $1,010,000.

Aggregation: When financial distress leads to early termination of a number of swaps between two counterparties, some master swap agreements call for the aggregation or netting of the positive and negative values of the swaps affected by the early termination.

Agio: In Switzerland, a bond's market value premium over par, expressed as a percent. For example, if the bond is at 101, its agio is 1 percent. Agio reflects price increases after the offering. *See also Disagio.*

Agreement Value: A measure of the value of a swap, usually based on the value (cost) of the right to pay a specific fixed rate or to reestablish the swap position in the current market environment. Market value is determined by reference to previously agreed sources of price or swap rate quotations.

Algorithm: A formula or set of rules used to solve a problem. The algorithm usually simplifies a real world relationship. The Black-Scholes and binomial option models and the cost-of-carry model for pricing forward and futures contracts are widely used algorithms used to price risk management contracts.

All-In Cost: (1) The total implementation cost of a transaction or instrument including interest, spreads, commissions, fees, etc. Often expressed as a percentage of face or as an annual percentage rate. (2) In an interest rate swap, the all-in cost will be expressed as the value of a single period fixed rate payment as a percent of the notional principal amount.

All-In Premium: (United Kingdom) The warrant premium expressed as a percentage of the current price of the underlying. *See Premium (3).*

All-or-Nothing Option: An option with a fixed, predetermined payoff if the underlying instrument or index is at or beyond the strike at expiration. The value of the payoff is not affected by the magnitude of the difference between the underlying and the strike price. *Also called Digital Option.*

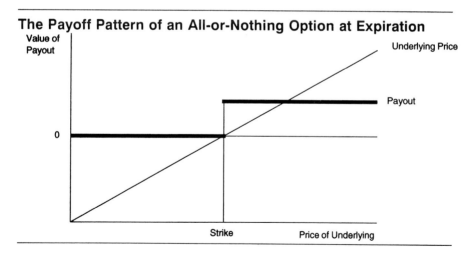

The Payoff Pattern of an All-or-Nothing Option at Expiration

All–Ordinaries Share Price Riskless Index Notes (ASPRINs):   Low or zero coupon equity index-linked notes with a specified percentage participation in the Australian All–Ordinaries stock index and minimum redemption at par. *See also Equity Index-linked Notes.*

Alligator Spread: Another name for a butterfly spread. This name suggests that the commissions and bid-asked spreads associated with the position will eat you alive. *See Butterfly Spread (diagram).*

Alpha Factor α: The net risk-adjusted premium return from a position or a portfolio. Calculated by subtracting (a) the risk-adjusted return consistent with the position or portfolio's place on the capital asset pricing model market line from (b) the actual return.

Measuring Alpha Relative to the Market Line

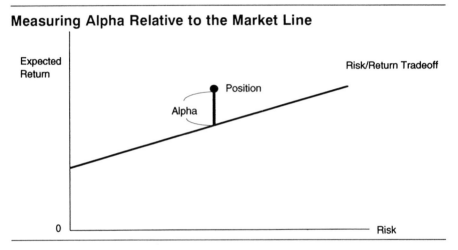

Alternative Currency Option: A currency option which, if exercised, settles in any one of two or more currencies at the choice of the option holder. Each currency has its own strike rate and the holder chooses the currency with the greatest option value at the time of exercise. *See also Dual Currency Option. Compare with Outperformance Option.*

Alternative Option: An option on the best (call) or worst (put) return of two or more securities or indexes during a designated measurement period. *Compare with Outperformance Option.*

American Depository Receipts (ADRs): Certificates traded in United States markets which represent an interest in shares of a foreign company. ADRs were created to make it possible for foreign issuers to meet United States security registration requirements and to facilitate dividend collection by dollar-based investors.

American Exchange Rate Quotation Convention: In currencies, the practice of quoting exchange relationships in terms of the number of dollars per unit of the foreign currency — as in dollars per Deutsche mark, dollars per pound sterling, etc. *See also European Exchange Rate Quotation Convention.*

American Option: A put or call that can be exercised at any time prior to expiration. Most listed stock options, including those on European exchanges, are American-style options. Important exceptions are certain low strike price options and/or options on shares with restricted transferability. Most listed options on other instruments are also American-style options, but a number of European-style options have been introduced in recent years, particularly on stock indexes and currencies. *See also European Option, Japanese Option, Bermuda Option, Quasi-American Option, Deferred Payment American Option.*

Americus Trust: Sponsor of a technique to separate certain common stocks into a five-year warrant and a five-year covered call warrant writer's position at relatively low cost. No Americus Trust instruments have been created since 1987 largely because of an adverse change in tax rulings. Although the remaining Americus Trust instruments terminated in 1992, the Americus Trust principle of decomposing a stream of returns has been widely incorporated in other derivative instruments. *See also Preference Equity Redemption Cumulative Stocks (PERCS), PRIME, SCORE, Termination Claim.*

Amortizing Cap: An interest rate cap with caplets covering declining notional principal amounts. This structure usually reflects repayment of principal on an underlying instrument.

Amortizing Collar: An interest rate collar which covers declining notional principal amounts. This structure usually reflects repayments of principal on an underlying instrument.

Amortizing Option: An interest rate or swap option (swaption) which covers declining notional principal amounts. This structure usually reflects repayments of principal on an underlying instrument.

Amortizing Swap: An interest rate swap with a declining notional principal amount reflecting the principal amortization of an underlying fixed or floating rate instrument. If the actual amortization schedules of the swap and the underlying are not set at identical levels in advance (as in a mortgage obligation), the fixed rate receiver faces significant prepayment or extension risk. *See also Index Amortizing Swap, Indexed Principal Swap, Interest Rate Swap.*

Amount at Risk: In a swap agreement, the present value of a replacement swap. This calculation implicitly assumes an effective netting agreement is in place.

Annuity Bond or Note: A fixed rate instrument which pays the investor an equal amount of cash each year over the life of the issue. Individual payments will contain increasing amounts of principal and correspondingly declining amounts of interest.

Annuity Swap: (1) A currency swap with an exchange of coupons or interest payments only. (2) Another name for a variety of amortizing swap.

Anomaly: An unexplained or unexpected price or rate relationship that seems to offer an opportunity for an arbitrage-type profit.

Anti-Crash Warrant: Call-type index warrant with a strike price equal to the lower of the index level at issuance or the index level at a predetermined future date, typically a few months into the life of the warrant. *Also called Partial Lookback Warrant, Reset Warrant, or Step-Down Warrant.*

Anticipatory Hedge: (1) A long derivatives position taken to provide participation in a market before an investor is ready to take a position in the related cash instruments or actuals. *Also called a Long Hedge.* (2) A short equivalent derivatives position taken to protect against a decline when tax or other considerations force a delay in the sale of the related long position.

Arbitrage: (1) Technically, arbitrage consists of purchasing a commodity or security in one market for immediate sale in another market (deterministic arbitrage). (2) Popular usage has expanded the meaning of the term to include any activity which attempts to buy a relatively underpriced item and sell a similar, relatively overpriced item, expecting to profit when the prices resume a more appropriate theoretical or historical relationship (statistical arbitrage). (3) In trading options, convertible securities, and futures, arbitrage techniques can be applied whenever a strategy involves buying and selling packages of related instruments. (4) Risk arbitrage applies the principles of risk offset to mergers and other major corporate developments. The risk offsetting position(s) do not insulate the investor from certain event risks (such as termination of a merger agreement or the risk of completion of a transaction within a certain time) so the arbitrage is incomplete. (5) Tax arbitrage transactions are undertaken to share the benefit of differential tax rates or circumstances of two or more parties to a transaction. (6) Regulatory arbitrage transactions are designed to provide indirect access to a risk management market where one party is denied direct access by law or regulation. (7) Swap-driven arbitrage transactions are motivated by the comparative advantages which swap counterparties enjoy in different debt and currency markets. One counterparty may borrow relatively cheaper in the intermediate- or long-term United States dollar market while the other may have a comparative advantage in floating rate sterling. A cross-currency swap can improve both of their positions. *See also Covered Interest Arbitrage, Index Arbitrage.*

Arbitrage Pricing Theory (APT): A model of financial instrument and portfolio behavior based on the proposition that if the returns of a portfolio of assets can be described by a factor structure or model, the expected return of each asset in the portfolio can be described by a combination of the covariances of the factors with the returns of the asset. The factors can be arbitrary (nonintuitive) or they can be macroeconomic variables such as interest rates, inflation, industrial production, etc. The resulting factor model can be used to create portfolios that track a market index, to estimate and monitor the risk of an asset allocation strategy, or to estimate the likely response of a portfolio to economic developments. Starting from an initial model proposed by Stephen Ross, APT models have been created for applications in most cash and derivatives markets.

Arkansas Best v. Commission, 485 U.S. 212 (1988): A tax case in which the United States Supreme Court upheld an Internal Revenue Service position that some types of hedging transactions result in capital rather than ordinary losses. This decision complicates many taxable entities' risk management procedures because capital losses are not fully deductible against ordinary income for United States taxpayers.

Arrangement Fee: A commission-like charge paid to a brokerage firm or other intermediary for its role in initiating or implementing a transaction.

Arrears Swap: *See In-Arrears Swap.*

As-You-Like Warrant: A warrant with a provision permitting the purchaser to designate it as either a call warrant or a put warrant for a limited period after the offering date. In general, the option to treat the instrument as a put warrant is of relatively little value. The underlying will have to decline substantially before a put will be worth more than the *initial* value of the call.

Asian Option: *See Average Price or Rate Option.*

Asked Price: Price at which an instrument is offered for sale.

Asset Allocation: (1) Dividing investment funds among markets to achieve diversification. (2) A value-oriented investment strategy which attempts to take long positions in markets or market sectors where prices appear to be low and to reduce positions, or take short positions in markets or market sectors where prices appear to be high. Tactical (TAA) or strategic (SAA) asset allocation advocates and value seeking portfolio managers often use similar techniques and policies. In contrast to momentum investors who accentuate market trends, most asset allocators' trades tend to offset destabilizing market movements and counteract price and rate fluctuations. The asset allocator tends to buy when prices decline and sell when prices rise. *But see also Dynamic Asset Allocation.*

Asset-Backed Security (ABS): Financial instrument collateralized by one or more types of assets including real property, mortgages, receivables, etc.

Asset-based Swap: Usually, an interest rate swap agreement in which the fixed rate payer holds a bond whose coupon rate is reflected in the swap terms. The term may also describe any swap initiated by the holder of an asset which generates the payment stream on one side of the swap.

Asset Class: An investment grouping or type of instrument with a return which is not conditional on the return of another grouping or type of instrument. More precisely, an investment grouping with risk and return characteristics that cannot be dynamically replicated in a continuous market with positions in another asset class and the risk-free asset. There has been a tendency in recent years to divide the world of investments into more asset classes than are warranted.

Asset/Liability Gap: Any shortfall in the projected ability of a financial institution to meet its contractual obligations from current holdings. Many institutions receive regular funding from outside sources, e.g., corporate contributions to a pension plan, so an asset/liability gap calculation that neglects expected contributions may cause unnecessary concern.

Asset/Liability Management: Any of a variety of techniques designed to coordinate the management of an entity's assets with the management of its liabilities. A simple example would be a financial institution's management of the duration of its fixed income assets to match the duration of its payment liabilities.

Asset Manager: A portfolio manager, corporate treasurer, or other individual responsible for the management of the risks and returns associated with a portfolio of securities or other instruments. *See also Liability Manager.*

Asset Risk Management: Techniques and procedures used by a holder of securities, commodities, or related instruments to offset or counteract possible adverse changes in the value of part or all of a portfolio.

Asset Swap: Another name for a fixed-for-floating interest rate swap. *See Asset-based Swap.*

Assign: *See Assignment.*

Assignment: (1) Notice to an option seller that an option has been exercised by the option holder. (2) Process by which exercise notices or decisions are allocated among the sellers (shorts) in a derivative contract market. (3) Transfer of rights in settlement of an obligation. (4) Transfer of a swap obligation to a replacement counterparty, usually with the consent of the opposite counterparty but occasionally as a result of legal processes. (5) Transfer of ownership in a structured product or other private placement with the consent of the issuer. A limited right of assignment is a common feature of many risk management instruments, but legal restrictions usually prevent totally free assignment.

Assumed Rate of Return: *See Actuarial Rate.*

Asymmetric Payoff: An irregular, often discontinuous, pattern of changes in settlement valuation that does not translate all linear changes in the value of the underlying instrument, index, or rate into a continuous, linear settlement value. Asymmetric payoff patterns are characteristic of traditional securities with embedded options and of option contracts themselves.

Asymmetrical Margining Agreement: A collateralization agreement between the counterparties to a swap or other OTC risk management contract that requires more stringent margin coverage from one counterparty, usually because of a difference in credit rating.

At the Money: The situation in which the market price or rate of the underlying and the strike price or rate of an at-the-money option are equal. An option to buy a stock at a strike price of $80 is at the money if the current market price of the stock is $80. With increasing frequency, particularly in currency markets, the phrase refers to the forward price associated with the current spot price, as in "at-the-money forward."

Atlantic Option: *See Bermuda Option.*

Auction Rate Note: A type of floating rate note with an interest rate reset on the basis of bids received at a Dutch auction conducted near the end of each rate period. *See also Dutch Auction Interest and Dividend Resets.*

Auction Rate Preferred Stock (ARPS): A floating rate preferred with the dividend rate reset by Dutch auction, typically every 49 days. The interest rate is usually subject to a maximum and the issue is puttable at each auction. *Also designated by the following names and acronyms: Auction Market Preferred Stock (AMPS), Auction Rate Preferred Stock (ARPS), Dutch Auction Rate Transferable Securities (DARTS), Money Market Preferred (MMP), and Short-Term Auction Rate (STAR).*

Authorized Futures and Option Funds (AFOFs): Publicly offered derivatives funds regulated by the Securities & Investment Board in the United Kingdom. The funds invest in derivatives and interest-bearing deposits. A few geared AFOFs offer leveraged market exposure through derivatives.

Auto-Correlation: A condition in which the random error terms in a sequence of observations are not independent. The significance of auto-correlation for securities markets is that if today's price change is independent of tomorrow's price change in direction and magnitude, a variety of statistical techniques can be used to value securities and measure risk — but technical analysis would be demonstrably worthless. If the direction and magnitude of today's price change has implications for tomorrow's, the statistician must exercise more care in making inferences from the data — and the technician cannot be discredited.

Automated Pit Trading (APT): A screen-based after-hours trading system on the London International Financial Futures Exchange, now called LIFFE-LTOM to reflect its merger with the London Traded Options Market.

Automatic Exercise: A procedure used by many option clearing organizations whereby expiring options that are in the money by a specified amount or that are cash settled are exercised without specific instructions from the option holder.

Average Price of an Option: *See Normal Price of an Option.*

Average Price or Rate Option (APO, ARO): An option whose settlement value is based on the difference between the strike and the average price (rate) of the underlying on selected dates over the life of the option, or over a period beginning on some start date and ending at expiration. The theoretical value of an average price or rate call will usually be less than the value of an otherwise identical standard option because the average price option acts like an option with a shorter expected life. The premium on an average price or rate option also will tend to be less than the combined premiums of a strip of options expiring on each measurement date, because prices or rates on the wrong side of the strike will reduce the average price or rate and, hence, the expected settlement value of the average price or rate option. With a strip, observations on the wrong side of the strike would make one piece of the strip worthless but would not drag down the value of the others. *Also called an Asian Option. See also Average Strike Rate Option.*

Average Rate Cap: A cap on the average interest rate over a period rather than on the rate on a single date. *See also Average Price or Rate Option.*

Average Strike Rate Option (ASRO): An option whose settlement value is based on the difference between the spot price or rate at expiration and an average strike price or rate determined over the life of the option. These options are often embedded in employee stock purchase plans and pension plans. *Also called Floating Strike Option.*

B

Back Bond: A bond obtained through exercise of an option or warrant.

Back Contract: Most distant expiration futures contracts currently trading.

Back Month: Any futures contract maturity beyond the nearest expiration month.

Back Spread: (1) Any complex position including at least one separate or embedded net long option position which causes the entire position to increase in value in response to a significant price or rate move up or down. (2) A vertical or diagonal option spread with net premium received, usually because the short option is further in the money or less out of the money than the long option. *Also called a Credit Spread.* (3) A reverse option hedge or any variable or ratio spread where more option contracts are purchased than sold.

Back-to-Back Loan: Originally designed to overcome currency restrictions, the initial back-to-back borrowing and lending arrangements were offsetting loans between two parties in two different currencies. For example, a United States firm might make a dollar loan to a United Kingdom company in the U.S., and the U.K. company would make an equal value loan (at spot exchange rates) in sterling to the U.S. firm in the U.K. Each party gets the currency it needs without going through the exchange rate mechanism. This structure has been replaced by currency swaps in major markets, but it is still used where exchange restrictions apply. Back-to-back loans are also used in credit enhancement, with or without the dual currency feature.

Back-to-Back Swap: A swap agreement that reverses the cash flow pattern of a simple swap, modifying the net paying or receiving position of the back-to-back counterparties. Back-to-back swaps have been used to extend the effective maturity of an issuer's fixed rate debt or to enhance the credit of a financial intermediary's derivative products subsidiary.

Back End Set Swap: *See Reset Swap.*

Backwardation Market: A futures/spot market relationship in which the futures price is *lower* than the spot price. Agricultural commodity markets with a harvest due before the settlement date of the futures contract will often be characterized by backwardation. John Maynard Keynes argued that backwardation was normal in speculative markets, but this position has few adherents today. *See also Carrying Charge Market, Contango.*

Balloon: The final payment on a bond or note that is substantially larger than preceding amortization payments. Balloon instruments feature an amortization schedule intermediate between a level payment amortized loan and a bullet loan in which the entire principal is paid at maturity.

Band: The range of acceptable exchange rates between two currencies, as in exchange rate bands under the Exchange Rate Mechanism (ERM).

Bank Capital Adequacy Requirements: An international set of credit risk weighted capital charges and capital minimums for banks scheduled to become effective in 1993. Often linked with the Bank for International Settlements. *See Basle Convergence Agreement.*

Bank Deposit Agreement (BDA): Same as Bank Investment Contract (BIC). *See Guaranteed Investment Contract (GIC).*

Bank Guarantee: A form of credit enhancement in which a bank lends its own credit to assure timely payment of another party's obligation(s).

Bank for International Settlements (BIS): An organization of central banks concerned with international payments. *See also Bank Capital Adequacy Requirements, Basle Convergence Agreement.*

Bank Investment Contract (BIC): *See Guaranteed Investment Contract (GIC).*

Banker's Acceptance Swap: An interest rate swap with a banker's acceptance rate as the floating rate. Banker's acceptances are the most common base for floating rate swaps in Canada.

Bargain: (United Kingdom) An agreement to trade.

Barrier Discontinuity: A standard barrier option has an "in" or "out" condition triggered by touching or trading through an instrike or outstrike price. If the barrier condition can be satisfied only at certain times (e.g., the market close), or on certain dates, there is a barrier discontinuity, and evaluation of the option is more difficult.

Barrier Options: Path-dependent options with both their payoff pattern and their survival to the nominal expiration date dependent not only on the final price of the underlying but on whether or not the underlying sells at or through a barrier (instrike, outstrike) price during the life of the option. Examples of barrier options include down-and-out and up-and-in puts and calls, early exercise trigger CAPS options, and a variety of similar instruments.

Barrier Price: The instrike or outstrike price that activates or deactivates a barrier option. The barrier price must only be touched under the provisions of some contracts, while others require the barrier to be touched or breached at a market close (CAPS) or several times.

Base Currency: The currency in which an investor or issuer maintains its books of account.

Baseball Option: *See Touch Option.*

Basis: (1) The difference between the forward price or yield and the spot price or yield of an instrument such as a futures contract or the forward component implicit in an options contract. Alternately expressed as the cost minus the benefits of holding the hedged spot underlying until the forward or futures settlement date. *See Fair Value Basis.* See figures on next page. (2) The uncertain relationship between price or rate in two or more related but not identical markets. In a cross hedge, this uncertain relationship creates basis risk. *See Basis Risk.* (3) A convention for interest rate calculation. *See Bond Basis, Money Market Basis.*

Basis Point (BP, BIP): 1/100 of a percentage point, also expressed as 0.01 percent. The difference between a yield of 7.90 percent and 8 percent is 10 basis points. When applied to a price rather than a rate, the term is often expressed as annualized basis points.

Basis Price: A reference price or rate.

Basis Rate Swap: A swap in which counterparties calculate swap payments relative to different floating rates. One rate may be a very short-term rate, the other an intermediate rate. Differences in credit quality may be

Futures and Option Basis

Futures Basis

Call Option Basis

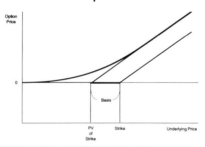

reflected in a premium or discount on one side of the swap. A Treasury/EuroDollar (TED) swap illustrates a credit quality basis rate swap. *Also called a Basis Swap.*

Basis Risk: (1) The possibility of loss from imperfectly matched risk offsetting positions in two related but not identical markets. Examples might be the risk of loss from using a Deutsche mark position to offset Swiss franc exposure or using an intermediate instrument to hedge long-term interest rate exposures. (2) Exposure to loss from a maturity mismatch caused, for example, by a shift or change in the shape of the yield curve.

Basis Trade: (1) A portfolio or basket trade in which the price for the position is determined by a spread against the price of an exchange-traded derivative, usually a futures contract. *See Exchange of Futures for Physicals (EFP).* (2) An arbitrage-type transaction which attempts to profit from changes in the relative prices of derivative and underlying instruments. (3) A cash and carry trade or its reverse.

Basket: A set of related instruments whose prices or rates are used to create a synthetic composite instrument which trades as a unit or serves as the underlying for a derivative instrument.

Basket Hedging: The use of a basket of currencies to offset the risk of all the nonbase currencies in a portfolio. Typically the basket will have fewer currencies than the portfolio, but, because of close correlations among many of the currencies, the basket should provide a close, low-cost (and usually more liquid) hedge of the currency risk.

Basket Option or Warrant: A third party option or covered warrant on a basket of underlying stocks chosen because they represent an industry, economic sector, or other group designed to appeal to option or warrant buyers. Some of these basket contracts are settled by physical delivery and some are settled for cash.

Basket Trade: A portfolio trade. *See Portfolio Trade, Program Trading.*

Basle Convergence Agreement: An international compact to establish and implement common standards for bank capital adequacy by January, 1993. The capital adequacy rules have encouraged banks to embrace disintermediation with the object of cleaning up their balance sheets. In addition, banks have tried to replace interest rate spreads with trading spreads and fees. There has been an overall tendency to transfer credit risk from banks to other financial market participants. *Also called Capital Adequacy Directive.*

Bear or Bearish: (1) A person who expects a market to decline. (2) A position which will profit if the market declines.

Bear Floaters: A floating rate note which resets at a multiple of the floating reference index rate minus a fixed rate. The floating rate increases or decreases by a multiple of the actual change in the floating rate index, but the multiplication of the floating rate and the subtraction of the fixed rate causes the rate on the note to multiply changes in the reference index rate. The figure on the next page illustrates a bear floater that calls for a variable rate payment of twice LIBOR minus the fixed rate. If floating rates rise, the floating rate receiver will obtain a leveraged benefit.

Anatomy of a Five-Year Bear Floater

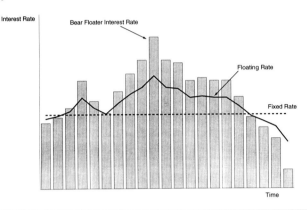

Bear Spread: A combination of options whose value increases (within limits) when the value of the underlying declines and declines when the underlying advances. *See also Bull Spread, Reverse Risk Reversal.*

Profit/Loss Pattern of a Bear Spread at Expiration

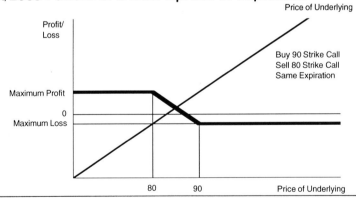

Bells and Whistles: Unusual or unique features of a financial instrument designed to appeal to a specific issuer or investor. Often used as a pejorative reference to features of an offering that seem to be added solely to attract attention.

Benchmark: (1) A reference index return or rate which serves as a basis for performance comparison or return calculation. (2) A standard specification for a physical commodity or financial instrument underlying a derivative.

Bermuda Option: Like the location of Bermuda, this option is located somewhere between a European-style option which can be exercised only at maturity and an American-style option which can be exercised anytime the option holder chooses. The Bermuda option typically can be exercised on a number of predetermined occasions as stated in the option contract. *Also known as Atlantic Option, Limited Exercise Option, and Quasi-American Option. See also Deferred Payment American Option, Japanese Option.*

Best Buy Option: A partial or full lookback call option.

Best Execution: In the United States, investment advisors have a fiduciary obligation to obtain the best possible net execution for the accounts they manage. In the United Kingdom, a similar obligation falls on a broker acting as the investment manager's agent. Determining what constitutes the best execution is often difficult.

Beta Factor: A measurement of stock price volatility *relative* to a broad market index. If a stock moves up and down twice as much as the market, it has a beta of 2. If it moves one half as much as the market, its beta is 0.5. Because it measures volatility *relatively* (to an index) rather than absolutely, the beta factor can be seriously misleading if used in stock option evaluation.

Better-of-Two-Assets Option: *See Alternative Option.*

Bid: The price at which a trader is willing to buy a security.

Bid-Asked Spread: The difference between the bid and offer price or rate. The most widely used comparative measure of market quality.

Bid-to-Cover Ratio: The ratio of the number of bids in a United States Treasury securities auction to the number of successful bids. Used as a rough measure of the success of the auction.

Bifurcation in Derivatives Taxation: Proposed Internal Revenue Service regulations that would treat hybrid instruments held by taxable United States investors as separate instruments for tax purposes. The effect would be to accelerate tax payments and create a risk that some losses might be unusable capital losses.

Biger and Hull Model: *See Garman-Kohlhagen Model.*

Bilateral Margining Agreement: A collateralization arrangement to assure both parties' performance on a swap or other OTC risk management contract. The agreement requires each counterparty to deposit margin with the other counterparty or a third party depending on the value of its net obligations. *See also Asymmetrical Margining Agreement.*

Bilateral Netting: An arrangement between two parties in which they exchange only the net difference in their obligations to each other. The primary purpose of netting is to reduce exposure to credit/settlement risk. *See also Netting by Novation.*

Bill: A debt instrument with an original life of less than one year. Usually issued at a discount to face value (e.g., United States Treasury bills) and redeemed at par.

Binary Option: *See All-or-Nothing Option (diagram).*

Binomial Model: A model of the form suggested by Cox, Ross, and Rubinstein and Sharpe which is based on the tendency of a binomial distribution to approach normality as a limit. The structure of the model is a branch network in which the underlying price or rate can rise or fall by a limited amount at each node. The weighted present values of the terminal node values are summed to determine option value. The binomial model is useful when the underlying distribution is normal or lognormal yet adjustments for cash flows and early exercise are necessary, and when option payoffs are path dependent. Efforts to use a binomial model to approximate results of non-normal distributions should be viewed with suspicion. By the central limit theorem, a binomial distribution will converge to the normal distribution despite efforts to delay convergence by varying up and down probabilities.

BIP, BP: *See Basis Point.*

Black-Scholes Equation: The primary differential equation used to determine the appropriate price or theoretical value of an option on the basis of a neutral hedge created with risk offsetting positions in the option and the underlying. Parameters or inputs to the equation include: spot price of the underlying, strike price of the option, interest rate, time until option expiration, and volatility of the underlying. The elegance and simplicity of the Black-Scholes model and its consistency with the capital asset pricing model of portfolio theory are responsible for its widespread adoption. The model's weaknesses are its restrictive assumptions. It requires modification or the use of alternative formulations in many real world circumstances. The Black-Scholes equation for the fair value of a European call option on a nondividend paying stock is*

$$C = SN(d_1) - Xe^{-rt} N(d_2)$$

where

C	= call option price
S	= current stock price
X	= exercise price
r	= short-term risk-free interest rate
e	= 2.718
$1n$	= natural logarithm
t	= time remaining to the expiration date (as a fraction of a year)
s	= standard deviation of the stock price
$N(.)$	= the cumulative normal probability

$$d_1 = \frac{1n\ (S/X) + (r + 0.5s^2)t}{s\sqrt{t}}$$

$$d_2 = d_1 - s\sqrt{t}$$

*Fischer Black and Myron Scholes, "The Pricing of Options and Corporate Liabilities." *Journal of Political Economy* 81 (May 1973), pp. 637–654.

Blended Interest Rate Swap: A combination of two or more interest rate swaps, usually one with a spot start and one with a forward start. The result of this structure is that payments are calculated on a weighted average of rates.

Blue-Sky Laws: The securities laws of individual states in the United States which regulate new securities issues and many secondary market transactions. The name comes from unrealistic promises made by some promoters of new securities.

Board Broker: An employee of the Chicago Board Options Exchange (CBOE) who handles customer limit orders to buy or sell options at prices away from the market.

BOATs: Yield differential warrants with a value tied to the yield spread between the French **OAT**s and the German **B**unds, a relationship that is often called the Maginot spread. *See International Spread Option, Warrant, or Note.*

Boiler Room: A high pressure securities or commodities sales operation often characterized by a high noise level designed to communicate excitement and urgency to customers at the other end of a telephone line.

Bond with Attached Warrant: A combination of a traditional bond or note and a call warrant on shares of the issuing firm. The warrant usually can be traded separately after the underwriting period. The structure differs from the traditional convertible bond in that the life of the warrant continues in the event the bond is called. Usually, the valuation of the bond with attached warrant is slightly different from that of a convertible bond, because the issuer's bond call provision would be used on the straight bond component of the bond with warrant issue under different circumstances than it would be used to call a convertible bond. The interest rate on the bond will be below market rates at issuance because of the value of the warrant, making a bond call unlikely. Unless the bond were usable at a premium to exercise the warrant, a bond call would not affect the life of the warrant.

Bond Basis: A method of interest calculation using a day count fraction equal to actual days divided by actual days in a year (usually 365). *See also Money Market Basis.*

Bond Option: An option with a bond or note as the underlying.

Bond-Over-Stock (BOS) Warrant: Outperformance warrant with a return based on the performance of a bond index less the return on a stock index. These instruments are issued on a variety of fixed income and equity indexes. *See also Stock-Over-Bond (SOB) Warrant.*

Bond Ratings: *See Appendix.*

Bond Warrant: *See Contingent Take Down Option.*

Book Entry Securities: Instruments represented in computer records rather than by traditional engraved certificates.

Bookout: A negotiated payment or settlement made in connection with the cancellation of a risk management agreement.

Borrower Option: A cap on a forward rate agreement.

Borrower's Option – Lender's Option (BO-LO): A debt instrument with embedded options giving the issuer (borrower) the right to change the coupon and the investor (lender) the right to put the instrument to the issuer if the rate is not acceptable.

Boston Option: (1) *Another name for Break Forward (diagram). Also called Cancellable Option, Forward Break, Forward with Optional Exit (FOX).* (2) Less frequently used to name a deferred premium option where the premium is deducted from the proceeds at exercise or paid at expiration if the option is not exercised. *Contrast with Contingent Premium Option.*

Bought Deal: (1) A securities underwriting characterized by a firm price or a rate guaranteed by the underwriting firm(s). This United Kingdom term describes a procedure relatively new in the United Kingdom but long standard in the United States. (2) The term is also used in the United Kingdom to describe secondary market transactions that would be called block trades in the United States.

Boundary Conditions: In the context of financial markets, boundary conditions are limitations on the value of an option or any other instrument determined by the provisions of the instrument and by the structure and value of any underlying instrument. Relevant boundaries for an option contract include relationships among the underlying price, the intrinsic value or forward intrinsic value of the option, and the stock price. Boundary conditions are usually expressed as equations that describe minimum and maximum values of the instrument under all possible circumstances. If boundary conditions are violated in the market, a risk-free arbitrage opportunity is created.

Box Spread: (1) This position can be visualized most easily as a combination of a long synthetic stock or index position (long call plus short put) and a short synthetic stock position (long put plus short call) which expire simultaneously and which have different strike prices. An alternate view of a box spread might combine put and call spreads. Box spreads were once used almost exclusively to transfer gains from one tax year to the next in the early days of options. Today they are used primarily to "borrow" or "lend" money because they are evaluated essentially on the basis of returns on the cash they tie up or free up. Index options which have European-style exercise provisions are used most frequently. Early exercise of American-style options destroys the box. (2) Offsetting long and short synthetic stock positions with different expirations. Often used to roll a position to a more distant expiration. If all the transactions opened new positions, the result would be a box spread. If one synthetic opened a distant position and the other closed a near position, it would be a jellyroll. *See Jellyroll, Synthetic Stock, Time Box.* (3) An over-the-counter interest rate spread contract.

Break Forward: An option-like mechanism used primarily in the currency markets to obtain full participation in a move in the underlying beyond a specified level without payment of an explicit option premium. The party long the break forward contract typically agrees to sell the underlying forward at a discount, or load, below the prevailing forward rate. The expected present value of this load pays for an option to cancel the forward agreement should the underlying rise above a predetermined level. The greater the load, the lower the price at which the holder of the option can cancel the forward agreement. *Also called a Boston Option (1), Cancellable Forward, Forward with Optional Exit (FOX).*

The Structure of a Break Forward

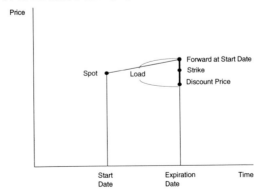

Break-Even Point: (1) The price at which a transaction produces neither a gain nor a loss. (2) A price on the underlying instrument at which two derivative strategies or a cash and a derivative strategy produce comparable gains or losses.

Break-Even Time: A simplistic technique used to evaluate the relative attractiveness of a convertible security and its underlying. Break-even time is calculated by dividing the premium over conversion value by a convertible's current yield advantage over the underlying, giving the time needed for the convertible's yield advantage to "cover" the premium. This calculation rarely gives an unequivocal indication of the relative attractiveness of a convertible.

Break Out: The process of undoing a conversion or a reversal, reestablishing the option buyer's original position. For example, an investor who sells stock short to convert a long call into a synthetic long put may cover the short stock position to "break out" the call.

Bretton Woods Agreement of 1944: A currency agreement which set fixed exchange rates for major currencies, provided for central bank intervention in currency markets, and set the price of gold at US$35 per troy ounce. The agreement controlled currency relationships for nearly 30 years.

British Bankers Association Interest Rate Swap (BBAIRS) Terms: A set of standardized terms for interest rate swaps, largely supplanted by the International Swap Dealers Association (ISDA) documentation.

Broken Dates: Settlement dates for forward currency contracts that fall within standard contract periods.

Broker: A financial market intermediary who acts as agent for one or both parties to a transaction. It is important to understand the difference between a broker who does not commit capital to a transaction and a dealer who may take one side of a trade for his firm's account. The broker receives a commission for service while the dealer hopes to find the other side of the transaction and earn a spread by closing out the position at a profit in a subsequent trade with another party.

Brokerage: Commissions. This usage is most common in Europe.

Brownian Motion: The name given to the irregular movement of pollen suspended in water. The phenomenon allegedly was observed by a botanist, Robert Brown, in 1828. This prototypical random movement was attributed to the effect of water molecules striking the pollen and dispersing it throughout the water. Although more recent work has suggested that Brown's optical equipment was not up to the observations he reported, the random process is the basis of many security price models. Also called a Wiener or Wiener/Bachelier process, Brownian motion is a type of Markov process. *See also Martingale, Stochastic Process.*

Bucket Shop: Prior to passage of securities legislation in the United States in the 1930s, many securities firms sold one-day or other short-term, over-the-counter, down-and-out calls or up-and-out puts. This practice was called *bucketing,* and the firms were called *bucket shops.* The term, which apparently originated in the practice of carrying beer into brothels in buckets, now characterizes any disreputable securities firm. Many states in the United States have bucket shop laws which impinge on the ability of financial intermediaries to create and trade certain types of over-the-counter instruments.

Bull or Bullish: (1) An individual who expects a market to rise. (2) A position that will benefit from a rising market.

Bull and Bear Notes: Terms used loosely to describe various tranches of interest rate or equity-linked instruments issued at the same time. A bear note can be a more "conservative" unit providing a higher minimum return and a lower ceiling than a bull note (which provides a wider range of returns). Alternatively, the bull and bear notes can be direct offsets of one another in which the return to the bear note is essentially the mirror image of the return to the bull note. Thus, the bear note benefits from a decline in the underlying or an increase in the rate structure over a range of underlying values, while the bull note benefits from rising prices and/or falling rates.

Bull-cum-Bear Options: A zero coupon note made up of a deep in-the-money call and a deep in-the-money put, either of which can be closed out prior to maturity to convert the overall position into either a call or a put. Because both options are so deeply in the money, the structure could almost be viewed as a bond attached to offsetting long and short forward contracts, either of which can be terminated early to provide desired market exposure.

Bull Floater: *See Reverse Floating Rate Note.*

Bull Spread: A partially risk offsetting option spread position which will be profitable if the underlying instrument rises in price. In one for one spread positions, the profit will be limited on the upside, and the downside risk will be limited to the net premium paid.

Profit/Loss Pattern of a Bull Spread at Expiration

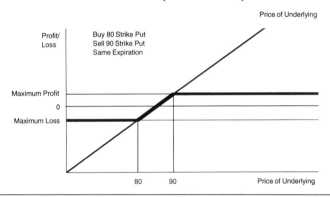

Bullet Maturity: A coupon paying debt instrument with no repayment of principal until maturity.

Bullet Swap: A swap with a constant notional principal reflecting a constant risk-offset requirement and/or the use of a debt security with full repayment of principal at maturity.

Bunds: German government bonds underlying the primary bond futures and options contracts denominated in Deutsche marks.

Bunny Bond: A coupon bond giving the investor the right to receive coupon payments in cash or in additional bonds with the same coupon as the underlying bond. The purpose of the structure is to offer the investor protection from reinvestment risk. *See also Guaranteed Coupon Reinvestment Bonds, Reinvestment Risk.*

Butterfly Spread: Although a few traders use different definitions, the most common butterfly spread combines a vertical bull and a vertical bear spread with the same expiration date on all options and the same strike price on all short options. The often sought, but unobtainable, "perfect butterfly" requires no net premium payment, assuring the buyer of profit at any price between the upper and lower strike prices with no possibility of a loss. *This structure is sometimes known as an Alligator Spread or a Sandwich Spread.*

The Profit/Loss Pattern of a Long Butterfly Spread

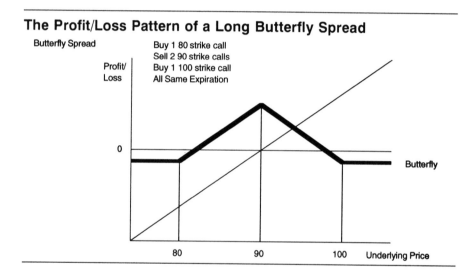

Buy Back: Purchase of a position to cover or offset a previously established short position.

Buy In: (1) When a call is exercised against an option writing account that does not hold a sufficient position in the called security, the broker may *buy in* the necessary position for delivery to the option holder. (2) Also, in short selling, if no securities can be borrowed to continue a short position, the broker will *buy in* securities for delivery, forcing the short seller to cover. This type of buy in occurs in issues with large short interests and/or small floats.

Buying the Basis: Buying a deliverable instrument or index-equivalent position and selling a futures position in an attempt to profit from a narrowing of the basis or from an attractive low-risk, interest-like return. *Also called a Cash and Carry Trade.*

Buy-Write: A covered call position created by simultaneously buying the underlying and selling the call.

Buy-write Option UNitary DerivativeS (BOUNDS):   An Americus Trust PRIME-like companion to the option exchanges' SCORE-like LEAPs proposed by the American Stock Exchange to fill the gap created by the expiration of the Americus Trust components. The functional equivalent of a covered call writer's position. Futures exchanges and the CFTC may challenge this instrument on grounds similar to those used to challenge index participations. *See also Americus Trust, Long-term Equity AnticiPation Securities (LEAPS).*

C

Calculation Agent: The party designated to calculate the amounts payable under a swap agreement.

Calendar Roll: An offset procedure by which a futures or option position is closed in one contract month and opened on the same side of the market in a more distant calendar month.

Calendar Spread: The option purchased in a calendar spread expires after the option sold. The number of contracts purchased equals the number sold and both options have the same strike price. For example, an investor who buys a December 80 call and sells a September 80 call is said to buy the Sept–Dec 80 call (calendar) spread. A calendar spread will be most profitable when the price of the underlying is very close to the strike on the expiration date of the short option.

Value of a Calendar Spread

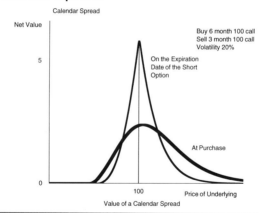

Value of a Calendar Spread

Call-adjusted Yield: The noncallable bond-equivalent yield on a callable bond. Obtained by subtracting the expected opportunity loss (due to exercise of the issuer's call privilege) from the basic yield to maturity. Similar adjustments are made in the calculation of call-adjusted duration and call-adjusted convexity. *See also Option-adjusted Spread.*

Call Feature: *See Call Provision.*

Call Loan Rate: The interest rate on short-term secured loans that can be cancelled (called) on 24 hours' notice.

Call Option: An option to buy. Call options on securities are ordinarily issued for a period of less than one year, but the term is now commonly applied to longer contracts. *See Option, Terms of Option Contract, Warrant.*

Long and Short Call Option Profit/Loss Patterns

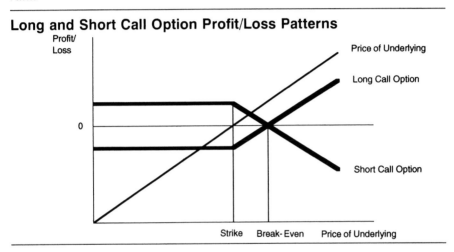

Call Or Put (COP):   *See As-You-Like Warrant.*

Call Premium: *See Premium, Call Price (1).*

Call Price: (1) The market price of an exchange-traded or over-the-counter call option. (2) The price at which a callable security can be retired by the issuer. In many cases, the call provision is a sequence of call prices which change over the life of the security.

Call Protection: Provisions in a bond or preferred stock indenture which provide for a length of time during which the issuer cannot call an issue or during which the issuer must pay a premium over parity to retire the issue.

Call Provision: A term in a bond indenture that gives the issuer of a bond the right (option) to call the bond for redemption and/or refunding at certain prices and at certain times. This option can be evaluated using techniques similar to those used in evaluating other options. *See Embedded Option.*

Call Risk: The lender's potential opportunity cost associated with unscheduled premature prepayment of principal on a debt instrument. Call risk is a special case of reinvestment risk, because it will usually be impossible to reinvest the funds in a similar instrument with an equal yield.

Call Spread: A spread consisting of partially risk offsetting long and short positions in at least two different calls on the same underlying stock. *See also Bull Spread, Calendar Spread, etc.*

Callable Securities: Typically, bonds or preferred issues, but occasionally warrants, which may be retired at the option of the issuer. The right to call an issue is often subject to certain conditions such as a time delay and/or the payment of a call premium. If a security is called, the holder may lose some of the market value of the position. The terms under which the issue may be called are described in the call feature or call provision section of the issuance documentation.

Callable Swap: A swap agreement in which the fixed rate receiver has the right to terminate the swap on one or more dates prior to its scheduled maturity. Like a puttable swap, this early termination provision is designed to protect a party from adverse effects of large changes in fixed rates. In this case, the receiver would be protected from a large increase in rates which would reduce the present value of his cash flow from the swap. The strike price might be stated in terms of a point on the swap yield curve. *See also Puttable Swaps.*

Called Away: The receipt of cash in return for the elimination of an underlying security position through the exercise of a call option (exercised against the position). Examples include a common stock position called away through the exercise of a short call option and a bond position called by the issuer under call provisions embedded in the bond indenture.

Cancellable Option: *See Break Forward. Also called Boston Option (1), Forward with Optional Exit (FOX).*

Cancellation of a Swap: Early termination of a swap agreement, usually accompanied by the payment by one counterparty to the other of an amount equal to the net present value of the swap. *See also Bookout.*

Cap: (1) A provision of a debt contract or a separate option agreement that, in effect, puts a ceiling or "cap" on an interest rate. For example, a floating rate borrower may buy an interest rate cap that limits interest cost to, say, eight percent even if rates go much higher. The form of the ceiling may vary. An embedded cap may actually impose a rate ceiling. A separate contract may pay the holder of the cap an amount equal to the amount by which market rates exceed the cap rate (times the notional principal). A cap usually consists of a strip or series of caplets — options putting a ceiling on rates for each rate reset period over the life of the cap. *See also Caplet.* (2) A similar option which puts a ceiling on rates or returns in foreign exchange or equity markets.

The Effective Interest Rate With and Without a Cap

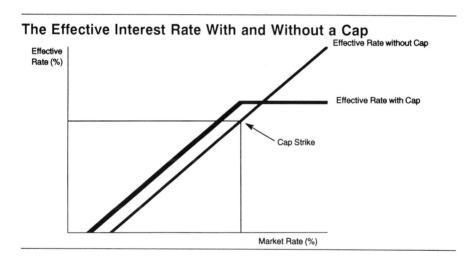

Cap and Floor: *See Interest Rate Collar, Risk Reversal.*

Cap and Floor Certificate: A packaged cap and floor on rates. The cap and floor typically bracket a series of readings in a floating reference index rate over the life of the certificate.

Cap Rate: The strike rate of a cap contract.

Capacity to Trade: The ability to enter into a binding contract of the specific type contemplated and to perform all fixed and contingent obligations under the contract. *See also Ultra Vires Act.*

Capital Adequacy Directive: *See Basle Convergence Agreement.*

Capital Asset Pricing Model (CAPM): A formal financial pricing/valuation model describing the relationship between expected risk and expected return for marketable assets. Although this classic model embodied in the security market line is not always empirically affirmed, it is the most widely used approach to relative asset evaluation. *Also called Mean Variance (MV) Portfolio Model and Modern Portfolio Theory (MPT).*

The Market Line of the Capital Asset Pricing Model

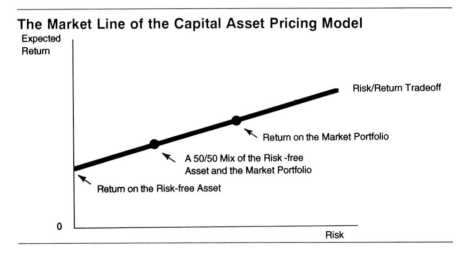

Capital Change: A stock split, stock dividend, merger, or spin-off that affects the number of shares of stock owned by an investor without necessarily affecting their aggregate value.

Capital Guarantee Notes: *See Equity-linked Notes.*

Capital Requirements: Equity or subordinated debt funding of a financial intermediary required by regulators to assure the stability and soundness of the institution. After a long period of relaxing capital requirements, recent trends have been in the direction of increasing capital and adjusting requirements to reflect the relative riskiness of an institution's assets and liabilities.

Capitalized Option: *See Contingent Premium Option.*

Caplet: One of the interim period cap components in a multiperiod interest rate cap agreement.

Capped Call: A long call position with a maximum payout — analogous in structure to a vertical bull spread position or a risk reversal. The terms under which the cap is exercised and the maximum call value may vary in different contracts and markets and should be checked carefully. *See, for example, Bull Spread, Capped Index Options (CAPS) for payoff diagrams.*

Capped Floating Rate Note: A floating rate note whose maximum rate is fixed in terms of the reference index rate, holding the issuer's interest payment down in a high rate environment. The premium received from sale of the cap increases the yield at rates below the cap rate plus the cap premium (in basis points).

Capped Index Options (CAPS): An exchange-traded, single contract, vertical option spread with European-style exercise plus an early exercise price trigger. CAPS incorporate in a single contract either two index calls or two index puts with the same expiration date and with strike prices 30 points apart. The two options are traded as a single, inseparable option spread contract. The early exercise price trigger terminates the contract and provides for settlement at the maximum value of the CAPS if the underlying closes at or through the cap or outstrike price (the upper strike price on call CAPS and the lower strike price on put CAPS) at any time during the life of the CAPS contract. If the early exercise trigger does not terminate the CAPS sooner, automatic European-style exercise occurs at expiration. The subtlety of some features of this contract suggests a careful reading of exchange literature. See figures on next page.

Capped Lookback Calls: A call option with a lookback strike and a ceiling on the settlement price or rate or on the total value of the settlement.

Capped Swap: An interest rate swap with an embedded cap on the floating rate payment.

Caption: An option to buy a cap. At the expiration of a caption, the holder has the right to purchase a cap with a contractual strike rate for a prespecified premium. *See also Cap, Compound Option.*

Carrying Charge Market: A forward or futures market in which the forward price is *higher* than the spot price by approximately the net cost of purchasing the spot commodity or security and storing and/or financing it

The Payoff Patterns of Put and Call CAPS

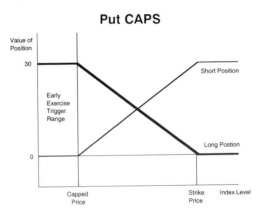

Put CAPS

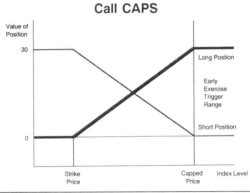

Call CAPS

until the settlement date of the futures contract. The opposite of a Backwardation Market. *Also called a Contango Market. See Basis.*

Cash-and-Carry Trade: An arbitrage-type position — typically consisting of a long position in an underlying and a short position in a futures contract — whose risk offsetting features transform the net position into the equivalent of a short-term money market instrument maturing at the expiration of the futures contract. *See also Index Arbitrage, Buying the Basis.*

Cash Enhancement Strategy: Any of a number of techniques designed to create the risk equivalent of a short-term money market portfolio with a superior return. Arbitrage techniques are used to obtain a higher rate of return at this very low level of risk. *See Buying the Basis, Cash-and-Carry Trade, Index Arbitrage.*

Cash Extraction Strategy: Any transaction or series of transactions in which an underlying position is exchanged for an approximately risk-equivalent derivative position that permits the investor to remove cash from the account. Adding back the cash return, the revised position should retain a return pattern that replicates the original position very closely.

Cash Flow Matching: A risk management technique which attempts to match assets and liabilities by purchasing a portfolio with periodic cash flows equal to expected liabilities for each period. *Also called Dedicating a Portfolio or Immunization of a Portfolio.*

Cash Flow Swap: A swap with irregular cash flows.

Cash-Futures Swap: *See Exchange of Futures for Physicals (EFP).*

Cash Index Participation (CIP): *See Index Participations.*

Cash Market: The market for securities, physical commodities, or other traditional investments, many of which serve as underlying instruments for derivative risk management contracts.

Cash Or Titles Option (COTO): A convertible instrument issued in Switzerland that let investors avoid the dividend withholding tax and let corporations raise capital. COTOs typically had an expiration date up to 12 months in the future and gave the holder the right to receive a cash dividend or exchange the COTO for new shares at a fixed price. COTOs ran into Swiss government opposition as a tax avoidance device.

Cash Settlement: (1) In contrast to traditional stock and bond option contracts and most commodity futures, many currency, fixed-income, and stock index options and financial futures contracts are settled with a cash payment based on the difference between the settlement price and the strike (options) or the settlement price and the previous settlement price (futures). (2) An alternative to activating a swap at the expiration of a swaption is to survey the market and calculate the cash value of the swaption which is paid to the holder upon exercise. (3) Delivery of securities against cash for settlement on the trade date. *Also called Same Day Settlement.*

Cash Settled Option: Although traditional option contracts call for delivery of the underlying in settlement following exercise of the option, many currency, fixed-income, stock index and basket options, and some options on stocks with restricted transferability are settled for cash equal to the difference between the strike price and the spot price of the underlying at the time of exercise.

Ceiling: *See Cap.*

Central Limit Theorem: The proposition that the distribution of a sum of independent, random variables that are not themselves normally distributed will approach a normal distribution if the number of observations in the sum is large enough. This theorem has been misused by advocates of certain option strategies by applying it to truncated return distributions. The sum of these truncated returns will require more time than any investor can count on to approach normality. *See also Binomial Model.*

Centrale de Lívraíson de Valuers Mobiliéres (CEDEL): One of two clearing houses for Euromarket securities. *See also Euroclear.*

Certificate of Accrual on Treasury Securities (CATS): Zero coupon instruments created by stripping United States Treasury securities. *See also Stripped Treasury Securities.*

Certificate for Amortizing Revolving Debt (CARD): Securitized credit card debt. *See Asset-Backed Security (ABS).*

Certificate for Automobile Receivables (CARs): Securities backed by a pool of automobile loans. *See also Asset-Backed Security (ABS).*

Certificateless Clearing: In contrast to the securities markets where physical delivery of certificates evidencing ownership of stocks and bonds is now giving way to electronic book entry of positions, options and futures have always been traded with no more than a broker's confirmation slip as evidence of most transactions.

Cheapest to Deliver (CTD): On certain commodity and fixed income derivatives contracts, a variety of "grades" of the underlying can be delivered at any of several delivery points, or a number of eligible bonds or notes can be delivered in satisfaction of the short's obligation. The market price of the derivative contracts reflects the assumption that the delivery requirement will be met by the short in the form of the cheapest instrument to deliver.

Cherry Picking: A practice in some bankruptcy proceedings of enforcing contracts favorable to the bankrupt and abrogating related obligations to unsecured creditors. Swap offset agreements and recent changes in United States law are designed to tie the two sides of a swap together and prevent cherry picking. United Kingdom law revisions to permit swap offsets in insolvency are under consideration.

Chinese Wall: In United States securities regulation, a set of procedures designed to segregate some components of the information flow within an organization to prevent nonpublic information held or developed in one part of the organization from being used illegally in another part of the organization. For example, a Chinese wall usually isolates information in an investment banking operation from trading and investment management.

Chooser Option: *See As-You-Like Warrant.*

Churning: Trading more for the sake of generating commissions or trading spreads than for the benefit of the account where the activity takes place.

Circuit Breakers: A complex and frequently changed series of rules adopted by securities and futures exchanges in the aftermath of the 1987 market break in an attempt to slow down market activity during major stock price movements.

Circus Swap: A currency coupon swap with $/LIBOR as the floating rate. Often used to link fixed rate swaps in two currencies which do not have active swap markets. *See Currency Coupon Swap.*

Class of Options: All listed option contracts of the same type covering the same underlying security, e.g., all listed Texas Instruments common stock call options.

Clearing: The process of settling a trade — including the deposit of any necessary collateral with the clearing corporation and exchange of any cash payments between the parties.

Clearing Corporation: The affiliate or subsidiary of a futures or options exchange which clears trades and holds performance bonds posted by dealers to assure performance on their own and customers' futures and options obligations. Called a clearing house in the United Kingdom.

Clearing House: The British term for clearing corporation.

Clearing Member: An exchange member authorized to deal directly with the clearing corporation when settling a trade executed on the exchange floor or through an electronic order matching system. Parties to every trade exchange names or other information identifying their clearing member. The clearing member is responsible for any collateral or cash exchanges with the clearing corporation, carries the position, and is responsible for its ultimate settlement or disposition.

Cliquet Option: (1) Originally a ratchet option (from *vilbrequin à cliquet*—ratchet brace). *See Ladder Option or Note.* (2) Less commonly, a rolling spread with strike price resets, usually at regular intervals. (3) An exploding or knockout option such as CAPS (from *cliqueter*—to knock). *See Exploding Option.* As this list of definitions suggests, the French like the sound of "cliquet" and seem prepared to apply the term to almost any option structure.

Close: (1) The price of the final trade or, alternately, the closing trading range in a trading session. (2) The time period near the end of a trading session. (3) To eliminate a position through an offsetting purchase or sale.

Closing Date: The date on which a transaction is completed with the transfer of ownership and the payment and receipt of funds.

Closing Purchase Transaction: A transaction in which an investor terminates his short option or futures obligation by purchasing a fungible contract having the same terms as a contract previously sold.

Closing Range: The range of prices within which a buy or sell order can be executed near the end of a futures market trading session.

Closing Rotation: *See Rotation.*

Closing Sale Transaction: A transaction in which an investor liquidates a long option or futures position by selling a fungible contract having the same terms as the contract previously purchased.

CMO Swaps: Collateralized mortgage obligation swaps with amortization of the notional principal linked to the repayment rate of a mortgage pool or the principal prepayment rate of a specific CMO tranche.

Cocktail Swap: A complex transaction involving several swaps of different types and more than two counterparties.

COFI Swap: An interest rate swap with the floating payment stream linked to the 11th District Cost of Funds Index (COFI). This rate is often used in swaps with savings institutions as counterparties.

Collar: (1) A feature of a debt contract or a separate agreement that puts both a cap (ceiling) and a floor (minimum) on the interest rate. (2) An option contract or set of contracts that limits downside risk in the underlying below a floor price and eliminates upside participation beyond a cap price. *See Interest Rate Collar, Risk Reversal.*

Collar Swap: An interest rate swap with an embedded collar on the floating rate payment.

Collared FRN: A floating rate note with an embedded collar.

Collateral: An obligation or security linked to another obligation or security to secure its performance. For example, an option writer may deposit with his bank or broker common stock in the company on which an option is written as collateral to guarantee performance on the option. He may also deposit securities convertible into the underlying stock or completely unrelated securities with an appropriate market value. Collateral is also posted as a performance bond to guarantee performance on listed futures contracts and on various over-the-counter contracts.

Collateralized Bond Obligation (CBO): A multitranche debt structure similar to a collateralized mortgage obligation (CMO) structure with low-rated bonds rather than mortgages as the collateral. *See also Collateralized Mortgage Obligation, Tranche.*

Collateralized Increasable Yield Notes: A combination of medium-term notes and a commodity futures pool which is designed to produce a guaranteed minimum return (often zero) and upside participation linked to the performance of the futures pool.

Collateralized Mortgage Obligation (CMO): A generic term for a security backed by real estate mortgages. CMO payment obligations are covered by interest and/or principal payments from a pool of mortgages. In addition to its generic meaning, the term CMO usually suggests a nongovernmental issuer. *See also Government National Mortgage Association Pass-through Certificates (GNMAs), Interest Only Obligation (IO), Principal Only Obligation (PO), Real Estate Mortgage Investment Conduit (REMIC).* CMOs are also known as *Fast-Pay/Slow-Pay Bonds and Serialized Mortgage-backed Securities* because they usually have a multitranche structure with interest and principal payments prioritized and segmented.

Collateralized Security: A debt instrument secured by an asset or a pool of assets.

Combination Option: Traditionally, an option consisting of at least one put and one call. The component options may be exercised or resold separately, but they are originally traded as a unit. The term is now applied loosely to any package of several different options. *See Spraddle, Spread, Straddle, Strangle, Strap, Strip.*

Commercial Real Estate-backed Bonds: Asset-backed securities with a single property or a real estate portfolio as collateral. This structure is used to increase the liquidity of real estate loans.

Commission: A transaction fee charged by a broker for acting as agent in a transaction. *Also called Brokerage, Courtage. See also Broker.*

Commodity Futures Trading Commission (CFTC): The regulatory agency charged with regulation of futures and futures option markets in the United States.

Commodity Index Notes: A traditional note with some or all of its positive return tied to the performance of a specific commodity or commodity index such as oil, gold, silver, the CRB index, etc. The participation in the commodity price may be in the form of either an option or a forward component. Often issued by a producer of the underlying commodity. *Also called Commodity-linked Notes or Bonds.*

Commodity Option: An option to buy (call) or sell (put) a specific commodity or commodity futures contract at a given strike price within a specified time.

Commodity Swap: A swap in which counterparties exchange cash flows based on a commodity price on at least one side. *See Swap.*

Commodity Trading Advisor (CTA):   The approximate futures market equivalent of a Registered Investment Adviser in the securities market in the United States.

Companion Collateralized Mortgage Obligation: Volatile CMO tranches that, for example, get principal first or interest last to stabilize the cash flows to other tranches. *Also called Support CMOs.*

Competitive Currency Risk: Currency exchange rate risk that affects a firm's competitiveness in a product line also produced by a competitor whose costs are incurred in a foreign currency. If the competitor's currency weakens, his relative competitive position improves because his costs decline relative to international competition. A producer facing competition of this sort can use currency contracts to match the competitor's cost structure.

Complete Markets: Markets in which investors have a full range of risk/return choices. Investment opportunities are presented in the form of basic components which the investor can assemble on a customized basis to conform to a personal utility function. One of the important contributions of derivative instruments is to increase investor utility by increasing the range of choices.

Completion Portfolio or Fund: A selection of stocks or, less frequently, bonds which fills "gaps" in a portfolio and improves its tracking with a designated benchmark index. Completion funds are often used by pension plan sponsors or endowment investment funds to add asset categories not covered by active managers.

Complex Option: An option with a change in the exercise price and/or whose underlying quantity may change over time. *Examples include Quantos and Step-Up or Step-Down Options.*

Compliance Procedures: Policies designed to ensure that a securities or futures firm's personnel follow rules imposed by government regulators and exchanges.

Component (COM) Bond: A collateralized mortgage obligation composed of non-detachable components. The principal pay type and/or sequence of principal pay of each component may vary.

Compound Average Rate Option: An option to buy a currency average rate put or call. *See also Average Price or Rate Option, Compound Option.*

Compound Option: (1) As the name implies, a compound option is an option on an option, such as a put on a call, a call on a put, a call on a call, or a put on a put. These options are used primarily in fixed income and currency markets when the need for the risk protection afforded by an option is not certain and the buyer of the compound option would like to pay a reduced initial premium. The contingency on the first option usually determines the need for the protection provided by the second option. (2) The term is occasionally used to refer to a call option on the shares of a leveraged company. Common shareholders, in effect, have a call option to "buy" the firm by paying off its debt. Alternately, shareholders cannot lose more than the cost of their shares if they abandon the firm to the debt holders. Robert Geske and others have used such examples to demonstrate that a call option on common stock can be usefully valued as an option on an option. Compound option techniques are often useful in evaluating early exercise options and in a variety of fixed-income option valuation applications. *See also Caption, Floortion, Split-Fee Option.*

Comptant: Cash transaction on a Swiss or French stock exchange.

Concertina Swap: A variable notional principal swap that uses the present value of an existing fixed-rate paying swap position to increase an issuer's near-term protection from high floating rates by reducing the fixed rate payment period and increasing the notional principal or increasing both the fixed rate and the notional principal. Reversing these transactions when rates drop will reduce the notional principal.

Conditional Forward Purchase Contract: A forward agreement under which the long side of the contract has the right to cancel the purchase by paying a fee to the short on the contract maturity date. Alternatively, the cancellation fee can be eliminated if the long guarantees a trade price sufficiently lower than the forward price. This contract and the conditional forward sale contract are variants of the break forward contract. *See also Break Forward Contract.*

Conditional Forward Sale Contract: The mirror image of a conditional forward purchase contract. The short side of the contract has the right to abandon the agreement by paying a fee or by guaranteeing a sale at a price sufficiently above the forward price.

Condor: A complex option spread that is similar to a butterfly except for the fact that the two short options have different strikes. Extinct in transaction cost-sensitive portfolios. *See Butterfly Spread.*

Long Condor Profit/Loss Pattern

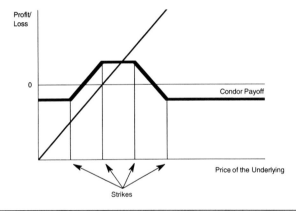

Confidence Intervals: An estimate of the probability (confidence) that an observation will fall within or outside a range designated by standard deviation intervals. The development of confidence intervals is based on the value of the cumulative normal density function between two points, so care must be taken that the underlying distribution is normal. *See Normal Distribution for a more detailed discussion.*

Constant Elasticity of Variance Model: A probability-type option evaluation model which incorporates a variance adjustment that causes the absolute level of the variance to decline as the stock price rises and causes the variance to rise as the stock price declines. Empirically, most volatilities do respond to price changes in approximately this way.

Constant Maturity Treasury (CMT): An interest rate benchmark index based on the yield of a synthetic security of appropriate maturity as interpolated from the Treasury yield curve.

Constant Maturity Treasury Option (CMT Option): A put or cap structure created for payers of annuities that pays off if the synthetic one-year Treasury rate rises above a strike rate. The CMT option holder benefits from any rate decline after deduction of the CMT option premium.

Constant Proportion Portfolio Insurance (CPPI): A portfolio insurance technique that exposes a constant multiple of a cushion over an investor's floor value to the equity market. Unlike other portfolio insurance models, CPPI is consistent with traditional utility functions and with the capital asset pricing model. *See Portfolio Insurance.*

Construction Loan Swap: *See Accreting Principal Swap.*

Contango: *See Carrying Charge Market.*

Contingent Cap: An interest rate cap contract for which the buyer of the cap pays no upfront premium but agrees to pay a predetermined premium if the cap has any value on its effective date. The premium for a contingent cap will be much greater than the premium on an ordinary cap but the premium will be paid only if the cap is in the money at expiration. *See Contingent Premium Option.*

Contingent Claim: A derivative asset whose value at any settlement date is determined by the value of one or more other assets. *See also Derivative Instrument or Product.*

Contingent Currency Risk: Currency exchange rate risk associated with a transaction that may or may not occur. A contract proposal, for example, may be hedged with a traditional option or with one of several specialized options designed for this problem. *See, for example, Contingent Hedge with an Agreement for Rebate at Maturity (CHARM), Shared Currency Option Under Tender (SCOUT).*

Contingent Hedge with an Agreement for Rebate at Maturity (CHARM): A currency option designed for companies bidding on foreign contracts. If the company wins the contract, the option may be exercised like any other currency option. If the company loses the contract, the option is void, but the issuer rebates a portion of the premium. Consequently, the value of the payoff depends on the buyer's ability to obtain business requiring currency protection as well as on currency movements. The rebate serves the dual function of relating the net premium to the value of the hedge and facilitating the hedging position taken by the currency option dealer.

Contingent Immunization: A fixed-income portfolio management technique that has some characteristics in common with portfolio insurance in equity markets. The manager of a contingently immunized portfolio may have considerable flexibility in the yield and duration of the positions used in the portfolio as long as the positions perform well relative to the associated liability. If the portfolio performs poorly, the manager will move to a portfolio that matches (immunizes) the duration and return requirements of the liabilities.

Contingent Order: An order to purchase or sell one security whose execution depends on the execution and the price of an order in another instrument. Contingent orders are frequently used in the execution of futures rolls and option spread transactions and in the establishment and liquidation of buy-writes.

Contingent Premium Option: A contract in which the buyer of the option pays no premium up front but agrees to pay a predetermined premium if the option has *any* value at expiration. The premium for a contingent premium option will exceed that of an ordinary option, but the premium will be paid only if the option is in the money at expiration. *Contrast with Deferred Premium Option.*

The Premium, Payoff, and Profit/Loss of a Contingent Premium Option

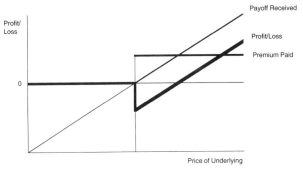

Contingent Premium Swaption: A contract conferring the right to buy or sell a swap on fixed terms. As with any contingent premium option, the holder pays a premium only if the option is in the money at the time of exercise or expiration. Because of the contingent premium feature, the premium will exceed the premium on a standard swaption. *See also Contingent Premium Option.*

Contingent Swap: A swap agreement that takes effect only if some designated event occurs, such as an acquisition or an interest rate move. Usually one party, needing the risk adjustment of the swap in the event of this contingency, will pay an option premium to the other party. A swaption is a specific type of contingent swap with its value and exercise contingent on an interest rate. *See also Swaption.*

Contingent Takedown Option: An option to buy a fixed-income security, usually issued as a "kicker" (attached to another fixed-income security). This option gives the buyer of a bond or note an option to acquire a second bond with a similar coupon.

Contingent Value Rights (CVRs): A contingent instrument issued in an acquisition to give selling shareholders a stake in the surviving company. CVRs may take the form of a put spread to guarantee that the total proceeds from the exchange of stock reach a certain value or the form of a call warrant with a payoff tied to the revenue or earnings of the acquired business.

Contract: (1) An over-the-counter risk management agreement. (2) The unit of trading on an option or futures exchange. The terms of the contract are set by the exchange with the concurrence of its regulator. Although mini-contracts are sometimes introduced for the retail market, it is not possible to trade fractional contract units.

Contract Grade: A cash market instrument or commodity eligible for delivery in settlement of a futures contract.

Contract Month: The settlement or expiration month of an exchange-traded option or futures contract.

Contract Period: A reference to the life of any risk management agreement but especially to the effective term of a forward rate agreement (FRA).

Conventional Option: An over-the-counter *stock* option issued in the United States. With nearly 1,000 stocks covered by exchange-listed options, the conventional stock option market continues to shrink. *See Put and Call Brokers and Dealers Association.*

Conventions of a Market: Most risk management products and markets have adopted standard terms or default provisions that are part of any agreement unless parties agree to a different provision (examples include $/LIBOR as the default reference index rate in interest rate swaps and Telerate as the standard source of Treasury rates). In contrast to the over-the-counter market, the conventions of an exchange market ordinarily cannot be modified by a simple agreement of the parties to a contract.

Convergence: One of the tests of the quality of a derivative market is how closely the derivative forward price converges to the spot price at expiration. Some markets, such as the market in S&P-500 futures, are characterized by almost perfect convergence: An arbitrager can be confident that a long stock index replicating portfolio sold at the opening on expiration day will match the value of the cash settlement on the related futures contract almost exactly. In other markets where an investor cannot be certain of trading at the settlement price, convergence is less certain, and the pricing relationship between the underlying and the futures contract is more tenuous. Other things equal, markets with good convergence and close spot/futures trading relationships tend to be liquid markets.

Conversion: (1) The process by which a put can be changed to a call and a call to a put. To convert a put to a call, the converter buys the put and the cash underyling and issues a call. To convert a call to a put, the converter buys the call, sells the cash underyling short and issues a put. *See also Break Out, Reversal.* (2) The exchange of a convertible security for the underlying instrument. (3) Selling a call against a long outright forward currency position. See figures on next page.

The Conversion Equation: Long Put + Long Stock = Long Call

Long Put

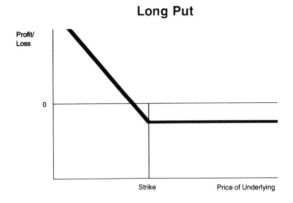

Plus

Long Stock

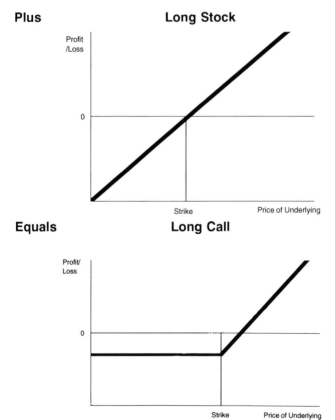

Equals

Long Call

Conversion Premium (on a Convertible Bond): The additional amount or percentage that the purchaser of a convertible bond pays over parity with the underlying. Note the analogy to the concept of premium in the United Kingdom warrant market. *See Premium (3) and (4).*

Conversion Premium on a Convertible Bond

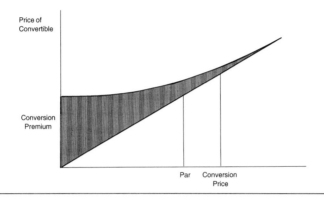

Conversion Price: The share price at which the face amount of a convertible bond or convertible preferred is converted into stock.

Conversion Ratio: The number of shares which an investor receives in exchange for a convertible bond or convertible preferred.

Convertible Adjustable Preferred Stock (CAPS): A floating rate preferred issue, convertible on dividend payment dates into a variable number of the issuer's common shares. The number of shares is equal in market value to the par value of the preferred (usually subject to a cap). The convertible feature is designed to give the adjustable rate preferred investor greater liquidity and to protect principal if necessary.

Convertible Adjustable Rate Mortgages (Convertible ARMs): Adjustable rate mortgages that are convertible into fixed rate mortgages upon payment of a service charge.

Convertible Exchangeable Preferred Stock: A convertible preferred issue that is exchangeable at the issuer's option for convertible debt with identical yield and identical conversion terms. Designed to permit an issuer to switch to a lower cost (tax deductible) obligation when its earnings become taxable.

Convertible Gilts: United Kingdom government bonds that give the holder an option to convert them into longer maturity bonds on specified terms.

Convertible Money Market Units (CMM): Unlike the more popular equity-linked notes, convertible money market units provide a high return if an equity-linked instrument appreciates but provide full participation (less the accumulated yield) in a downside move if the value of the equity instrument or index declines *(see diagram)*. Whereas an equity-linked note provides a return pattern often reminiscent of a long call, the convertible money market unit provides a return pattern similar to that experienced by a covered call writer. Someday a philosopher will analyze why institutional investors generally sell covered calls rather than buy puts against their portfolios but tend to buy equity-linked notes rather than convertible money market units.

Return Pattern of Convertible Money Market Units

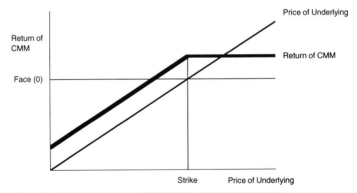

Convertible Option Contract: A currency option with a trigger price feature that converts the option into a forward foreign exchange contract when the exchange rate trades to or through the trigger price.

Convertible Reset Debentures: A convertible bond with a required upward interest rate adjustment, typically effective several years after issuance. The issuer is required to reset the coupon high enough to give the debentures a market value at least equal to their face or par value. The purpose of the reset is to compensate the bond holder for any credit deterioration. The reset will frequently encourage the issuer to refinance or, perhaps, to force conversion.

Convertible Security: A bond, preferred stock, or warrant that is convertible under prescribed circumstances into the common stock of a corporation or into some other security with or without a supplementary payment of cash or "useable" securities.

Convertible Stock Note: A "debt" instrument which pays coupons and principal in common stock of the issuer. A variety of mandatory convertible bond.

Convexity: (1) In a fixed-income instrument, convexity is a measure of the way duration and price change on a particular instrument when interest rates change. A bond or note is said to have positive convexity if the instrument's value increases at least as much as duration predicts when rates drop and decreases less when rates rise. Positive convexity is desirable because it makes a position more valuable after a price change than its duration value suggests. (2) In an option position, convexity is a measure of the way the value of the position changes in response to a change in the volatility or price of the underlying instrument. A position with positive convexity (gamma) maintains or increases its value better than delta predicts when volatility increases or when prices change by a large percentage in either direction. A position with negative convexity loses value relative to delta's prediction when prices change in either direction. *See also Gamma.*

Convexity Hedge: Another name for a reverse option hedge or a long straddle. The name comes from the tendency of these positions to increase in value with increasing volatility or a large one-time price movement.

Core Liquidity Provider: A large scale market maker which is such a large factor in a market that bid/asked spreads would widen if it withdrew from the market.

Corner: (1) The act of gaining control of enough of the items trading or available for trading in a market to dictate prices and terms to other market participants. (2) The state of such control.

Correlation Coefficient: A statistical measure of the extent to which two variables (usually prices or rates in financial market applications) move together. Correlation coefficients are widely used in arbitrage-type activities and in index replication strategies. A correlation coefficient of 1.0 implies that prices or rates track perfectly. A figure of 0.0 suggests the absence of any measurable direct relationship. A negative correlation coefficient of −1.0 indicates a perfect offsetting relationship.

Corridor: (1) A combination of two caps, one purchased by a borrower at a set strike and the second sold by the borrower at a higher strike to, in effect, reduce the price of the first cap. The two cap structure limits interest costs unless rates rise through the strike on the upper cap. At that rate, the borrower's interest costs begin rising again. (2) A collar on a swap created with two swaptions — the structure and participation interval is determined by the strikes and types of the swaptions.

Effective Interest Rate Paid by a Borrower with a Corridor

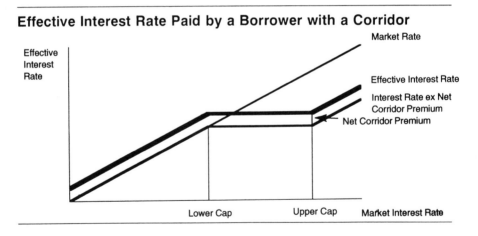

Cost of Carry: (1) The net out-of-pocket cost of holding a cash market position. (2) A model for the pricing of futures contracts, particularly financial futures, which describes the fair value of the futures contract in terms of the net cost incurred to hold a long cash position and a short futures position through the settlement date of the futures contract.

Cost of Funds Index (COFI):   An interest rate reference index based on the cost of funds to 11th District (United States) savings and loan associations. *See COFI Swap.*

Counterparty: One of the participants in a swap agreement or any other risk management contract.

Counterparty Risk: The expected cost of possible credit and "moral hazard" losses associated with the chance that a risk management agreement counterparty will default on contractual obligations. *See also Moral Hazard.*

Country Limit: A risk management policy that limits exposure to borrowers or counterparties in a particular country.

Country Risk: Legal, political, settlement, and other risks associated with a cross-border transaction.

Coupon: (1) The nominal annual rate of interest on a bond or note usually expressed as a percentage of the face value. (2) A piece of paper which is detached from a bearer bond and exchanged for a quarterly, semi-annual, or annual interest payment.

Coupon Stripping: *See Stripped Treasury Securities.*

Coupon Swap: A traditional fixed-for-floating interest rate swap.

Courtage: Brokerage or commission charges on a French or Swiss stock exchange.

Covariance: A measure of the correspondence between the movement of two random variables such as securities prices or returns. The correlation coefficient is a normalized covariance measure that is independent of the units of measurement. *See also Correlation Coefficient.*

Covariance Assets: Categories of investments added to a portfolio because their returns are not highly correlated with returns on the domestic stocks and bonds which are the fund's principle holdings. These low covariance assets may not improve average returns, but they reduce return variation and, consequently, often increase compound returns. Examples of covariance assets include real estate, foreign stocks and bonds, and gold mining shares.

Covenant: A provision of a loan or risk management agreement that requires or prohibits certain actions by a borrower or a risk management agreement counterparty. Covenants may limit dividends, require maintenance of working capital, set a ceiling on compensation, etc. If a covenant is violated, the instrument is considered in default. *See also Negative Pledge Agreement.*

Cover: (1) To buy back instruments previously sold. Typically used to describe the closing of a short position. (2) A hedge position purchased from a third party to offset the market risk of a derivative issuance or OTC risk management agreement. For example, many investment banks purchase cover for the option components of equity or index-linked instruments from one or more of the major financial intermediaries specializing in risk management products.

Coverage: Any of several ratios of cash flow or income available to meet obligations to the size of the total or immediate obligations.

Coverage Period: The interim period in a swap or other periodic reset agreement during which a specific set of terms are effective. The aggregate of the interim coverage periods is the total coverage period of the agreement.

Covered Arbitrage: Creation of a synthetic foreign exchange forward contract with a pair of zero coupon debt instruments denominated in each of the two currencies.

Covered Call: A short call option collateralized by a long position in the underlying. *Also called a Buy-Write. See Covered Writer (diagram).*

Covered Interest Arbitrage: A simple currency swap in which the counterparties exchange currencies at both the spot and forward rates simultaneously. The forward swap restores currency exposures to the original position without a currency gain or loss making this a way of adjusting exposure to a narrowing or widening of interest rate differentials rather than adjusting currency exposures.

Covered OPtion Securities (COPS): A short-term note with a high coupon and an embedded put giving the issuer the right to pay interest and principal in a foreign currency at an exchange rate fixed at issuance.

Covered Warrant: A stock, basket, or index warrant issued by a party other than the issuer of the underlying stock(s) and secured by the warrant issuer's holding in the underlying securities or the warrant issuer's general credit standing. Covered warrants are most common in Europe and parts of Asia. Often they are issued by investment banks when transfer of the underlying security is temporarily or permanently restricted, when traditional warrants are not available, or when buyers want security and currency warrant combinations not otherwise available in the market.

Covered Writer: A call option writer who owns the underlying stock which is subject to option. An investor setting up an option hedge or writing multiple options may be covered with respect to part of the option position and uncovered with respect to the rest. *See Option Hedge, Uncovered Writer.* See figures on the next page.

Crack Spread: An oil refiner's operating margin embodied in the relative prices of crude oil and refined products spot, futures, or forward contracts.

Credit Card Receivable-backed Securities: Asset-backed instruments with consumer credit card obligations as the securitized collateral. *Also called Certificate for Amortizing Revolving Debt (CARD).*

Credit Enhanced Debt Securities: Bonds or notes with special investor protection that gives them a better credit standing than ordinary debt of the issuer would have. To obtain enhanced credit, an issuer may pay a guarantor or endorser for a letter of credit or a surety bond which lends the guarantor's higher credit to the issuer. The purpose of credit enhancement is to achieve a lower net borrowing cost.

Credit Equivalent Amount: The result of translating the off balance sheet liabilities of a financial intermediary into the approximate risk equivalent of loans.

Credit Exposure in a Swap: Net credit exposure is the reduction in the present value of the net swap cash flows if the swap had to be replaced at current market terms for the remaining life of the original swap. This calculation assumes an enforceable netting agreement is in place.

Credit Quality Rating: *See Table of Bond Ratings in the Appendix.*

The Covered Call Writer's Profit/Loss Position at Expiration

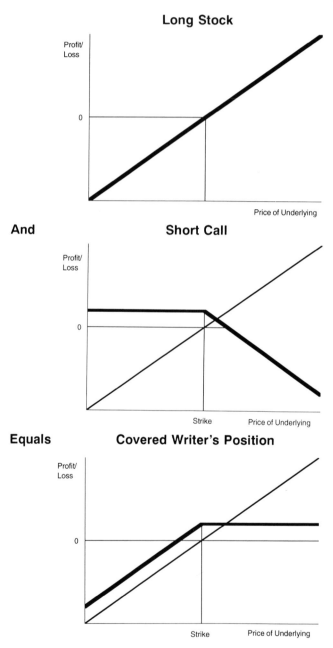

Credit Risk: (1) Exposure to loss as a result of default on a swap, debt, or other counterparty instrument. (2) Exposure to loss as a result of a decline in market value stemming from a credit downgrade of an issuer or counterparty. Credit risk may be reduced by credit screening before a transaction is effected or by instrument provisions which attempt to offset the effect of a default or which require increased payments by the issuer in the event of a credit downgrade.

Credit Risk Premium: The component of a debt instrument's yield (or price discount) that reflects the expected value (cost) of the risk of a possible default. The credit risk premium is usually expressed in basis points. (It is occasionally as much as several hundred basis points.)

Credit Sensitive Note: Fixed or floating rate note with an interest rate reset in the event of a change in the issuer's credit rating.

Credit Spread: (1) *See Quality Spread.* (2) An option spread which generates a net cash inflow into the investor's account when it is initiated.

Credit Watch: An alert or warning issued by a credit rating agency in anticipation of a credit upgrade or downgrade. *See Table of Bond Ratings in the Appendix.*

à la Criée: (France and Switzerland) Open outcry.

Cross-Currency Basis Swap: An interest rate swap with both counterparties as floating rate payers in their respective currencies.

Cross-Currency Cap: An option which pays the holder any positive difference between the spread on two different currency base (LIBOR) rates and a strike spread.

Cross-Currency Option: An outperformance option struck at an exchange rate between two currencies. Often the premium is in a third currency.

Cross-Currency Option or Warrant Bonds: *See Dual Option Bonds.*

Cross-Currency Settlement Risk: The risk that one party to a currency swap will default after the other side has met its obligation, usually due to a difference in time zones. *Also called Herstatt Risk* after a failed German bank which generated such a default on a large scale. *See also Settlement Risk.*

Cross-Currency Swap: *See Currency Coupon Swap.*

Cross Default: A provision of a loan or swap agreement stating that any default on another loan or swap will be considered a default on the issue with the cross-default provision. The purpose of this provision is to protect a creditor or counterparty from actions favoring another creditor.

Cross Hedging: A technique used in a variety of markets in an attempt to offset the risk of one instrument by taking a risk offsetting position in another instrument whose risk characteristics do not perfectly offset the position to be hedged. Examples include hedging the risk of a 100 stock portfolio with futures contracts on the S&P-500 or doing a currency hedge on a portfolio of German stocks with Swiss franc futures. Among the risks in a cross hedge are that different maturities of the offsetting positions will lead to a mismatch, that the market for one of the instruments will be highly illiquid with correspondingly larger price fluctuations, or that differences in credit quality will affect the cross-hedge basis.

Cross-Indexed Basis (CRIB) Swap: *See Rate Differential Swap.*

Cross Rate: The exchange ratio between any two currencies. In practice, the term is most frequently applied to currency relationships that are nonstandard in the country where the currency relationship is quoted. In United States markets, a yen/D-mark rate would be a cross-rate, but in Tokyo or Frankfurt, it would be one of the primary currency relationships traded.

Cross-Rate Options: Currency options on a currency pair that is not standard in the market where the options are traded. For example, in the United States market, standard options would include sterling/dollar options, D-mark/dollar options, and options on any other currency relative to the U.S. dollar. A sterling/D-mark option would be a cross-rate option in the United States market. In London or Frankfurt, this would be a standard option.

Cross-Rate Swap: *See Rate Differential Swap.*

Crossing: An agency transaction in which the same broker represents both parties.

Crowd: A group of exchange members organized around a specific floor location. Although members of the crowd may have a variety of functions, they trade a common list of securities, futures, or options.

Crush Spread: The soybean processor's operating margin—embodied in the relative prices of soybeans, soybean meal, and soybean oil.

Currency Average Rate Option: *See Average Price or Rate Option.*

Currency Coupon Swap: A variant on the standard currency or interest rate swap in which the interest rate in one currency is fixed, and the interest rate in the other is floating. The only difference between a traditional interest rate swap and a currency coupon swap is the combination of the currency and interest rate features.

Currency Exchange Warrants (CEWs): A cash settled, American-style warrant typically issued in conjunction with straight debt by a corporate issuer. The holder of the warrant is entitled to a cash payment at exercise if the spot rate in the target currency exceeds the rate designated as the strike.

Currency Forward: *See Outright Forward Currency Transaction.*

Currency Insurance: The currency market analog of portfolio insurance or contingent immunization, currency insurance is created either through dynamic hedging in cash or futures contracts or, more frequently, by using a basket of short-term currency options to replicate the characteristics of a longer-term option.

Currency-linked Notes: Any of a wide variety of structures with returns determined by changes in currency rates and, correspondingly, by interest rate differentials across currencies. Currency-linked instruments are available in isolation or combined with a variety of interest rate, equity, or index structures.

Currency-linked Outperformance Units (CLOUs): A note with its return tied to an embedded outperformance option that increases in value in proportion to the relative change in two currencies.

Currency Option: Generically, the right, but not the obligation, to buy (call) or sell (put) a currency with another currency at a specified exchange rate (strike rate) during a specified period ending on the expiration date.

Currency Overlay Management: The use of a separate currency manager to optimize currency exposures for an entire asset portfolio or corporate liability structure rather than delegate currency decisions to managers of various equity or fixed income portfolio segments or the divisional financial managers. *See also Overlay Risk Management.*

Currency Protected Instruments: The return from a foreign market or instrument is translated back to the investor's home currency at an embedded exchange rate. *See also Rate Differential Swap.*

Currency Protected Swap (CUPS):   An interest rate or other swap with one of the payment rates or returns denominated in a currency different than the currency used to state the notional principal amount. Both rates or returns are calculated against the base currency. *Also called Cross-Indexed Basis (CRIB) Swap, Cross-Rate Swap, Diff or Difference Swap, Differential Swap, Interest Rate Index Swap, LIBOR Differential Swap, Rate Differential Swap.*

Currency Risk: The component of return volatility in a cross-border asset class that is due to changes in foreign exchange rates.

Currency Swap: In its simplest terms, the counterparties to a currency swap exchange equal initial principal amounts of two currencies at the spot exchange rate. Over the term of the swap, the counterparties exchange fixed or floating rate interest payments in their swapped currencies. At maturity, the principal amount is reswapped at a predetermined exchange rate. In contrast to the parallel loan structure which swaps have largely replaced, netting agreements usually limit the exposure of the parties to each other's credit to a single period *net* exchange and any increase in the "residual" value of its side of the swap.

Currency Swap Agreement: Generically, an exchange of payments converting a loan from one currency to another. In practice, currency swap agreements are frequently combined with other swap agreements or risk management transactions.

Currency Swap Option: An option to buy or sell a currency swap at a specific exchange rate. The option is typically priced off the forward rate curve with European-style exercise.

Custodian: A financial institution that holds securities in safekeeping for clients.

Custody Cost: Payment to a custodian for safekeeping and some record keeping services. *See also Holding Cost.*

Cylinder: *See Risk Reversal.*

D

Daily Price or Trading Limit: The maximum amount that the price of a security, future, or option is permitted by an exchange to rise or fall in one day. The purpose of trading limits — much like the purpose of circuit breakers — is to impose a cooling-off period on a turbulent market.

Day Count Basis: *See Money Market Basis, Bond Basis.*

Day Trade: A day trade occurs when a security, option, or futures position is bought and sold during the same trading session.

Daylight Exposure: The risk associated with nonsimultaneous settlement of related transactions, especially securities lending or currency transactions that may settle in different time zones. *See also Overnight Delivery Risk, Settlement Risk.*

Deal: (United Kingdom) A transaction.

Dealer: A financial market intermediary who trades as a principal rather than as an agent. *See also Broker.*

Dealing: Trading, usually as a principal.

Debit Spread: An option spread which generates a net cash outflow in an investor's account when it is initiated.

Debt-Equity Swap: A refinancing device which gives a debt holder an equity position in exchange for cancellation of the debt.

Debt Instrument or Debt Security: Generically, an obligation to repay a fixed amount, usually with periodic interest. A lump sum interest payment at maturity may be substituted for periodic payments in the case of a zero coupon debt instrument.

Debt with a Mandatory Common Stock Purchase Contract: Notes with an embedded contract requiring holders of the debt instrument to buy sufficient common stock from the issuer to retire the debt issue in full at its scheduled maturity date. Before a change in the law, these notes were used as primary bank capital in the United States. *See also Mandatory Convertible.*

Debt Warrant: *See Contingent Takedown Option.*

Decline Guarantee: A put option.

Dedicating a Portfolio: *See Cash Flow Matching, Immunization of a Portfolio.*

Default: Failure to meet an obligation such as timely payment of interest or principal, maintenance of minimum working capital levels, etc. Upon an event of default, a creditor is usually permitted to take steps to protect his interests.

Default Risk: (1) The chance that a particular interest, principal, or swap payment or set of payments due from an issuer or a counterparty will not be forthcoming on schedule. (2) The cost of a payment default. Different financial transactions have different default probabilities and, because of different magnitudes of associated net cash flows and principal exposures, different costs associated with the same probability of default.

Defeasance: A technique of liability immunization which permits a debtor to offset and eliminate a liability with the purchase of government securities or a special risk management contract.

Deferred Coupon Note or Bond: Debt instrument which pays no interest for a fixed period and then pays interest at a relatively high rate for the remainder of its life. *See also Deferred Interest Bond.*

Deferred Interest Bond: A bond that pays interest only at a future date or dates. A zero coupon bond is the ultimate deferred interest bond, because it pays all interest and principal at maturity. *See also Deferred Coupon Note or Bond.*

Deferred Payment American Option: This structure, far more common with puts than calls, permits an option holder to freeze the underlying price at which an option will be exercised prior to the option's maturity. Under the deferred payment feature, the intrinsic value of the "exercised" option is not paid out until the scheduled maturity (expiration) of the option. The actual or implied carrying cost of the long underlying position which makes American puts more expensive than European puts remains with the put holder until expiration. This contract usually costs approximately the same as a European put but provides some of the market timing possibilities of an American put. *Also called a Deferred Payout Option and may be* *embedded in a Deferred Payment Note or Bond (2) and a Fixed Assurance Note.*

Deferred Payment Note or Bond: (1) A bond issued to investors with payment to the issuer deferred for a fixed period, usually to facilitate the investor's use of the bond as collateral for a loan. (2) An equity-linked note or bond with an embedded deferred payment American option which permits early designation of a spot price as the price to be used in calculating the payout but defers the payout until maturity of the bond or note.

Deferred Premium Option: An option without an upfront premium. At expiration, the premium is paid or netted against any option payoff. The only difference between a deferred premium option and a standard option is the timing of the premium payment. *See Boston Option (2). Contrast with Contingent Premium Option.*

Deferred Start Options: Any of a variety of options traded before their lives commence and, perhaps, even before their strikes and other terms are set. Typically, these options provide for selection of the strike and start date at the holder's option, constrained by a formula built into the option contract. Sometimes the terms are set entirely by formula based on spot prices or rates on selected dates. *See, for example, Barrier Options, Deferred Strike Price Option.*

Deferred Strike Price Option: An option that permits the buyer of the contract to set the strike price at a fixed ratio to the spot price at any time during an interval after the trade date. If the buyer does not set the strike earlier, it is determined by the spot price at the end of the deferred start period. A deferred strike price option is usually purchased when the buyer feels that current levels of volatility are relatively low, and there is an opportunity to obtain a commitment to issue an option at a lower implied volatility than the buyer expects to be available when he wants to fix the strike price on the option. The deferred strike price option's premium as a percent of the forward price on the trade date and the other terms of the option contract are determined on the trade date.

Deferred Swap: Any swap in which some or all payments are delayed for a specific period after their magnitude is determined — usually for tax or accounting purposes.

Delayed Convertible: A convertible security which cannot be converted immediately.

Delayed Reset Swap: *See In-Arrears Swap.*

Delayed Settlement: A provision of a risk management agreement that provides for a longer than usual time between the determination of settlement terms and the accounting and funds exchange of the settlement process.

Delayed Start Swap: A swap with a forward start date.

Deliverable: A financial instrument or commodity that meets the settlement requirements of a futures contract. *See also Cheapest to Deliver, Contract Grade, Delivery Option.*

Delivery: The exchange of funds for a cash instrument, commodity, or cancellation of a cash settlement obligation.

Delivery Day: The day on which the short in a futures contract makes delivery of the appropriate cash or underlying.

Delivery Factor: A coefficient which is multiplied by the settlement price of a financial futures contract to obtain the invoice price for a specific deliverable instrument. Delivery factors for interest rate contracts in the United States commonly are based on an eight percent yield.

Delivery Option: In settlement of a futures contract, the seller often has a choice of tendering one of several instruments or grades of a commodity to satisfy his obligation. *See also Cheapest to Deliver.*

Delivery Price: *See Settlement Price.*

Delivery Risk: In a currency transaction, it is often impossible to settle both sides simultaneously, putting the full principal amount of the transaction at risk for a short period. *See Settlement Risk.*

Delivery Specifications: The provisions of a futures, forward, or option contract that details the characteristics of the financial instruments or commodities that are accepted as good delivery in settlement of the contract at expiration or exercise.

Delivery Versus Payment (DVP):   A settlement procedure that coordinates the exchange of cash for securities to eliminate most settlement risk.

Delta Δ: The change in option price for a given change in the price of the underlying. The neutral hedge ratio. *See Black-Scholes Equation.*

The Effect of Maturity on Call and Put Deltas

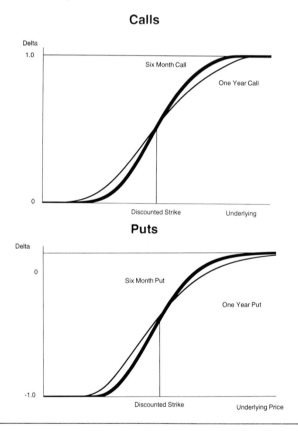

Delta Hedge: A risk offsetting position that matches the market response of the base or underlying position over a narrow range of price or rate changes. Because one side of the net position has option characteristics, the position must be modified to maintain delta neutrality if the price or rate moves beyond a narrow range. *See also Delta/Gamma Hedge.*

Delta/Gamma Hedge: A risk offsetting position — consisting in part of short-term option contracts — that neutralizes the market risk of an underlying position in an instrument with some embedded option features. The hedge offsets the current delta within a narrow range and attempts to match the change in delta (gamma) of the underlying position over a wider range of possible prices. In contrast to dynamic hedging or delta hedging, which relies on a series of transactions in the underlying, forward, or futures to match changing deltas, a delta/gamma hedge has an option payoff pattern built in.

Delta Neutral: A series of related instruments or a portfolio consisting of positions with offsetting positive and negative deltas which eliminate or neutralize the aggregate response to market movements over a range of prices or rates.

Depo Rate: A deposit rate in the interbank market. As LIBOR is an offered rate, the corresponding depo rate is a bid rate.

Déport: (French) *See Backwardation Market.*

Deposit: Money or other liquid assets left at a depository institution to earn a return, as a liquidity reserve or in compensation for services provided by the institution.

Deposit Notes: A term deposit in a bank. Deposit notes, like medium-term notes, may serve as the basis for an equity or currency-linked risk management structure. *See Currency-linked Notes, Equity-linked Notes.*

Depository Institution: A financial institution which, usually among other businesses, accepts cash deposits for which it pays interest or provides services (e.g., checking) in return for the opportunity to invest or lend the proceeds from the deposits at a higher return than its cost of funding. Examples include commercial banks, credit unions, and savings banks.

Derivative Instrument or Product: (1) A contract or convertible security that changes in value in concert with and/or obtains much of its value from price movements in a related or underlying security, future, or other instrument or index. (2) A security or contract, such as an option, forward, swap, warrant, or a debt instrument with one or more options, forwards, swaps, or warrants embedded in it or attached to it. The value of the instrument is determined in whole or in part by the price of one or more underlying instruments or markets. *Also called a Contingent Claim.*

Designated Order Turnaround (DOT) System: (1) An electronic order entry system developed and used by the New York Stock Exchange to expedite the execution of small market and limit orders by routing them directly to the specialist post on the floor. This system is actively used in program or portfolio trading in NYSE stocks. The proper name of the NYSE system is SuperDOT. (2) Generically, an electronic system that delivers orders to an exchange floor or other order matching system for automatic or semi-automatic execution.

Designated Primary Market Maker (DPM): A floor trader responsible for maintaining a two-sided market for a specific product on the Chicago Board Options Exchange. The DPM's responsibilities are much like those of a specialist on other exchanges. Creation of this category of floor member is a recognition of the advantages the specialist system enjoys when two exchanges are competing for order flow in the same product.

Detachable Warrants: Warrants originally issued with a bond or other security but which may be separated, traded, and/or exercised independently of the other security.

Diagonal Bear Spread: Regardless of whether puts or calls are used, this position involves the purchase of a relatively long-term option contract and the sale of a shorter-term contract with a lower strike price. Ordinarily, the number of contracts purchased equals the number of contracts sold. As the diagram indicates, the investor profits from a market decline, within limits.

Value of a Diagonal Bear Spread

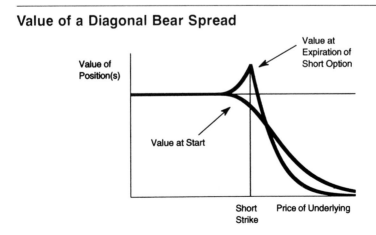

Diagonal Bull Spread: Regardless of whether puts or calls are used, the option contract purchased expires later and has a lower strike price than the option sold. Ordinarily, the number of contracts purchased equals the number of contracts sold. As the diagram indicates, the investor profits from a market advance, within limits.

Value of a Diagonal Bull Spread

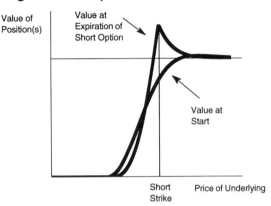

Diff or Difference Option: (1) An option on the forward interest rate differential (DIFF) between comparable instruments denominated in different currencies. (2) A spread or outperformance option with a payout linked to the price or rate difference between two underlyings. *See, for example, Yield Differential Warrants, Outperformance Option, Spread Option.*

Diff or Difference Swap: *See Rate Differential Swap.*

Difference Check: The form of payment for a net settlement such as the periodic net payment under a swap agreement where counterparty obligations are offset (netted).

Digital Option: *See All-or-Nothing Option.*

Dilution: The process by which the participation of equity owners in the earnings of a company is reduced through the issuance or prospective issuance of new common stock or participating preferred stock. Warrants or other convertible securities issued by a corporation have a potential diluting effect on earnings per share, because they can lead to new share issuance.

Exchange-traded options or third party options or warrants do not dilute earnings because they are exercised into existing shares. In practice, unless a warrant or convertible issued by the company is quite large (relative to the common stock equivalent capitalization), the dilution effect is not a major consideration in the valuation of the underlying or derivatives on the underlying. Except in rare cases where a warrant or other convertible is sold at less than a fair market price, dilution gets more analytical attention than it deserves.

Disagio: In Switzerland, the discount on a bond relative to par, expressed as a percent. *See also Agio.*

Discontinuity Risk: Exposure to loss from failure of market prices or rates to follow a "smooth" or continuous path. A classic example was the risk portfolio insurers faced in the October 1987 market break.

Discount: (1) A debt instrument selling at less than parity because its coupon, if any, is below market rates. (2) A security selling at less than its theoretically fair or expected value.

Discount Currency: A currency whose debt market is characterized by interest rates higher than the rate prevailing in the reference (domestic) currency. For many years, sterling was a discount currency with respect to most of the world's major currencies. High interest rates in sterling denominated instruments and low forward exchange rates implicitly predicted that a holder of pounds would be able to buy fewer dollars or D-marks at a future date than he could buy in the spot market. *See also Interest Rate Parity, Premium Currency.*

Discount Swap: A swap based on the coupon of a discount bond or note as the fixed rate payment. Rather than add a spread to the fixed rate payment, the parties may agree to a balloon payment by the fixed-rate payer at maturity, based on the size of the current discount. *Compare with Low Coupon Swap.*

Disintermediation: A broad change in financial relationships characterized by a decline in the traditional deposit and lending relationship between banks and their customers and an increase in direct relationships between the ultimate suppliers and users of financing. The securitization of collateral, the rise of money market funds for investment of cash reserves, and the growth of communications networks have all contributed to this trend. Disintermediation has drastically changed the roles played by various financial intermediaries and non-financial firms in the risk management process. *See also Intermediation, Securitization.*

Diversification: An approach to investment management analyzed and popularized by Harry Markowitz and encouraged by widespread acceptance of the usefulness of the capital asset pricing model. With diversification, risk can be reduced relative to the average return of a portfolio by distributing assets among a variety of asset classes such as stocks, bonds, money market instruments, and physical commodities, as well as by diversifying within these categories and across international boundaries.

Dividend Arbitrage: Any of several techniques used to obtain part or all of an investor's return in the form of dividend payments. These techniques are often referred to as dividend capture when practiced in the United States. Dividend capture may be practiced if dividends are treated more favorably than other forms of investment return for tax, regulatory, or accounting purposes.

Dividend Capture Program: Any of a number of techniques designed to take advantage of the relatively favorable tax treatment accorded intercorporate dividends in the United States. Stock may be traded frequently to "capture" as many quarterly dividends as possible subject to holding period requirements in the tax code. Dividend capture strategies have been less common in the United States since the 1986 tax law changes. *See also Dividend Arbitrage.*

Dividend Stripping: A misnamed reference to the process by which German investors take maximum advantage of the favorable tax treatment of German corporate dividends received by domestic investors.

Dividend Washing: *See Dividend Stripping.*

Dollar Bond Index-Linked Securities (Dollar BILS):   Floating rate, zero coupon notes with an effective interest rate — determined retrospectively by the change in the value of a specific index — which measures the total return on a long-term bond. Used primarily for asset liability matching or portfolio immunization.

Dollar Roll: A special repurchase agreement transaction where the security transferred to the investor as collateral is a mortgage-backed instrument. Because mortgage securities are more diverse than Treasury securities, the borrower may receive different securities than he delivered when he repays the loan. Dollar rolls are an inventory management tool for mortgage securities dealers as well as a short-term/financing lending instrument. *See also Repurchase Agreement.*

Don't Know (DK): A refusal to settle a trade by one counterparty because its operations department has no record of or instructions to complete the trade. In a volatile market, DK's can be an important source of settlement risk.

Double Barrier Option: An option which has two instrikes, outstrikes, or trigger prices. *See also Barrier Options.*

Double Option: (1) An option to buy (call) or sell (put) but not both. Exercise of the call causes the put to expire and exercise of the put causes the call to expire. Double options have been used primarily in unlisted commodity option trading, but they are also found in OTC financial structures. (2) In the operation of a bond sinking fund, the issuer is often permitted to purchase "double" the mandatory number of bonds for the sinking fund at par.

Double Rated: (United Kingdom) Callable securities.

Double Taxation Agreement: One of numerous bilateral treaties that reduces the tax bill in a stockholder's home country by eliminating or reducing the domestic tax on foreign dividends or giving a tax credit for dividend withholding taxes paid abroad.

Down-and-In Call: A contract that becomes a standard call option if the underlying drops to the instrike price. The strike price of the resulting standard option may be identical to the instrike price or it may be at any other level the parties to the contract agree on. *See Barrier Options.*

Down-and-Out Call: A call option that expires if the market price of the underlying drops below a predetermined expiration (outstrike) price. *See Barrier Options.*

Drawdown Swap: *See Accreting Principal Swap.*

Dressed Option: A short futures option collateralized by a risk offsetting position in the underlying futures contract. A dressed call option — comparable to a covered call — is a short call collateralized by a long position in the underlying futures contract.

Drop-Lock Floating Rate Notes: A floating rate instrument that converts into a fixed rate note when the reference index rate drops below a pre-set trigger rate.

Drop-Lock Swap: A deferred start interest rate swap with a provision that resets the fixed rate payment if fixed rates have changed by an agreed amount.

Dual Coupon Swap: A fixed-for-floating interest rate swap with an embedded call option giving one party the right to require that periodic settlements be made in an alternate currency if exchange rates move against the base currency used in the swap.

Dual Currency Bond: Generically, a fixed income instrument which pays a coupon in a base currency (the currency of the investor) and the principal in a non-base currency (typically the currency of the issuer). This generic structure is subject to many variations. *See also Indexed Currency Option Notes (ICONS), Principal Exchange Rate-Linked Securities (PERLS), Reverse Dual Currency Bond.*

Dual Currency Option: An option which settles in either of two currencies at the choice of the option holder.

Dual Currency Swap: A swap used to hedge the issuance of a dual currency bond, it incorporates an option and other components to transfer the unwanted features of the dual currency bond from the issuer to a financial intermediary who, in turn, will probably disaggregate and reassemble the components.

Dual Option Bonds: A bond with an embedded option giving the investor a choice of currencies for interest and principal payments. *Also called Cross-Currency Option or Warrant Bonds.*

Dual Options: *See Outperformance Option.*

Duet Bond: A bond with interest and principal payments linked to the exchange rate between two currencies on the date of payment. An exchange rate movement may have a leveraged rather than a simple percentage impact on the size of the payments.

Dumbbell Strategy: A duration-matching method that attempts to take advantage of the shape of the yield curve to improve performance while meeting an average duration target with a combination of instruments which have shorter and longer durations than the target duration.

Duration: *See Macaulay Duration, Modified Duration, Effective Duration, Option-adjusted Duration.*

Duration Bogey: The level of asset or liability duration sought in the management of a portfolio.

Duration Gap: The difference between the duration of an asset portfolio and its associated liabilities.

Duration Matching: *See Immunization of a Portfolio.*

Duration Risk Management: The use of modified duration measurements for a group of assets and/or liabilities to quantify and control exposure to long-term interest rate risk.

Dutch Auction Interest and Dividend Resets: Provisions of some floating rate notes and adjustable rate preferreds that determine rates by reoffering the securities in the market place on each reset date. The organization conducting the Dutch auction accepts bids and allocates notes or preferred shares to successful bidders at the highest market clearing price (lowest successful bidder's yield).

Dynamic Asset Allocation: Typically used as a synonym for dynamic hedging or portfolio insurance.

Dynamic Hedging: A technique of portfolio insurance or position risk management in which an option-like return pattern is created by increasing or reducing the position in the underlying (or forwards, futures, or options on the underlying) to simulate the delta change in value of an option position. For example, a short stock index futures position may be increased or decreased to create a synthetic put on a portfolio, producing a portfolio insurance-type return pattern. Dynamic hedging relies on liquid, continuous markets with low to moderate transaction costs. *See also Delta Hedge, Delta/Gamma Hedge, Portfolio Insurance.*

Dynamic Overwriting: A call option writing strategy which mandates an increase in the short call position as the price of the underlying rises. The dynamic overwriter may begin by selling calls covered by 10 percent of the underlying position. If the price of the underlying rises, he may re-purchase these calls at a loss and sell calls with a higher strike and a greater aggregate premium against 20 percent of the underlying position and so on. In effect, the dynamic overwriter counts on mean reversion in the price of the underlying as he increases a short position most aggressively when the position is proving most unprofitable. Results of this strategy — measured by the performance of the option position alone — are characterized by long periods of modest profitability interrupted by enormous losses when the market rises sharply.

E

Early Exercise: Exercise of an American-style put or call option before its expiration date.

Early Exercise Price Trigger: The provision of CAPS contracts under which the CAPS option terminates early with settlement at its maximum value if the underlying index is priced at or through the cap or outstrike price at the close of any trading session. *See also Capped Index Options (CAPS).*

Early Redemption (Put) Option: An embedded feature of some bonds with both fixed and floating rates that permits the holder to sell the bonds back to the issuer or to a third party at par or close to par in the event interest rates rise and/or the quality of the issuer's credit declines. *Bonds with these options are usually called Put Bonds.*

Early Termination Date: The date on which the final obligations of the parties to a risk management agreement are calculated in the event of a default.

Écart: (Swiss) The difference between the price of a company's bearer shares and its registered shares. The latter can be owned only by Swiss nationals and generally trade at a discount to the bearer shares.

Econometric Model: As applied to options and other convertible securities, a series of mathematical relationships, usually derived by multiple regression analysis or a similar technique, that describe the relative price movements of derivatives and underlyings. The resulting model is designed to predict the average or normal price of an option or other convertible security when the underlying's price and other relevant variables are inserted in the equations that make up the model. Deservedly, probability models have enjoyed greater popularity than this type of econometric model.

Economic Hedge: Most commonly a currency hedge to offset the advantage of a competitor with a depreciating currency. *See Competitive Currency Risk.*

Economic Risk: Exposure to changes in exchange rates, local regulations, product preferences, etc., that favor the products or services provided by a competitor. *See also Competitive Currency Risk.*

Effective Date: *See Start Date.*

Effective Duration: The ratio of the proportional change in bond value to the infinitesimal parallel shift of the spot yield curve. Equal to modified duration if the yield curve is flat. *See also Modified Duration.*

Effective Rate or Yield: The net interest rate an investor receives (or a borrower pays) after the premium of a cap or floor is added to or subtracted from the contractual rate of interest.

Efficient Market: A market in which prices accurately and promptly reflect all information available to investors. In such a market, past price and volume patterns cannot provide meaningful predictions of future price movement. These minimum features describe a weak form efficient market. More stringent requirements describe semi-strong and strong forms.

Elasticity: (1) A measure of the response of one value to a relative change in another. For example, if volume is not affected materially by a given percentage change in price, volume is said to be inelastic to price. If volume increases greatly when prices are cut slightly and drops sharply with a small price increase, volume is highly elastic to price. (2) Used colloquially as an equivalent of delta or neutral hedge ratio. Note that delta is an absolute change measured in currency units, so this usage is not strictly consistent with the origins of the term in economics. (3) Delta times the underlying price divided by the option or warrant price. *Equivalent to Effective Gearing or the Leverage Factor.*

Electricity Forward Agreement (EFA):   A contract calling for the delivery of and payment for electric power in a future period. EFAs are used much like oil derivative contracts to fix or hedge energy costs.

Embedded Option: An option that is an inseparable part of another instrument. Most embedded options are conversion features granted to the buyer or early termination options granted to the issuer of a security by the buyer. A common embedded option is the call provision in most corporate bonds which permits the issuer to repay the borrower earlier than the nominal maturity of the bond. The home owner's option to repay mortgage principal early — resulting in early liquidation of a mortgage-backed security — is another common embedded option.

Embeddo: *Another name for Embedded Option.*

Emerging Market Warrants: Covered or guaranteed options or warrants on common stocks, stock indexes, or government bonds traded in an immature market often characterized by some combination of restrictions on foreign ownership, discontinuous trading, inadequate investor protection, and/or limitations on currency convertibility. The creator or writer of these warrants insulates the buyer from some of these undesirable market characteristics in return for an above average premium.

Empirical: Based on the analysis of actual data or experience. A conclusion based on observation rather than speculation or deduction. Empirical studies are undertaken to test or to suggest a hypothesis.

Employee Retirement Income Security Act (ERISA): The legislation that established regulation of the investment and risk management policies of pension (defined benefit) and profit sharing (defined contribution) employee benefit plans in the United States. *See also Prudent Expert Rule of ERISA.*

Endorsement: In over-the-counter transactions, a creditworthy guarantor sometimes endorses a derivative contract to guarantee performance. Clearing corporations perform an analogous function for listed options and futures.

Enhanced Derivative Product Companies (EDPCs): AAA- or AA-rated subsidiaries of lower-rated financial intermediaries that serve as counterparties or issuers of risk management products.

Enhancement of a Position: The use of arbitrage-type techniques to improve the return from a position without materially changing its risk characteristics.

Equitize Cash: To purchase an equity futures, forward, or options synthetic position and collateralize it with a previously held cash equivalent position.

Equity Contract Notes: Debt issued by a bank with mandatory convertibility into common stock. Counted as primary bank capital under earlier capital rules. *See also Mandatory Convertible.*

Equity-enhanced Dedication: A form of portfolio insurance using a dedicated bond portfolio as the reserve asset and common stocks or stock index futures as the risky asset. This technique is designed to maintain a minimum pension surplus (or a ceiling on underfunding) while providing equity exposure and a chance to increase the ratio of assets to liabilities.

Equity Index-linked Notes: *See Equity-linked Notes.*

Equity Index Warrants: *See Index Warrants.*

Equity-linked Debt Placements: *See Equity-linked Notes.*

Equity-linked Foreign Exchange Option: A variable quantity currency option that provides full equity exposure and an option to limit currency exposure. *Compare to Quantity Adjusting Options (Quantos) (1).*

Equity-linked Notes (ELN):   Securities which combine the characteristics of a zero or low coupon bond or note with a return component based on the performance of a single equity security, a basket of equity securities, or an equity index. In the latter case, the security would typically be called an equity index-linked note. Equity-linked notes come in a variety of flavors. The minimum return may be zero with all of what would normally be an interest payment going to pay for upside equity participation. Alternatively, a low interest rate may be combined with a lower rate of equity participation. The participation rate in the underlying equity instrument may be more or less than dollar for dollar over any specific range of prices. The participation may be open ended (the holder of the note participates proportionately in the upside of the underlying security or index, no matter how high it goes), or the equity return component may be capped. Other things equal, a capped return will be associated with a higher rate of participation up to the cap price. *Various versions of this instrument are known as Equity Participation Notes (EPNS), Guaranteed Return Index Participations (GRIPS), Guaranteed Return on Investment Certificate (GROI), Index Growth-Linked Units (IGLUs), Index Participation Certificate, Protected Equity Notes (PENs), Protected Equity Participations (PEPs), Protected Index Participations (PIPs), Safe Return Certificate or* *as a variety of "money back" certificates.* While the names may provide a clue to the structures, each issuer seems to have at least one proprietary name for some version of these instruments. Investors must look at the structure and pricing of the units offered and compare them with more familiar names and structures.

Return Patterns for Capped and Participating Equity-linked Notes

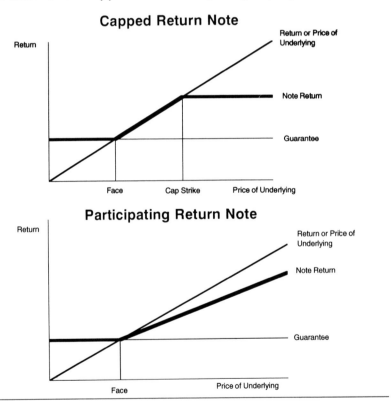

Capped Return Note

Participating Return Note

Equity-linked Swap: A swap with payments on one or both sides linked to the performance of equities or an equity index.

Equity Participation Indexed Certificates (EPICs):   *See Equity-linked Notes.*

Equity Participation Notes (EPNs): *See Equity-linked Notes.*

Equity Yield Enhancement Securities (EYES): An equity-linked instrument with a single stock as the underlying, a coupon that exceeds the dividend on the underlying stock, and a capped return. The higher coupon is purchased with the proceeds from the cap. A synthetic preference equity redemption cumulative stock (PERCS). *See diagram under the PERCS listing.*

Escalating Swap or Escalating Principal Swap: *See Accreting Swap.*

Escrow Receipt: A document providing evidence of the existence of collateral. An escrow receipt may be used to protect a securities firm carrying a customer's short option position. The escrow receipt certifies that collateral adequate to protect the broker and the clearing corporation has been deposited with the bank or trust company issuing the escrow receipt.

Euroclear: One of two clearing houses for securities traded in the Euromarkets. *See also Centrale de Lívraison de Valuers Mobiliéres (CEDEL).*

Eurocurrency: Dollars, D-marks, yen, pounds, or any other currency deposit or instrument which is outside the formal control of the issuing country's monetary authorities. The Euro prefix describes only the geographical origins of the first markets in securities denominated in these unregulated currencies.

Euromarkets: Markets in securities and futures denominated in Eurocurrencies and sold to investors based outside the country which is home to the currency used as the unit of payment and valuation for the instrument.

European Currency Unit (ECU): A weighted basket of currencies of members of the European Economic Community (EC). Over time, the composition and weighting of the ECU will become increasingly stable if current agreements remain in force.

European Exchange Rate Quotation Convention: In currency markets, the practice of quoting exchange relationships in terms of the number of units of the foreign currency per dollar. Quotations in French francs per dollar or D-marks per dollar would be expressing the exchange rate relationship in the European convention. *See also American Exchange Rate Quotation Convention.*

European Monetary System (EMS): A set of rules establishing the European Currency Unit (ECU) and the Exchange Rate Mechanism (ERM) by which most members of the European Economic Community are committed to maintain exchange rate relationships within narrow bands.

European Monetary Union: A plan which would replace the currencies of member countries with the European currency unit (ECU). The outlook for plan adoption was clouded in mid-1992 by defeat of the plan in a Danish referendum.

European Option: A put or call that can be exercised only on its expiration date. The term has nothing to do with where the option is traded or what underlies it. Stock options listed on European option exchanges are usually American-style options in the sense that they can be exercised prior to the expiration date. *See American Option, Bermuda Option, Deferred Payment American Option, Japanese Option.*

Eurowarrants: Warrant contracts traded in the Euromarkets, primarily in London and Zurich.

Event of Default: *See Default.*

Event Risk: Exposure to loss from a change in the credit quality of an issue or issuer resulting from a merger or acquisition, a leveraged buyout, a product failure, or some other development with a major impact on the issuer's business or capitalization.

Ex-Dividend Date: The date on which the buyer of a stock is no longer able to purchase the stock the regular way and still receive a specific dividend payment. A holder of the stock who sells on the ex-dividend date will be entitled to retain the dividend when it is paid.

Ex-Pit Transaction: *See Exchange of Futures for Physicals (EFP).*

Ex-Warrants: An instrument sold without the warrants which were attached to the instrument at the time of its issuance.

Exchange: A formal marketplace or procedure for trading tangible or intangible property. The trading process is usually accompanied by standard procedures for settling trades.

Exchange of Futures for Physicals (EFP): A technique (originated in physical commodity markets) whereby a position in the underlying is traded for a futures position. In financial futures markets, the EFP bypasses any cash settlement mechanism that is built into the contract and substitutes physical settlement. EFPs are used primarily to adjust underlying cash market positions at a low trading cost. An EFP by itself will not change either party's net risk position materially, but EFPs are often used to set up a subsequent trade which will modify the investor's market risk exposure at low cost. *Occasionally called a Cash-Futures Swap or an Ex-Pit Transaction.*

Exchange Option: An option to surrender one asset in exchange for another.

Exchange Rate Agreement (ERA): A synthetic agreement for forward exchange (SAFE), much like a forward rate agreement in the interest rate market, that increases or decreases in value as the spread between two forward currency exchange rates, say, three months and six months forward, moves up or down. Note that in contrast to a forward exchange agreement (FXA), the ERA is settled with reference to two forward rates rather than a forward and the spot rate on settlement. Usually related to some other risk position rather than a stand-alone position. *See also Forward Rate Agreement (FRA), Forward Exchange Agreement (FXA), Synthetic Agreement for Foreign Exchange (SAFE).*

Exchange Rate Mechanism (ERM): A commitment on the part of members of the European Monetary System (EMS) — most members of the European Economic Community (EC) — to maintain relatively fixed currency exchange rates. For most currencies, fluctuations around a bilateral central rate with regard to each other currency in the ECU will be maintained at plus or minus 2 1/4 percent from an agreed upon relationship. Tables of current minimum and maximum exchange rate parity relationships are used to predict exchange rate intervention and central bank monetary policies.

Exchange-traded Contracts: Standardized options and futures listed and traded on an organized exchange. These contracts meet many end user risk management needs and are used by major financial intermediaries as risk management tools for their diverse positions. *See also Over The Counter (OTC).*

Exchangeable Auction Rate Preferred Stock: An auction rate preferred stock that is exchangeable at the issuer's option for auction rate notes on any dividend payment date. The purpose of this form is to permit the issuer to replace the preferred dividend paid from after-tax earnings with tax deductible interest when the issuer's income becomes taxable.

Exchangeable Debt: A bond or note issue which is "convertible" into the shares of a company other than the issuer of the debt instrument. This structure has been used primarily by corporations to sell a large position in the shares of another company.

Execution Cost: Usually the directly measurable cost of trading — less comprehensive than transaction cost. *See also Transaction Cost.*

Execution Risk: The chance that a desirable transaction cannot be executed within the context of recent market prices or within limits proposed by an investor. Unless a financial intermediary is willing to act as a dealer (principal) and guarantee a specific execution — within the rules of a marketplace — investors face execution risk in virtually all exchange-traded instruments. *See also Unwinding Risk, Roll Over Risk.*

Exercise Limit: A limit on the number of exchange-traded option contracts that can be exercised by one holder within a specified time period. Related to position limits.

Exercise Notice: A notification — ultimately reaching the option seller — that the buyer of an option wishes to exercise and obtain the appropriate cash settlement or physical delivery of the underlying.

Exercise of an Option: Purchase or sale of the underlying at the strike price by the holder of a call or put. In cash settled option markets, exchange of the option position for cash.

Exercise Price: *More commonly called Strike or Strike Price.*

Exotic Options: Any of a wide variety of options with unusual underlyings, strike price calculations, strike price determinations, payoff mechanisms, or expiration conditions. *Also called Non-Standard Options. See, for example, Average Price or Rate Option, Barrier Options, Compound Option, Contingent Premium Option, Deferred Strike Price Option, Dual Currency Option, Lookback Option, etc.*

Expectation Model: A theory of forward or futures price determination that emphasizes the importance of price or return expectations. While expectations may play a role through the interest rate structures that determine cost of carry, few observers today assign an independent role to expectations in financial forward or futures price determination.

Expected Credit Loss: The long-term average cost of defaults anticipated in a swap or debt instrument investment program. Theoretically, this cost should be recovered from swap spreads and interest rate premiums.

Expected Value: For any investment instrument, the probability-weighted sum of all possible outcomes.

Expected Volatility: The value for the underlying's volatility that a risk manager anticipates in the period covered by a risk management operation.

Expiration Cycle: One of three cycles which United States stock option exchanges used from the mid-1970s to the mid-1980s. Beginning in 1985, the exchanges began to modify the traditional cycles to allow four rather than three expiration months to trade at once and to allow at least two near-term expiration months at all times. Other markets usually have relatively simple rules for listing new expiration months.

Expiration Date: (1) The date after which an option is void. An option buyer must decide whether or not to exercise on or before this date. *See also Extension.* (2) The final settlement date of a futures or forward contract.

Expiration Price: An outstrike price in a barrier or exotic option.

Expiry: The British term for (1) the expiration process and (2) the expiration date.

Exploding Option: A collar or risk reversal structure in which the short option "explodes" (expires), and the long option pays off at maximum value when the underlying trades through the outstrike price either instantaneously or as of the close of a trading session. *See also Barrier Options, Capped Index Options (CAPS), Up-and-Out Call.*

Exposure Management: *See Risk Management.*

Extendable Notes: (1) An open-ended debt obligation which resets every few years to a new interest rate based on negotiations between the issuer and the investor. At each renegotiation date, the investor has the option to put the notes back to the issuer if the new rate the issuer proposes is unacceptable. (2) A combination of a traditional bond or note and an embedded option which gives the issuer (or less frequently the holder) the right to call or to extend the maturity of the note at a prespecified interest rate.

Extendable Swap: One or both parties to a swap have an option to extend the swap for an additional period beyond the original maturity date.

Extension: (1) An agreement between the buyer and the writer of an over-the-counter derivative instrument to lengthen the life of the contract beyond the original expiration date. Extensions are not common because both parties have to agree to the extension and to the price to be paid for it. There is no mechanism for extension of a specific listed option or futures contract. (2) The tendency of some mortgage pools to prepay principal more slowly than average or than predicted by standard formulas.

Extension Risk: The risk or cost associated with slower than anticipated repayment of mortgages either because the underlying mortgage pool has unusual characteristics or because interest rates have remained too high to stimulate repayment or refinancing.

Extension Swap: A swap with a forward start date which coincides with the termination date of an existing swap with otherwise similar terms. The forward start date swap extends the life of the initial swap.

Extinguishable Option: *See Barrier Options.*

F

Face Value: (1) Value of a bond or other debt instrument at maturity. *Also called Par.* (2) Notional principal amount.

Facility: An open line of credit or a lending arrangement.

Fail: A trade that does not clear on the settlement date. *See also Settlement Risk.*

Fair Value Basis: The value or range of values of the difference between the forward or futures price and the spot price that offers no opportunity for profitable arbitrage at current carrying costs. For example, if the maximum risk-free lending rate is 6.0 percent and the minimum borrowing rate is 6.2 percent, the fair value basis of a zero coupon bond future 1-year out would be a range between 6.0 percent and 6.2 percent over spot. In real markets, participants' opportunity sets will be different and the fair value basis may range between a single point and a relatively wide interval.

Fair Value of an Option: The option value computed by a probability-type option valuation model. The fair value of an option is the price at which both the buyer and the writer of the option should expect to break even, neglecting the effect of commissions and other trading costs and after an adjustment for risk. Fair value is an estimate of where an option *should* sell in an efficient market, not where it *will* sell. The fair value of an option is also defined as parity plus basis plus insurance value. *See also Black-Scholes Equation, Parity, Insurance.*

Fair Value Premium: *See Fair Value Basis, Fair Value of an Option, Forward Intrinsic Value.*

Fence or Fence Spread: *See Risk Reversal.*

Fiduciary: A person or institution standing in a relationship of trust to one or more entities. In the financial risk management context, a fiduciary manages money or property for another and must exercise a high standard of care imposed by law or contract.

Fiduciary Call: A call is purchased and the present value of its aggregate exercise price is invested in money market instruments which are placed in escrow to cover the cost of possible exercise. The implication is that the cash deposit reduces overall portfolio risk by preventing call purchases that will increase leverage.

Fiduciary Put: A put is written and its aggregate exercise price is invested in money market instruments which are placed in escrow to assure that adequate cash will be available in the event of exercise. As with the fiduciary call, the cash deposit prevents the use of options to increase leverage.

Financial Accounting Standards Board (FASB): The professional organization with primary responsibility for determination of financial reporting standards in the United States. The Securities and Exchange Commission has the power to override FASB standards.

Financial Engineering: The art (with contributions from science) of creating desirable cash flow and/or market value patterns from existing instruments or new instruments to meet an investment or risk management need. The creations of financial engineers are typically based on traditional instruments such as bonds and notes with forward and futures contracts, options, and swap components added.

Financial Futures Contract: A regulated, exchange-traded futures contract with a financial instrument as the underlying. Examples include futures contracts on debt instruments, currencies, and stock indexes. *See Futures Contract.*

Financial Institutions Recovery, Reform, and Enforcement Act (FIRREA): An act that made thrift institutions subject to Federal Reserve Board capital requirements and, together with revisions in the federal bankruptcy code, assured the enforceability of netting for swap agreements subject to United States law.

Financial Instrument: Cash, evidence of an ownership interest in an equity, or a contract that is *both:*

- a (recognized or unrecognized) contractual right of one entity to (1) receive cash or another financial instrument from another entity or (2) exchange other financial instruments on potentially favorable terms with another entity.

- a (recognized or unrecognized) contractual obligation of another entity to (1) deliver cash or another financial instrument to another entity or (2) exchange financial instruments on potentially unfavorable terms with another entity. (From a Financial Accounting Standards Board exposure draft.)

Financial Intermediary: A bank, securities firm, or other financial institution that collects deposits and makes loans, facilitates fund transfers and risk management transactions, and/or facilitates the flow of capital between operating units and the economy.

Firewall: Barrier designed to prevent losses or risks taken in one part of a financial institution from weakening other parts of the institution.

Firm Price: A price at which a trader is willing to trade for a limited period of time. *Compare to Indicative Prices.*

First Loss Guarantee: A form of credit enhancement in which an investor has additional recourse to a third party for a stated percentage of any obligation or a percentage of any losses. A common feature of securitized loan packages.

Fixed Assurance Notes (FANs):   *See Deferred Payment Note or Bond (2).*

Fixed Exchange Rate Foreign Equity Option: *See Quantity Adjusting Options (Quantos).*

Fixed Exchange Rate System: The currency exchange rate structure under the Bretton Woods agreement which called for central bank intervention to maintain exchange rates within a very narrow band.

Fixed-Fixed Currency Swap: Both sides of the swap are fixed rate payers in the respective currencies.

Fixed-Floating Swap: A basic interest rate swap of fixed rates for floating rates in the same currency.

Fixed Interest Rate Substitute Transaction (FIRST): A two tranche floating rate note with one tranche a reverse floater. The net effect of the offsetting tranches is to make the issuer a fixed rate payer.

Fixed Rate Payer: (1) A party to an interest rate swap whose payment is based on the coupon of a long-term fixed income instrument or is otherwise set at the same level during each payment interval. Often called the buyer of the swap or said to be long the swap. (2) The issuer of a fixed coupon note or bond.

Fixing: (1) Setting a price or rate for a future period based on the relationship of market prices or rates and contractual terms. (2) (United Kingdom) Short selling.

Floating Exchange Rates: The currency exchange rate structure since the collapse of the Bretton Woods agreement. Exchange rate relationships have been constrained by bilateral and multinational agreements, but the rigid rate parity of the former fixed rate structure is not in force.

Floating-Floating Swap: *See Basis Rate Swap.*

Floating Rate Note (FRN): A fixed principal instrument, often utilized in swaps, which has a long or even indefinite life and whose yield is periodically reset relative to a reference index rate to reflect changes in short- or intermediate-term interest rates.

Floating Rate Payer: (1) A party to an interest rate swap who is required to make variable interest rate payments determined by the reference index rate named in the swap contract. Often called the seller of the swap or said to be short the swap. (2) The issuer of a floating rate note (FRN) or adjustable rate preferred stock (ARPS).

Floating Rate Rating-Sensitive Notes: A type of floating rate note in which the quarterly reset is based on a spread over the reference index rate. The spread increases if the issuer's debt rating declines. *See Table of Debt Ratings in the Appendix.*

Floating Strike Option: *See Average Strike Rate Option*

Floor: (1) A feature of a debt contract or a separate agreement that puts a minimum or floor on the interest rate of a floating rate instrument. (2) A

long put that limits the downside risk in a long equity position or portfolio.
See also Cap, Collar.

The Effect of an Interest Rate Floor

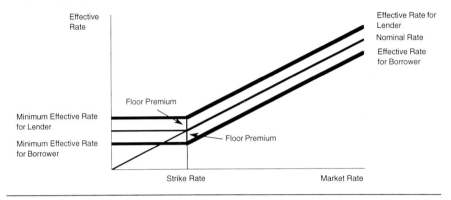

Floor/Ceiling Swap: A swap with a built-in interest rate collar which
constrains the floating rate payment between floor and ceiling rates as in a
separate interest rate collar structure.

Floor Rate: The strike rate of a floor contract.

Floored Put: A put position whose maximum payout is limited by contract — analogous to a vertical put spread and similar in form to a reverse
risk reversal. The terms on which the floor provision comes into effect will
vary considerably by market and should be checked carefully. A put CAPS
with its "exploding" early exercise price trigger is a variety of floored put.
Compare with a Capped Call or Corridor. Also called a Limited Put.

Value of a Floored Put at Expiration

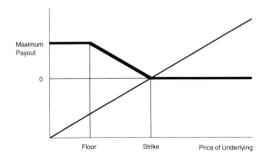

Floorlet: One of the interim period floors in a multiple period floor agreement.

Floortion: An option on a floor. The holder of a floortion has the right to buy a floor at a contractual strike price for a prespecified premium at the expiration of the floortion. *See also Floor, Compound Option.*

Force Majeure Clause: A contract provision that excuses one or both parties from part or all of their obligations in the event of war, natural disaster, or some other event outside the parties' control.

Forced Conversion: Involuntary conversion of a warrant or convertible instrument undertaken to preserve the value of the holder's position. Forced conversion occurs when the issuer exercises a bond call provision or is acquired by another firm for cash.

Forecast Volatility: *See Expected Volatility, Implied Volatility.*

Foreign Currency Bond: A debt instrument with a coupon paid in a different currency than the proceeds of issuance. The principal payment at maturity will be in the same currency as the coupon or converted to the currency of issuance at the spot rate of exchange at maturity. *See also Dual Currency Bond.*

Foreign Exchange Markets (FX, Forex):   Cash, forward, futures, and options markets in currencies.

Foreign Exchange Risk: *See Currency Risk.*

Foreign Interest Payment Securities (FIPS):   A perpetual reverse dual currency bond with a periodic put back to the issuer at par. Coupons are in the currency of the issuer and the put is at par in the currency of the investor. *See also Dual Currency Bond, Reverse Dual Currency Bond.*

Foreign Property Rule: A Canadian law that limits the percentage of a pension fund that may be invested in foreign assets. Historically, the percentage was 10 percent, but it is rising gradually to 20 percent in 1994.

Foreign Stock Index Options, Warrants, and Futures: These exchange-traded contracts, most common in the United States, provide exposure to CFTC/SEC-approved foreign stock indexes (typically the Nikkei or Japan index, the FTSE-100, or the CAC-40). The index level is translated into dollars for pricing and settlement purposes and, in most warrants and options, the exchange rate is fixed at issuance for the life of the contract. *See also Covered Warrant, Guaranteed Exchange Rate Warrant, and Guaranteed Warrants.*

Forward: A contractual obligation between two parties to exchange a particular good or instrument at a set price on a future date. The buyer of the forward agrees to pay the price and take delivery of the good or instrument and is said to be long the forward, while the seller of the forward, or short, agrees to deliver the good or instrument at the agreed price on the agreed date. Banks are often involved as credit intermediaries and collateral may be deposited, but cash is not exchanged until the delivery date. *See also Futures Contract.*

Forward Band: A zero cost interest rate collar.

Forward Break: *See Break Forward.*

Forward Cap: An interest rate cap with a deferred start date.

Forward Currency Swap: A currency swap with a forward start on terms agreed upon in advance. Used to hedge or lock in some combination of interest rates and currency rates relative to an expected change in financing or operations.

Forward Exchange Agreement (FXA): A contract whose value at maturity is based on differences between the forward rate on the start date and the spot rate at settlement.

Forward Intrinsic Value: Parity plus basis. The intrinsic value of an option (parity) plus the fair value basis on the forward underlying the option contract. A European option should not sell for less than its forward intrinsic value in an efficient market. The forward intrinsic value of a call will always be above the traditional intrinsic value measurement except in some cases when there is a dividend to be paid prior to expiration. The forward intrinsic value of a European put will always be less than the put's traditionally measured intrinsic value except in cases where there is an impending dividend. *See also Basis (diagram).*

Forward with Optional Exit (FOX): *See Break Forward. Also called Boston Option (1), Cancellable Option.*

Forward Outright Rate: The actual forward exchange rate as distinguished from the swap rate premium or discount. The rate used in an outright forward contract. *See Outright Forward Currency Transaction.*

Forward Plus: *See Participating Range Forward.*

Forward Point Agreement: A swap agreement under which one party pays fixed forward points set at the time of agreement and the other party pays floating forward points based on relative interest rates in the two currencies at a series of future dates.

Forward Points: A number added to or subtracted from the spot currency exchange rate to calculate a forward price.

Forward Rate: *See Forward Yield Curve.*

Forward Rate Agreement (FRA): A contract determining an interest rate to be paid or received on a specific obligation beginning at a start date in the future. A notional principal contract like an FRA need not be with the party on the other side of the obligation that the FRA contract is linked to. Any gain or loss on the FRA is like a gain or loss on an option or futures contract in terms of its impact on the return of an underlying position.

Forward Rate Bracket: A contingent forward contract often used in currency markets. The investor can take advantage of favorable price moves to the upper end of the contract range while remaining protected against moves below the lower end of the contract range. Within the range, the contract settles at the spot rate and the customer pays no option premium. The payoff pattern is similar to an interest rate collar or risk reversal in fixed income and equity markets respectively. *Also called a Range Forward Contract (diagram) in currency markets.*

Forward Rate Curve: *See Forward Yield Curve.*

Forward Spread Agreement: (1) A specialized forward rate agreement which settles at the index rate (usually LIBOR) at the time of settlement plus or minus the agreed spread. (2) A forward which settles at the basis between two agreed-upon rates on settlement day.

Forward Start Agreement: A risk management agreement whose effective life does not start until a future date set by agreement or contingent on a specific event. Ordinarily, all terms of the contract are set at the trade date. *Contrast with Spot Start.*

Forward Swap: A swap agreement with the period covered by the exchange beginning at a future date. Often priced as two partially offsetting swaps—both starting immediately, but one ending on the deferred start date of the forward swap.

Forward Yield Curve: An interest rate curve derived point by point from the traditional yield curve, the forward curve is used to price many interest rate derivative instruments. The forward curve shows the implied forward interest rate for each period covered by the yield curve. The diagrams under the listing for yield curve illustrate forward rate curves for both normal and inverted yield curve environments.

Fourchette Option: (French) Any of a variety of spread- or range-contingent option payout structures.

Fourth Market: Direct trading between institutional investors, either without the services of a broker or dealer or using a broker's back office only to clear the trades.

Fraption: An option on a forward rate agreement. *Also called an Interest Rate Guarantee.*

Free Collar: A zero cost collar or risk reversal with the premium on the cap and the floor offsetting one another. *See Interest Rate Collar, Risk Reversal.*

Free Of Tax to Residents Abroad (FOTRA):   Certain United Kingdom securities which are exempt from withholding taxes to holders filing proof of non-United Kingdom residency.

Frequency: The periodic schedule of rate or price readings used to calculate the payoff of an average rate or price option.

Frogs: Floating rate notes with coupons reset quarterly or semiannually to the coupon on the current 30-year Treasury bond. Used in yield curve swaps.

Front Contract or Front Month Contract: The near month futures contract.

Front Spread: An option spread with a net premium outflow, usually because the long option is further in the money, closer to the money, or has a longer life than the short option.

Frontrunning: The practice (illegal in the United States) of effecting a transaction on the basis of material nonpublic information about an impending order or trade. Regulators have introduced the fuzzy concept of intermarket frontrunning to emphasize the relationships among options, futures, and cash markets.

Fulfillment Fund: *See Completion Fund.*

Full Floating Rate Note: *See Reverse Floating Rate Note.*

Full Investment Note (FIN): An equity-linked note which mirrors the performance of the stocks in a mutual fund portfolio and extends that performance to the fund's cash reserves. A FIN permits the fund to perform as if it were fully invested at all times in spite of the fact that the fund keeps an adequate reserve for possible shareholder redemptions. The FIN also helps reduce problems caused by the short-short rule. *See also Short-Short Rule.*

Full Two-Way Payment Clause (FTP): An optional settlement clause in the ISDA swap agreement that requires settlement of a swap at its full value even if that requires a net payment to a defaulting counterparty. *See also Limited Two-Way Payment Clause (LTP).*

Fundamental Financial Instruments: As identified by the Financial Accounting Standards Board, these include unconditional receivables (payables), conditional receivables (payables), forward contracts, options, guarantees, or other conditional exchanges, and equity instruments. Most risk management practitioners would list equity, debt, forwards, swaps, and options.

Funding Risk: The potential for unanticipated costs or losses due to a mismatch between asset yields and liability funding costs. The risk may be due to different maturities of assets and liabilities, changes in credit quality, or a variety of other causes.

Funds: Cash or equivalents such as federal funds or clearing house funds used to settle a transaction.

Fungibility: The standardization and interchangeability of listed option and futures contracts and certain other financial instruments. Fungibility permits either party to an opening transaction to close out a position through a closing transaction in an identical contract. All financial contracts with identical terms are not necessarily fungible, a fact that can increase risk in some markets.

Future Rate Agreement: *See Forward Rate Agreement.*

Futures Commission Merchant (FCM): A broker who handles customer orders in a futures market.

Futures Contract: An agreement between two parties, a buyer and a seller, to exchange a particular good for a particular price at a particular date in the future, all of which are specified in a contract common to all participants in a market on an organized futures exchange. The contract must be for a specific amount of a good for delivery at a specific time as required by the exchange with the price determined in a public marketplace by "open outcry." Futures contracts can be traded freely with various counterparties without counterparty credit risk. After a trade is cleared, the exchange is the ultimate counterparty for all contracts, so the only credit risk is the credit worthiness of the exchange's clearing corporation. No credit intermediary is necessary, but margin deposits must be posted as performance bonds with the clearing broker and, in turn, with the exchange. Typically, variation margin payments mark futures positions to market at least once a day.

Futures and Options Funds (FOFs): Unit trusts offered in the United Kingdom which are able to make limited use of derivative instruments. *Also called Authorized Futures and Option Funds.*

Futures-style Options: A proposed contract to replace many traditional options on futures contracts. Unlike traditional options, the buyer of a futures-style option does not prepay the premium. Buyers and sellers post margin as in a futures contract, and the option premium is marked to the market daily. Valuation differs from traditional futures options primarily in the analysis of the timing of cash flows associated with the buyer's non-payment of the premium.

G

G-Hedge: An interest rate collar with an upfront premium and a symmetrical range on either side of the forward rate.

Gamma γ: The change in delta divided by the dollar change in the underlying instrument's price. The second derivative of the option price with respect to the price of the underlying. A measurement of the rate of change of the rate of change in the option price with respect to the underlying price. If the gamma of a position is positive, an instantaneous move either up or down in the underlying will give the position a higher value than the delta would predict. A positive gamma indicates a position with positive convexity. *See also Convexity.*

Gamma Distribution: One of a family of distributions suggested by Bookstaber as a possible form for certain securities' price behavior.

Gap Analysis: *See Maturity Gap.*

Garman-Kohlhagen Model: A currency option evaluation model similar in structure to the Black-Scholes option model with separate terms for foreign and domestic interest rates. Biger and Hull published essentially the same model at about the same time.

Geared Equity Capital Units (GECUs):   An open-ended, usually leveraged, equity-linked note. As the diagram indicates, the leverage is usually obtained by setting the minimum value of the note below the amount the buyer pays for it. *See also Guaranteed Index Units, Equity-linked Notes.*

The Return Pattern of a GECU

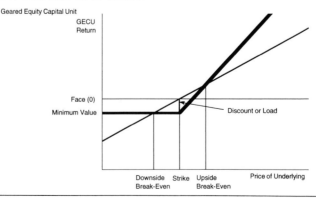

Geared Zero Coupon Convertibles: A complex variant of standard zero coupon convertibles (LYONS) with a minimum redemption value below par, leveraged exposure to the performance of the underlying common stock up to a capped price, no conversion premium or interim put provision, no call provision, and exercise only at maturity.

Gearing: The price of the underlying divided by the price of the call or warrant. The term, also called nominal gearing, is widely used in the United Kingdom warrant market and in other markets (such as the Japanese warrant market) which were developed on the United Kingdom model. The gearing ratio is of limited value in any analysis of option or warrant price relationships. A related concept, effective gearing is only slightly more useful. The latter is the traditional gearing measure multiplied by the call option or warrant delta. Effective gearing is also called elasticity. *See also Premium/Gearing Ratio*

Geld und Brief: Bid and asked in German. Note that the letter "g" designates a bid and the letter "b" an asked price in a German language price table.

Gensaki Rate: The repo rate on Japanese government bonds. The Gensaki rate rivals the yen LIBOR rate as an indicator of short-term rates in yen-denominated instruments.

Geometric Average: The nth root of the product of n observations or values.

$$\text{If } n = 3, x = \sqrt[3]{a * b * c}$$

Indexes based on geometric averages are uncommon since the index underlying the Value Line Index contracts was changed to an arithmetic average. A geometric average will be smaller than a corresponding arithmetic average unless all observations are equal. This feature is significant in evaluating options and performance records in terms of compound returns.

Gilts: Bonds issued by the government of the United Kingdom and named after the gilded edge on the bond certificate.

Global Asset Allocation: Active management of commitments to asset classes and markets in a number of countries, typically combined with passive or index management within markets. To keep trading costs at manageable levels, global asset allocation adjustments are typically made in futures and options markets.

Global Depository Receipts (GDRs): The Euromarket analog of American Depository Receipts (ADRs). GDRs are issued and cleared by the Euromarket depositories rather than by banks. *See also American Depository Receipts (ADRs).*

Global Hedge: A hedge covering the unwanted risks of a portfolio or an entire organization on an aggregate basis, taking advantage of any natural risk offsets and using broad spectrum hedging instruments. Global hedging is a low cost approach to risk management available only to large financial intermediaries. *See also Micro Hedge.*

Globalization: The trend toward looking at economic and financial issues, instruments, and portfolios from a worldwide rather than a single-country viewpoint.

Globex: An electronic "exchange" or trading mechanism designed to trade a variety of securities and derivatives. Initially, Globex will trade instruments when their primary markets are closed.

Good Delivery: Delivery at settlement of funds or instruments that meet the requirements of a market.

Governing Law: The legal system of the sovereign jurisdiction which interprets an agreement.

Government National Mortgage Association (GNMAs) Pass-through Certificates: Debt securities collateralized by residential mortgage debt and guaranteed as to payment of interest and principal by the Government National Mortgage Association, an agency of the United States government.

Grant Date: (1) The start date of an employee stock option. (2) The effective start date of a deferred start date option.

Gross Settlement: A method of making payments between parties in which each party makes a separate payment on each transaction between them. Gross settlement arrangements are giving way to various net settlement arrangements to reduce credit/settlement risk and expense.

Group of Seven (G7): A group of countries and an organization of national economic and monetary authorities committed to working out economic and currency exchange rate issues. Members are the United States, Japan, Germany, the United Kingdom, France, Italy, and Canada.

Group of Thirty (G30): An international task force that developed a plan for faster, standardized clearance and settlement of international securities transactions.

Guarantee: A contractual or statutory commitment to accept responsibility for repayment of a loan or similar obligation.

Guaranteed Coupon Reinvestment Bonds: A bond or note structure which gives the holder a series of options to receive each interest coupon in cash or to reinvest it in the same bond at par on the interest payment date. A holder electing to reinvest all coupons in this manner would create the equivalent of a zero coupon bond. The appeal of the guaranteed coupon reinvestment bond is that it gives a holder flexibility to avoid the reinvestment risk associated with having to reinvest coupons at lower rates than the original yield on the bond. *Also called Bunny Bond.*

Guaranteed Exchange Rate Warrant: Covered warrants on non-United States stock indexes issued in the United States by a sovereign or a financial intermediary with the currency exchange rate at maturity fixed at the spot rate in effect at issuance. *Also called Guaranteed Warrant, but all guaranteed warrants do not fix the exchange rate at issuance. See also Covered Warrant.*

Guaranteed Index Units: Zero coupon or low yield notes combined with capped or uncapped participations which provide upside exposure to changes in the value of an equity index. *See Equity-linked Notes.*

Guaranteed Investment Contract (GIC): An obligation issued by an insurance company in return for a payment by an investor. The terms of GICs vary greatly, but they typically offer a relatively high initial return guarantee and impose some restrictions on the investor's ability to withdraw funds. A similar contract offered by a bank is called a Bank Investment Contract (BIC). The failure of several insurance companies which were active issuers of GICs has led investors and marketers to look for synthetic GICs which offer a similar return pattern with lower risk. *See Synthetic Guaranteed Investment Contract, Participating Account.*

Guaranteed Return Index Participations (GRIPs): Equity index-linked notes, typically with less than 100 percent participation in the index. *See Equity-linked Notes.*

Guaranteed Return on Investment Certificate (GROI): A combination of a note and a collar or risk reversal position guaranteeing investors a minimum return with a cap on the maximum return. *See Equity-linked Notes.*

Return Pattern of a GROI

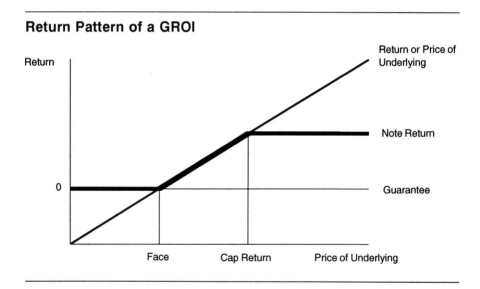

Guaranteed Return Structures (GRSs): Any equity structured product that guarantees a minimum value at maturity (e.g., most equity-linked notes) or guarantees a minimum return based on levels reached by the underlying during the life of the instrument (e.g., ladder options).

Guaranteed Warrant: A stock index warrant issued by a sovereign or a corporation in the United States market. *See also Covered Warrant, Guaranteed Exchange Rate Warrant.*

H

Haircut: (1) The margin or, more frequently, the capital tied up when a financial intermediary takes a position. (2) A commission or fee for execution of a transaction (uncommon).

Hammersmith and Fulham, London Borough of: A local government in the United Kingdom that was extremely active in sterling swaps between 1986 and 1989. Swap volume was very large relative to underlying debt, suggesting large scale speculation by the borough council. The speculation was unsuccessful and a local auditor ruled that the transactions were *ultra vires* — beyond the powers of the council. The House of Lords ultimately upheld the auditor's ruling. The "legal" risk of some risk management contracts was established at considerable cost to the London financial community.

Harmless Warrant: A warrant permanently attached to a callable bond.

Heaven and Hell Bond: A variety of dual currency bond with principal redemption linked directly to the change in the spot exchange rate from issuance to maturity.

Hebel: (German) Leverage.

Hedge: An action which reduces risk, usually at the expense of potential reward. Hedging is typically accomplished by making approximately offsetting transactions that will largely eliminate one or more types of risks. In the narrower sense, the term often indicates partially offsetting a long position in one security with a short or short equivalent position in a related security. *See also Long Hedge, Option Hedge, Option Writing, Reverse Option Hedge, Spread.*

Hedge Account: (1) An account in which a risk reduction position is carried. (2) Designation of a trader's futures position as a hedge account can be important in obtaining favorable margin requirements and an exemption from speculative position limits on futures contracts.

Hedge Accounting: A set of accounting principles which permits a related series of risk offsetting transactions to appear together on accounting records with the object of presenting a more realistic picture of the impact an investment strategy has on a portfolio of assets or on the management of liabilities. If the losses or gains on the items being hedged are deferred, gains or losses on the hedging instruments are deferred. If gains or losses in the hedged item are included in income or effect balance sheet values, changes in value of the hedging instrument(s) are also included as they affect the income statement or balance sheet. The purpose of hedge accounting is to provide a match of related gains and losses and to avoid distorting financial reports. The Securities and Exchange Commission and the Financial Accounting Standards Board are engaged in a complex disagreement over some aspects of the use of hedge accounting in financial reporting. This disagreement may lead to great differences between the economic effect of a risk management transaction and its reflection in financial reports.

Hedge Fund: A private pool of assets managed intensely — and often aggressively. A wide variety of financial instruments may be used and the managers of the fund are typically paid a percentage of any profits. In spite of the name, many such funds do little or no hedging, and risk exposures vary greatly. Funds offered in the United States have a limited number of holders (usually limited partners), and partners must meet certain requirements in terms of net worth, minimum investment, etc.

Hedge Ratio: *See Neutral Hedge Ratio, Delta.*

Hedge Wrap: *See Risk Reversal.*

Hedged Swap: An unmatched swap where one counterparty has undertaken transactions, perhaps in the futures market or in related instruments, to offset interest rate or other risks of its swap position.

Hedging Instrument: A contract, security, or other vehicle which can partially or fully offset some type or element of risk.

Herstatt Risk: *See Cross-Currency Settlement Risk.*

High Coupon Swap: A swap where a fixed rate payment is above the market rate (the underlying bond or note is selling at a premium). The receiver of the high coupon may pay an upfront fee as compensation for the higher cash flow. *Also called a Premium Swap.*

High-Low Floater: A floating rate note with a premium rate up to a cap level on the reference index rate. If the market rate is above the cap rate, the note becomes a reverse floater; its yield declines as the reference rate appreciates further. A high-low floater is a yield enhancement device for investors who expect no more than a modest rise in floating rates over the life of the agreement.

High-Low Option: A cash-settled call option contract with a payout equal to the difference between the high and the low price or rate touched during a period times the contract multiplier. Can also be created as a combination of a lookback call and a lookback put.

Hindsight Currency Option: An option giving the buyer the retroactive right to buy a currency at its low point (call) or to sell a currency at its high point (put) within the option period. Generically, a lookback option.

Historical Volatility: The variance or standard deviation of the change in the underlying's price, rate, or return during a designated period in the past. Historical volatility may or may not be a useful indicator of future volatility, but it is often used as such. *See also Implied Volatility.*

Hockey Stick Payoff Pattern: The traditional kinked return pattern of an option valued at expiration.

Holding Cost: Annualized expenses associated with maintaining an ongoing position in a security or market. Includes custody costs and any property or income tax, including withholding tax.

Horizontal Spread: *See Calendar Spread.*

Host Bond: A debt instrument originally issued with detachable warrants. Often useable at par to exercise the warrants. *See also Useable Security.*

Hybrid Debt: Any combination of a debt instrument and an equity, currency, or commodity forward, option, or swap. A variant of hybrid security. *See also Bifurcation of Derivative Taxation.*

Hybrid Security: Generically, a complex security consisting of virtually any combination of two or more risk management building blocks—bond or note, swap, forward or future, or option. *See also Bifurcation of Derivative Taxation.*

I

Immediate Repackaging of a Perpetual (IRP): Combining a newly issued perpetual floating rate instrument with a fixed rate or zero coupon bond to create cash flow/swap patterns of greater interest to investors.

Immunization of a Portfolio: A risk management technique to ensure that a portfolio of debt instruments will cover a liability coming due at a future date or over a period in the future. The typical approach to immunization is to invest in a portfolio with a Macaulay duration equal to the duration of the liabilities and a present value equal to the present value of the liabilities. This technique implicitly assumes that any shifts in the yield curve will be parallel shifts. *Also called Dedicating a Portfolio or Duration Matching. See also Cash Flow Matching.*

Implied Forward Interest Rate: The interest rate for a specific forward period calculated from the incremental period return in adjacent instruments on the spot zero coupon yield curve. *See Forward Yield Curve, Yield Curve, Zero Coupon Yield Curve.*

Implied Repo Rate: The maximum cost of financing a position which is consistent with or discounted by the return available from a cash/futures arbitrage position. For example, an investor evaluating a cash-and-carry trade, such as buying a stock portfolio and selling a stock index futures contract, will calculate the expected return (dividends plus futures basis) as a money market rate. The implied repo rate is the break-even financing rate for this arbitrage position.

Implied Standard Deviation (ISD): *See Implied Volatility.*

Implied Volatility (IV): The value of the price or rate volatility variable that would equate current option price and fair value. Alternatively, the value of the volatility variable that buyers and sellers appear to accept when the market price of an option is determined. Implied volatility is calculated by using the market price of an option as the fair value in an option model and calculating (by iteration) the volatility level consistent with that option price.

Implied Zero Coupon Swap Curve: A yield curve for zero coupon notes derived from the traditional yield curve and used to value swaps with a fixed rate payment. *Also see Zero Coupon Yield Curve.*

In-Arrears Swap: A structure much like a traditional interest rate swap except that the floating rate is set in-arrears—based on the reference index rate at the end of the reset period—and applied retroactively to the entire period. *Also called an Arrears Swap, Back-End Set Swap, LIBOR In-Arrears Swap, and Reset Swap.*

In the Money: A term referring to an option which has intrinsic value because the current market price of the underlying exceeds the strike price of a call or is below the strike price of a put. For example, a call exercisable at $100 is said to be 3 points in the money when the underlying bond is selling at $103. *See also At the Money, Out of the Money.*

In Option: An option that begins to exist as a conventional option only if a particular barrier price is reached prior to the expiration date of the option. Examples would include a down-and-in call, a down-and-in put, or up-and-in puts and calls.

Incentive Stock Options: Long-term (typically five years) call options offered by a firm to key employees to increase their compensation and encourage behavior consistent with the interests of shareholders. The tax and accounting treatment of these options is constantly under fire, but they are an established component of executive compensation in the United States.

Incentive Trade: A pre-trade agreement between a customer and a broker provides for the broker to share in any gain from a better than average order execution and to be penalized for an inferior execution.

Income Warrants: Warrants that pay interest and carry an exercise right.

Increasing Rate Notes: Debt obligations on which the coupon rate increases by predetermined amounts or to predetermined levels at specified time intervals. An increasing rate structure can be used to defer a portion of interest expense to later years or, when used in connection with a bridge loan, to compensate investors for increasing risk associated with the issuer's delay in redeeming the notes through refinancing or from the proceeds of asset sales.

Index: A number calculated by weighting a number of prices or rates according to a set of predetermined rules. A financial market index is a statistical construct that measures price changes and/or returns in stock markets, fixed income markets, or futures markets. The purpose of the index calculation is to provide a single number whose behavior is representative of the movements of a variety of prices or rates and indicative of behavior in a market. Indexes serve as underlyings for a number of risk management products, particularly in equity and fixed income markets.

Index Allocated Principal (XAC) Bond: A collateralized mortgage obligation whose principal paydown is allocated according to the value of some index. *See also Indexed Principal Swap.*

Index Amortizing Swap: An interest rate swap with a notional principal amount that declines at the rate of a short-term money rate such as LIBOR. The use of an index protects the fixed rate receiver from unanticipated prepayment risk. A flaw in the structure is that actual prepayment risk to the fixed rate payer—who often holds mortgage securities—is usually greatest when the reference index rate is lowest. *Compare with Indexed Principal Swap.*

Index Arbitrage: An investment strategy which attempts to earn higher than money market returns by taking risks comparable to the risks of a money market instrument or attempts to earn higher than stock index returns by taking risks comparable to those incurred by an investor in a stock index fund. The higher returns are made possible by a trading strategy which shifts cash between long and short stock positions and money market positions and buys and sells stock index futures contracts in response to deviations in the stock index futures basis from its fair value. *See also Program Trading.*

Index Fund: A fund designed to track the performance of a market index. Most common among stock funds but used in other markets as well.

Index Growth-Linked Units (IGLUs): A combination of a note and a collar or risk reversal position. As the name implies, the underlying is usually an index, but it may also be a small basket. *See Equity-linked Notes.*

Index-linked Bonds or Notes: Debt instruments with principal and/or interest payments linked to the performance of an inflation or stock market index. *See also Equity Index-linked Notes, Real Yield Security.*

Index Participation Certificate: An equity index-linked note — usually one which provides more or less than 100 percent participation in the movement of the index and less or more than a full return of principal at maturity. *See Equity-linked Notes, Participation.*

Index Participations: Instruments introduced by the Philadelphia Stock Exchange and the American Stock Exchange in 1989 to provide small investors with a low cost way to obtain an index equivalent portfolio. A federal court held that index participations were futures contracts and, hence, could not be traded on securities exchanges. The index participations, which had attracted fair investor interest, were delisted because of this regulatory obstacle. The AMEX is planning a replacement product, Standard & Poors Index Depository Receipts (SPIDRs, pronounced spiders), but the depository receipt structure of SPIDRs has an inherently higher cost than index participations.

Index Principal Return Note: *See Equity-linked Note.*

Index Tracking: A reference to the correlation between a portfolio's return and the return on a benchmark index or, alternately, to the portfolio's tracking error relative to the index. Many equity indexes and enhanced index portfolios are managed with close attention to index tracking. *See also Tracking Error.*

Index Warrants: Put and call options on an index or index futures contract with an original life of more than one year. Index warrants are issued by corporate or sovereign entities or cleared and guaranteed by option clearing corporations. Pricing of these instruments in the market place often depends on investors' ability or inability to sell the warrants short or on the ability of new issuers to license an index to supply new warrants.

Indexation: (1) A passive or nearly passive investment strategy that attempts to replicate the return of a benchmark index in a fund. (2) The practice of linking the return on a security to an index of inflation.

Indexed Currency Options Notes (ICONs): A variant of the dual currency bond with all payments in one currency but with the principal payment indexed to a currency exchange rate at maturity. If the exchange rate is less than an agreed rate, the bond holder receives the face value of the note minus an amount which (typically) increases as the exchange rate declines. Within this generic structure, a number of variations are possible, including a reversed version which provides that the principal payment increases with a decline in the exchange rate. This structure has attracted more publicity than users.

Indexed Notes: The generic combination of a zero coupon bond and an embedded index option feature "purchased" with the present value of what would normally be the periodic yield on the bond. The option provides the holder of the note with participation in the performance of the index. The participation can be either open-ended or capped and more or less than 100 percent of the movement of the index. The underlying can be any of a wide variety of indexes. *See also Equity-linked Notes, Participation, Real Yield Security.*

Indexed Principal Swaps (IPS): An amortizing fixed-for-floating rate swap with a fixed rate above the market rate for a constant notional principal swap, and an amortization rate that decreases as rates rise and increases as rates fall. The most common variety is the mortgage replication swap. *Compare with Index Amortizing Swap.*

Indicative Prices: (1) Bid and offer prices provided by a market maker for the purpose of evaluation or information, not as indicating firm bid and offer prices at which she is willing to trade. (2) A preliminary estimate of the price at which a financial instrument might be created. Indicative prices are quoted to customers for planning or valuation purposes, but they do not form the basis for an actual transaction without further discussion.

Inflation-linked Debt: *See Real Yield Securities.*

Inflation Risk: The opportunity cost incurred if the return from investing — typically in a note or bond — does not offset the loss in purchasing power due to inflation.

Initial Margin: The collateral deposit or performance bond deposited with a broker at the time a derivative position or an underlying security position is taken. Initial margin may be set by government regulators (the Federal Reserve Board on securities in the United States) or by the exchange where the instrument is traded (futures contracts). If the broker carrying the position and handling the trade feels the minimum margin does not give her firm and its customers adequate protection, she may set a higher minimum margin.

Instrike: The trigger or barrier price at which an in option — such as an up-and-in put or a down-and-in call — becomes a conventional option.

Insurance: (1) A risk/return pattern characteristic of options that limits (or insures against) price or rate movements through a predetermined (strike) price or rate in exchange for the explicit or implicit payment of an option (insurance) premium. (2) The component of an option or of a more complex instrument that provides this risk limitation feature. In contrast to a straight hedging transaction which eliminates risk symmetrically over all price ranges, an insurance position creates an asymmetric risk-return pattern. *See also Volatility Value.*

Integrity Risk: (1) In portfolio or basket trading, delivery of a portfolio that contains one or more highly illiquid positions that increase execution cost and risk. Portfolio traders usually guard against integrity risk by requiring general information on the size, trading activity, and volatility of each position in the basket. (2) *See Moral Hazard Risk.*

Interest Only Obligation (IO): A tranche of a collateralized mortgage obligation or similar instrument whose owner receives only the interest or some part of the interest paid on mortgages in the underlying pool. IO tranches are not uniform. The value of a protected income-only stream usually increases if rates decline slowly and moderately, but the holder of a companion or support IO tranche may receive interest payments only until repayments reach a certain fraction of the face value of the pool. Rapid repayment of mortgage principal in a sharply lower rate environment reduces the total value of a pool's interest payments. If a specific IO tranche is designed to be affected first by prepayments, the interest payments available for that tranche can disappear quickly. The mortgage prepayment option and payments dependent on its exercise or nonexercise have proven to be difficult to evaluate. *See also Collateralized Mortgage Obligation (CMO), Companion Collateralized Mortgage Obligations, Planned Amortization Class (PAC), Prepayment Option, Principal Only Obligation (PO), Tranche.*

Interest Rate Collar: An interest rate collar is a combination of an interest rate cap and an interest rate floor. The buyer of the collar purchases the cap option to limit the maximum interest rate he will pay and sells the floor option to obtain a premium to pay for the cap. The effect of the combination is to confine interest rate payments to a range bounded by the strike prices of the cap and floor options. On the other side of the trade, an asset manager might sell a cap and give up the potential for unlimited upside yield in return for the assurance of a minimum return obtained by using the proceeds from the cap to purchase a floor.

Interest Rate Differential (DIFF):   The yield spread between two otherwise comparable debt instruments denominated in different currencies.

Interest Rate Guarantee (IRG):   An option on a forward rate agreement (FRA). *Also called a Fraption.*

Interest Rate Index Swap: *See Rate Differential Swap.*

Interest Rate Option: A right but not an obligation to pay or receive a specific (strike) interest rate on a predetermined principal for a set interval.

Interest Rate Parity: The principle by which forward currency exchange rates reflect relative interest rates on default risk-free instruments denominated in alternative currencies. Currency forward rates and interest rate structures will reflect these parity relationships. Currencies of countries with high interest rates will tend to depreciate over time, and currencies of countries with low interest rates will tend to appreciate over time, reflecting (among other things) implied differences in inflation. These tendencies will be reflected in forward exchange rates as well as in interest rate structures. Any opportunity to earn a profit from small currency or interest rate discrepancies will be arbitraged away. *See also Purchasing Power Parity.*

Interest Rate Reset Notes: Interest on these notes is reset several years after issuance to the greater of the initial rate or a rate sufficient to give the notes a market value greater than the face amount. The reset provision is designed to protect the buyer of a long-term debt instrument from loss of principal due to rising interest rates or a decline in the issuer's debt rating.

Interest Rate Risk: Exposure to accounting or opportunity loss as a result of a relative or absolute change in interest rates. Varieties of interest rate risk include prepayment risk, reinvestment risk, volatility risk, call risk, and long-term rate risk. A variety of instruments are available to reduce or eliminate most kinds of interest rate risk.

Interest Rate Swap: Generically, a fixed rate for floating rate swap in a single currency. *See Swap.*

Intermediary: *See Financial Intermediary.*

Intermediation: Flow of funds from securities into the banking system. *See also Disintermediation.*

International Spread Option, Warrant, or Note: An instrument with a return pattern linked to cross-border interest rate spreads. The payoff at maturity can be set to increase as spreads increase or as spreads decline. *See, for example, BOATs.*

International Swap Dealer's Association, Inc. (ISDA): The principal swap industry trade group. The ISDA Master Swap Agreement is the industry standard documentation for all types of swaps, swap options, and related instruments.

Interquartile Range: The difference between the value of the observation that falls at the bottom of the first quartile in a population and the value of the observation that falls at the top of the fourth quartile. Often used as a measure of dispersion when a population does not match a standard normal or lognormal distribution.

Intrinsic Value of an Option: The amount, if any, by which an option is in the money. *See Basis, Forward Intrinsic Value of an Option, Parity.*

Inverse Floater: *See Reverse Floating Rate Note.*

Inverted Curve Enhancement Swap (ICE Swap): A swap agreement that places a floor under the floating rate (in an inverted yield curve environment) in exchange for a higher fixed rate.

Inverted Market: *See Backwardation Market.*

Inverted Yield Curve: *See Yield Curve.*

Investment Grade: A bond or note rated BBB or higher by Standard & Poor's or comparably by other rating agencies. *See Table of Bond Ratings in the Appendix.*

Issuer: The legal entity that issues and, usually, assumes any obligations of an investment instrument.

Issuer's Option Bond: A debt instrument which, in return for a higher yield than the issuer would otherwise have to pay, gives the issuer an unusual option. The option may range from a put on the issuer's common stock to the right to retire the issue at maturity, partly with cash and partly with a new issue of bonds. In the latter case, the issuer's option may be an option to extend maturity. *See also Mandatory Convertible.*

J

Japanese Option: At the time trading was initiated in TOPIX options on the Tokyo Stock Exchange and in Nikkei-225 options on the Osaka Stock Exchange, these options were exercisable each Thursday during the life of the option contract. In early 1992, the exercise was changed to European style on options expiring after June 1992.

Jellyroll: A transaction in offsetting long and short synthetic stock positions created from options with identical strike prices but different expiration dates. Closing transactions in the near expiration options and opening transactions in the distant expiration options are used to roll a synthetic stock position to a more distant expiration. *See also Box Spread, Synthetic Stock.*

Jump Process: A description of a stochastic price or rate change mechanism or process that includes occasional moves larger than traditional random processes would generate. Analytically, jump processes may be viewed as combinations of a traditional random process and a second process generating the larger moves.

K

Kappa κ: Change in option price in response to a percentage point change in volatility. Kappa measures the sensitivity of option value to a change in implied volatility. *See also Tau and Vega which are used more widely to describe this relationship.*

Keepwell Agreement: A special form of guarantee in the form of a promise by a corporate parent to keep a subsidiary solvent. *See also Guarantee.*

Kicker: A right, warrant, or other low value security added to a debt or stock offering to improve the market reception of the entire issue. *Also called a Sweetener.*

Knock-In Option: An infrequently used term to describe down-and-in or up-and-in barrier options activated at specific price or rate levels.

Knock-Out Option: A term descriptive of down-and-out or up-and-out puts and calls embedded in a structured risk management instrument or traded separately.

Kurtosis: A measure of the extent to which observed data fall near the center of a distribution or in the tails. A kurtosis value less than that of a standard, normal distribution indicates a distribution with a fat midrange on either side of the mean and a low peak—a platykurtotic distribution. A kurtosis value greater than that of a normal distribution indicates a high peak, a thin midrange, and fat tails. The latter, a leptokurtotic distribution, is common in observed price, rate, and return time series data. *See also Jump Process.*

L

Ladder Option or Note: An index or currency warrant or option or equity index-linked note that provides an upward reset of its minimum payout when the underlying touches or trades through certain steps or threshold levels or attains a certain level on designated reset dates. For example, if the underlying trades through a price 35 percent above the strike, the holder of the warrant may be guaranteed a minimum payout equal to the value of the warrant at that price even if the index subsequently declines. A series of steps can ratchet the minimum payout up the ladder, providing protection from a later decline in the index. *Also called a Lock-Step Option, a Step-Lock Option or Note, or a Cliquet Option.*

Lambda Λ: The percentage change in an option price divided by the percentage change in an underlying price. A measurement of the option's leverage — equivalent to the leverage factor. *See Leverage Factor.*

Latent Option or Warrant: *See Embedded Option.*

Law of One Price: The economic principle that the same item or closely equivalent items must sell for the same price in the marketplace. This is the essential principle behind most arbitrage-type transactions.

Leg: (1) One of several components of a combination option. (2) A phrase used by traders to describe a procedure in which one of two offsetting positions is taken in the hope that a subsequent change in the price of the other position will permit execution of the entire trade on favorable terms. When this procedure does not work, the trader "gets legged." If a trader "lifts a leg," he closes one of the offsetting positions in the hope of an unhedged profit on the other.

Legal Right of Set-Off: Under bankruptcy law, a right to net obligations with a bankrupt counterparty. In the United States, recent changes in the law have largely established netting rights in swaps and related risk management agreements. Other jurisdictions are moving in this direction in a competitive response. *See also Netting Agreement.*

Legal Risk: The most important legal risks in financial risk management are capacity or ultra vires risk (the risk that a counterparty is not legally capable of making a binding agreement) and regulatory risk (the risk that a statute or a policy of a regulatory body conflicts with the intended transaction). *See also Hammersmith and Fulham, London Borough of, and Ultra Vires Act.*

Lender Option: A floor on a floating rate agreement.

Lender's Option — Borrower's Option (LOBO):   A floating rate instrument which permits the lender to nominate a revised rate at periodic reset dates, and lets the borrower decide whether to pay the rate or redeem the bond. *Compare with other floating rate reset mechanisms.*

Leptokurtosis: A property of a probability distribution that gives a higher peak, a thinner midrange, and fatter tails than a normal distribution. *See also Kurtosis.*

Less Developed Countries (LDCs):   Countries with lower per capita incomes, greater dependency on commodity prices, less fully developed capital markets, and, often, less favorable credit ratings than major industrial countries.

Level Payment Swap: Converts the cash flows from an amortizing debt instrument into a fixed swap payment at the payment level of the amortizing debt.

Leverage: An investment or operating position subject to a multiplied effect on profit or position value from a small change in sales quantity or price. Leverage can come from high fixed costs relative to revenues in an operating situation or from debt or an option structure in a financial context.

Leverage Factor: The expected or actual percentage price change in value of an option or other derivative position in response to a one percent change in the cash value of the underlying. Equal to gearing if the option delta equals one. For all values of delta, leverage equals delta times underlying price divided by warrant or option price per underlying unit. Sometimes expressed as a ratio rather than as a percent. *See also Lambda, Gearing.*

Leveraged BuyOut (LBO):   Any of a variety of techniques used to replace much of the equity in a corporate capitalization with debt. LBOs in the 1980s have led to opportunities (and need) for risk management in the 1990s.

Leveraged Reverse Floating Rate Notes: A structure similar to a reverse floating rate note except that the multiplier of the fixed rate in effect at the time the position is established is greater than two, and the floating reference index rate is multiplied by that multiplier less one to give a payoff to the reverse floating rate note that responds more than proportionately in reverse to changes in floating rates. *See Floating Rate Note, Reverse Floating Rate Notes.*

Liability: An obligation to make a payment to another.

Liability-based Swap: A swap driven by a floating rate borrower's decision to transform a floating rate liability into a fixed rate obligation or a fixed rate borrower's decision to swap for a floating rate. In either case, the motivation for the decision to swap comes from a desire to modify liabilities.

Liability Manager: A pension plan administrator, corporate financial officer, or other individual responsible for the management of financial liabilities such as pension obligations, a corporation's liability structure, etc. *See also Asset Manager.*

Liability Risk Management: The application of risk control techniques to management of the payment obligations of a corporation, pension plan, insurance company, or any entity which is contractually obligated to make payments to debtors or beneficiaries over time.

LIBOR: *See London Inter-Bank Offered Rate.*

LIBOR Differential Swap: *See Rate Differential Swap.*

LIBOR Eurodollar (LED) Spread: A yield curve spread at the very short end of the yield curve.

LIBOR In-Arrears Swap: *See In-Arrears Swap.*

Lifetime: The term or tenor of a financial instrument or agreement.

Lifting a Leg: Closing out one of two or more risk offsetting positions in an attempt to increase profit by capturing a favorable trend in a market. *See also Leg.*

Limit Move: The maximum price change in a single session permitted by an exchange. Many futures exchanges impose limits on price changes in physical commodities except in the spot month. Except for the Japanese exchanges, daily price limits in financial instruments were uncommon and were being phased out until the 1987 market break led to renewed interest in circuit breakers and price limits. *See also Circuit Breakers.*

Limit Option: *See Barrier Option.*

Limited Exercise Option: *See Bermuda Option.*

Limited Put: *See Floored Put.*

Limited Two-Way Payment Clause (LTP): An optional clause in the ISDA swap agreement that permits the nondefaulting party to avoid any net liabilities to the defaulting party while claiming any net balance due from the defaulting party. This clause has been criticized as inequitable by market participants and bankruptcy litigants.

Liquid Asset-Backed Securities (LABS): *See Securitization.*

Liquid Yield Option Note (LYON): A zero coupon convertible, callable (by the issuer), puttable (by the investor) bond issued by a corporation. The combination of a LYON's features usually assures that an investor will earn a positive return—at least until the expiration of the last opportunity to put the security back to the issuer—and that the total return, if the company prospers and the common stock performs well, will be less than the return earned by common shareholders. The payout pattern of a LYON is roughly similar to some types of equity-linked notes.

Liquidate: Close a position.

Liquidity: A market condition in which enough units of a security or other instrument are traded to allow large informationless transactions to be absorbed by the marketplace without significant impact on price stability.

Liquidity Premium: An extra component of yield required to compensate an investor for the possibility that an adequate resale market may not develop in a given security.

Liquidity Risk: (1) The cost or penalty associated with an illiquid market. Liquidity risk is usually reflected in a wide bid-asked spread and large price movements in response to any attempt to buy or sell. (2) In a depository institution, the cost or penalty associated with unanticipated withdrawals or the failure to attract expected deposits. Liquidity risk is usually managed by limiting holdings of illiquid positions, by matching asset and liability maturities, and by limiting any maturity gap.

Listed Option: An option contract traded on a securities or futures exchange.

Load: A discount on a contingent forward sale or similar agreement which finances the implied premium "paid" for a break forward. *See also Forward.*

Loan-based Certificates: Asset-backed instruments with consumer loan paper as collateral.

Loan Participation: A synthetic debt instrument created when a bank sells a share in a loan with a life under one year to a nonbank investor. Sale of the loan participation reduces the assets the bank carries and provides attractively priced financing to a borrower too small to have its own commercial paper program. The loan participation also provides a slightly higher yield, administrative simplicity, and diversification to a buyer of short-term debt instruments. *See also Disintermediation, Intermediation.*

Local: A floor trader/market maker on an exchange (used most frequently in future markets).

Lock-Limit: An imbalance in supply and demand at a daily price limit. Trading is not possible because the futures contract has reached the daily price limit, and few orders are arriving on the unpopular side of the trade.

Lock-Step Option: *See Ladder Option or Note.*

Lognormal Distribution: Prices are said to have a lognormal distribution if the logarithm of the price has a normal distribution. To illustrate, if a stock is priced at $100 per share and prices have a normal distribution, the distribution of prices is the familiar bell-shaped curve centered at $100, but if the prices have a lognormal distribution, then it is the logarithm of the price which has a bell-shaped distribution about $\log_n 100 = 4.6051702$. The logarithm of the prices is equally likely to be 5.2983174 or 3.912023, i.e., $4.6051702 \pm .6931472$ corresponding to prices of $200 and $50, respectively. If the lognormal probability density curve is plotted as a function of price rather than as a function of the logarithm of price, the curve will appear positively skewed with tails more nearly depicting the observed behavior of stock prices. *See also Normal Distribution.*

The Shape of a Lognormal Distribution

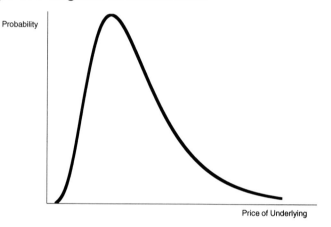

London Inter-Bank Offered Rates (LIBOR): The primary fixed income index reference rates used in the Euromarkets. Most international floating rates are quoted as LIBOR plus or minus a spread. In addition to the traditional Eurodollar and sterling LIBOR rates, yen LIBOR, D-mark LIBOR, Swiss franc LIBOR, etc., are also available and widely used. *See also listings under LIBOR.*

Long: (1) Ownership of an investment position, security, or instrument. (2) A position which will benefit from a rising market. (3) An investor whose position is such that she will benefit from a rising market.

Long the Basis: A hedged position consisting of a long position in the cash instrument or actual and a short position in a future or forward. The opposite position would be short the basis. *See also Basis.*

Long Bond Yield Decrease Warrants (Turbos): Originally, 2-year warrants struck at the interest rate on 30-year United States Treasury bonds.

The warrants act like put warrants on rates or call warrants on the bond price.

Long Dated Forward: A forward contract with a settlement date more than one year in the future.

Long Dated Option: Traditionally, any option with an initial life of more than a year. Today, the term is usually reserved for instruments with an initial life in excess of two or three years.

Long Hedge: A risk offsetting position which protects an investor or liability manager from an opportunity loss in the event of price appreciation in an underlying before a desired position can be established. An example might be a long call or a long futures or forward position taken in anticipation of a cash inflow which will finance a cash market investment.

Long Position: (1) The position of the holder or buyer of a security or other instrument. (2) A position that appreciates in value when market prices increase, such as owning stocks, bonds, futures, or call options or selling put options. Note that the holder of a put is long the contract but profits when the market declines.

Long-term Equity AnticiPation Securities (LEAPs): Exchange-traded options with an original life of about two years. Both puts and calls are available, and LEAPs become fungible with ordinary exchange-traded options as their remaining life falls into the range of traditional exchange-listed options.

Long-term Rate Risk: Exposure to adverse fluctuations in long-term interest rates. The exact nature of the risk depends on whether risk is viewed from the perspective of an asset manager or a liability manager and how the current asset or liability structure compares with the desired structure. Various instruments are available to manage long-term interest rate risks.

Lookback Option: An option giving the buyer the retroactive right to buy (sell) the underlying at its minimum (maximum) within the lookback period. *Also called Lookback Strike Option. See also Hindsight Currency Option.*

Lookforward Option: An option giving the buyer the prospective right to the difference between the spot (strike) price at the beginning of a period and its high (call) or low (put) over that period.

Low Coupon Swap: An interest rate swap with fixed rate payments below current market rates. The floating rate counterparty usually receives a frontend fee. Low coupon swaps are frequently tax motivated. *Compare with Discount Swap.*

Low Exercise Price Options (LEPOs):   An option introduced in Switzerland and Finland and under consideration in other countries to avoid the stamp duty imposed on stock trading, to facilitate the equivalent of short sales, and to create a risk transfer and financing instrument for shares which are not freely transferable. A LEPO will have a strike price very close to zero and, hence, will provide all of the features of ownership except voting rights and dividends. LEPOs may be cash settled if there are restrictions on transfer of the underlying to foreign investors.

M

Macaulay Duration: The present value weighted time to maturity of the cash flows of a fixed payment instrument or of the implicit cash flows of a derivative based on such an instrument. Originally developed as a risk measurement for bonds (the greater the duration or "average" maturity, the greater the risk), duration has proven useful in analyzing equity securities and fixed income options and futures. The diagram illustrates Macaulay duration as a balancing of present values of cash flows. *See also Modified Duration.*

Macaulay Duration of a Ten Percent Coupon, Four-Year Bond in an Eight Percent Yield Environment

Cash Flows

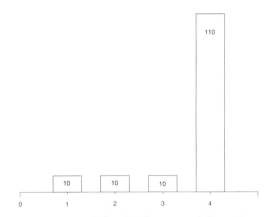

Present Value of Cash Flows and Duration

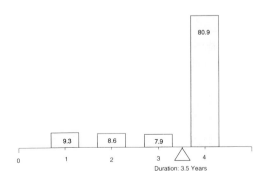

Macro Hedge: *See Global Hedge.*

Macroeconomic (Macro) Swap or Option: A risk management agreement designed to offset some element of quantity or business cycle risk by linking one or both payments to macroeconomic indexes.

Maginot Spread: The yield difference between German bunds and French OATs. *Also called BOAT Spread.*

Maintenance Margin: In addition to the initial margin or performance bond posted in futures, options, and securities markets, each of these markets requires participants to post additional margin if the initial margin is not adequate to ensure that participants will meet their obligations. There is usually no maintenance margin requirement on long option positions because they must be fully paid for in most markets. Maintenance margin is usually called variation margin in futures markets. *See also Variation Margin.*

Making a Market: Posting continuous two-sided (bid and asked) prices and being prepared to trade at those prices during normal market hours.

Mambo Combo: A combination of an in-the-money call and an in-the-money put, both long or both short. For example, a short 80 strike call plus a short 90 strike put is a short mambo combo. Few investors have a reason to put this number on their dance cards.

Managed Futures Accounts: An approach to fund management that makes only government securities, futures contracts, and options on futures contracts eligible for inclusion in a portfolio. Some managers specialize in physical commodity futures, but most managers find they must trade a variety of financial as well as nonfinancial contracts if they have much money under management.

Mandatory Convertible: An equity-like instrument which provides a higher yield or whose principal is denominated in a stronger currency than the underlying common stock at the time of issuance. On or before a contractual conversion date, the holder must convert this instrument into the underlying common stock. Mandatory convertibles are used when a traditional equity issuance would not be possible without placing severe market pressure on the underlying stock, or because the common stock yield or the stock's native currency is unattractive to potential purchasers.

Margin: The required equity or other performance bond that an investor must deposit to collateralize an investment position. *See also Initial Margin, Maintenance Margin, Margin Call, Variation Margin, Performance Bond.*

Margin Call: A demand from the broker or dealer carrying a customer's position for additional cash or collateral to guarantee performance on a position.

Margrabe Option: Named after the author of an article on how to value it. *See Outperformance Option.*

Mark to the Market: To price a position or portfolio at current market prices. A mark to the market can have a significant effect on a margin account. A margin investor will be required to deposit more margin if the market moves sufficiently against him. The mechanism and the nature of variation or maintenance margin requirements varies among markets.

Market: (1) Location (physical or electronic) where transactions take place. (2) Prices at which a market maker is willing to buy and sell a particular instrument. If a market maker is willing to buy XYZ at 10 1/2 and sell XYZ at 11, his market is "10 1/2 at 11" for XYZ.

Market on Close Order (MOC): A type of order frequently used in portfolio trading and in related futures and options transactions which instructs the broker to execute the order at the closing price for the day. In futures markets, a market on close order will be executed within the closing range. Under current New York Stock Exchange rules, a market on close order is assured of execution at the closing price if it is entered by a certain time. Investors using market on close orders should be aware of the probable effect a large order will have on the closing price.

Market Gapping: *See Discontinuity Risk.*

Market Impact: The effect on the price paid or received for a security that comes from the size of the positions bought or sold. For example, if the market for a single lot is 1/2 to 5/8 and a sale of 10,000 shares occurs at 1/4, the market impact is said to be the bid at 1/2 minus the sale price at 1/4, or 1/4. Market impact is often the largest component of trading cost for a large transaction or a large investor. *See also Transaction Costs.*

Market Index Deposits (MIDs): Bank certificates of deposit or deposit notes with a return linked to the performance of an index, usually a stock market index. *See also Equity-linked Notes.*

Market Index Target-Term Securities (MITTS):   *See Equity-linked Notes.*

Market Indexed NotEs (MINEs): *See Equity-linked Notes.*

Market Line: *See Capital Asset Pricing Model (CAPM).*

Market Maker: (1) Any dealer who regularly quotes both bids and offers and is ready to make a two-sided market. (2) A trader on the floor of an exchange who enjoys certain trading privileges in exchange for accepting an obligation to help maintain a fair and orderly market.

Market Risk: Exposure to (adverse) price change.

Marketability Risk: *See Liquidity Risk.*

Markov Process: *See Brownian Motion. See also Square Root Law.*

Martingale: A random process distinguished by the absence of a drift component or any expected change over an interval. *See also Brownian Motion, Stochastic Process.*

Master Swap Agreement: Comprehensive documentation of standard terms and conditions covering all swap transactions between two counterparties.

Matched Book: A portfolio of offsetting assets and liabilities with equal maturities.

Matched Swap: A swap covered on one side by an underlying bond or note with terms similar to that side of the swap.

Matrix Price: An estimated price or value for a fixed income security. Matrix prices are based on quoted prices for securities with similar coupons, ratings, and maturities rather than on specific bids and offers for the designated security.

Maturity: The date on which the life of a financial instrument ends through cash or physical settlement or expiration with no value.

Maturity Gap: An early approach to the measurement of interest rate risk. For each period out to the longest maturity, the market values of rate sensitive assets and rate sensitive liabilities are measured. The size of the gap in each period is multiplied by the change in interest rates to be evaluated. The results are summed to give the effect on the cumulative net interest income or expense. This approach has been largely abandoned for analyses based on asset and liability duration.

Maturity Mismatch Risk: The risk that, due to differences in maturities of the long and short positions in a cross hedge, the value of the risk offsetting positions will fail to move in concert.

Maximum Rate Notes: *Another name for Reverse Floating Rate Notes.*

Mean: Most commonly, the arithmetic average of a population or series of observations. *See also Geometric Mean, Median.*

Mean Reversion: The name given diverse processes by which variables such as prices, rates, and volatilities tend to return to a mean or average value after reaching extremes. *See also Volatility Auto Regressive Integrated Moving Average (VARIMA).*

Mean Variance Portfolio Model: *See Capital Asset Pricing Model (CAPM).*

Median: The middle observation in an ordered distribution. After the mean, the most common measure of central tendency.

Medium-Term Notes (MTN): Plain vanilla debt instruments with a fixed rate and a fixed maturity (typically less than seven years, but occasionally much longer). Medium-term notes are the basic component of the debt issuance programs of many investment grade borrowers. A medium-term note yield can serve as the base rate for a swap payment and an MTN component can be part of a hybrid security.

Micro Hedge: To offset risk on a position by position basis. *Compare with Global Hedge.*

Mini-Max Floater: A floating rate note with an embedded collar.

Mini-Max Strategy: Generically, any interest rate risk management structure that provides participation and protection while attempting to minimize any option premium payment. This is often accomplished by selling a cap or floor to offset the cost of a corresponding floor or cap.

Ministry of Finance (MOF): The principal regulator of financial markets in Japan.

Mirror Swap: A swap designed to cancel or offset the remaining payments of an earlier swap agreement.

Mismatched Payment Swap: A swap agreement under which the parties make payments at different times and/or at different intervals exposing one or both parties to settlement risk.

Modern Portfolio Theory (MPT): *See Capital Asset Pricing Model (CAPM).*

Modified Duration: A measurement of the change in the value of an instrument in response to a change in interest rates. The primary basis for comparing the effect of interest rate changes on prices of fixed income instruments. The formula shows the small difference between modified and Macaulay duration. Many applications are not sensitive to the difference, and modified and Macaulay duration numbers are often used interchangeably. *See also Macaulay Duration.*

$$D_{mod} = \frac{1}{1 + \frac{y}{f}} D_{mac}$$

Where D_{mod} = modified duration
$\quad\quad D_{mac}$ = Macaulay Duration
$\quad\quad y$ = yield to maturity
$\quad\quad f$ = frequency of coupon payment

If Macaulay Duration is 6, yield is 7 percent (.07), and the bond pays interest twice a year:

$$D_{mod} = \frac{1}{1 + \frac{.07}{2}} \times 6 = 5.8 \text{ years}$$

Modified Following: In a swap or other interim reset agreement, variable terms are usually "modified following" a designated date. *Compare with In-Arrears Swap.*

Modigliani-Miller Hypothesis: The proposition (which was largely responsible for earning its proposers Nobel prizes) that in an efficient capital market with no taxes, the relative proportion of debt and equity in a corporate capitalization does not affect the total market value of the firm. Corporate financial officers and financial engineers continue to search for market inefficiencies and tax-related opportunities in the real world.

Momentum Investor: A market participant who increases or reduces his level of market participation to "go with the flow" — increasing market exposure when the market is rising and decreasing market exposure when the market is falling. Trend-following technical traders and portfolio insurance practitioners are a few of the investors who use this approach. *For contrast, see Asset Allocation.*

Money Back Certificates: Any of a family of hybrid instruments which promises the investor the return of her original investment at a minimum. Cash that might ordinarily be paid as yield goes to pay for exposure to any of a variety of equity, interest rate, commodity, and/or currency exposures. These hybrids are usually best analyzed by dividing the original investment into a zero coupon bond that will appreciate to the value of the original investment over the life of the instrument and the balance which is used to buy an option, invest in a commodity pool, etc. *See, for example, Equity-linked Notes.*

Money Back Options or Warrants: Similar to money back certificates, but the warrant structure may permit only a partial refund of the warrant investment in the event of an adverse move in the underlying. *See Money Back Certificates, Redeemable Warrant.*

Money Market Basis: A day count fraction equal to actual days divided by 360 except in the United Kingdom and several Commonwealth countries where the denominator is 365 or actual days. *See also Bond Basis.*

Moneyness: The characteristic of being sufficiently like cash to be used as a medium of exchange in the settlement of transactions.

Monte Carlo Method: In option evaluation, a numeric probability approach to the valuation of path-dependent options which cannot be decomposed easily into a series of standard options with closed-form (analytic) solutions. The Monte Carlo technique is also used when there is reason to believe that the underlying return-generating process does not match a standardized distribution. In applying the Monte Carlo method, an analyst will generate a series of prices for the underlying(s) using a model that approximates the market's price-generating process. An average (expected) option value at expiration for each underlying or set of underlyings is determined. The quality of the result depends on the realism of the price- or return-generating process.

Moral Hazard: The risk that a party to a transaction has not entered into a contract in good faith, has provided misleading information about its assets, liabilities, or credit capacity, or has an incentive to take unusual risks in a desperate attempt to avoid losses.

Moral Hazard Risk: Exposure to loss resulting from a willful, improper, or illegal act by an agent or counterparty. *See also Moral Hazard.*

Mortgage-backed Securities: Debt instruments collateralized by residential, commercial, or industrial real estate mortgages. *See also Collateralized Mortgage Obligation (CMO), Government National Mortgage Association (GNMA) Pass-through Certificates, Interest Only Obligation (IO), Principal Only Obligation (PO), Real Estate Mortgage Investment Conduit (REMIC).*

Mortgage Over Treasury Option (MOTO): A cash-settled call on the spread between a specific mortgage-backed security or index yield and a selected Treasury security yield. The value of the option will be affected by the mortgage repayment rate and, hence, by the level and volatility of interest rates.

Mortgage Prepayment Cap: An OTC option contract that protects the holder of the cap from a return loss if the prepayment rate in a specific mortgage pool exceeds a strike expressed relative to a PSA prepayment rate. Although they are uncommon, prepayment floors are also available. *See also Prepayment Option, Public Securities Association (PSA).*

Mortgage Replication Swap: A variety of indexed principle swap in which the fixed rate side is based on a mortgage-style rate and amortization schedule. The rate is often a real mortgage rate or a premium over a benchmark Treasury issue. The amortization rate is a real or preset amortization schedule. *See also Indexed Principal Swap.*

Multi-Currency Swap Agreement: An exchange of payments covering a series of cash flows among several different currencies to be both paid and received. Analytically, a multi-currency swap agreement can be split into a series of separate bilateral currency swap agreements.

Multi-Factor Option: *See Alternative Option.*

Multi-Index Option: An outperformance option with a payoff determined by the difference in performance of two or more indexes. *See also Outperformance Option.*

Multi-Period Option: Any of a variety of option structures whose payout is based on the value of the underlying on several occasions (average rate or price option) or which is really a series or strip of separate options (most caps and floors).

Multilateral Netting: An arrangement among three or more parties in which each party makes payments to an agent or clearing house for net obligations due to other parties or receives net payments due from other parties. This procedure is used to reduce credit/settlement risk.

Multiple-Traded Option: Exchange-traded option contracts on the same underlying traded on different exchanges or in different countries. These contracts may or may not be fungible.

Municipal Over Bond Spread (MOB): The difference between the yield implicit in the municipal bond futures contract and the yield implicit in the Treasury bond futures contract. The spread is sensitive to the shape of the yield curve (the municipal contract components are usually shorter-term bonds) and the perceived credit quality of the municipals.

Mutual Offset: A cross-margining system that reduces initial margin requirements on one futures exchange if a risk offsetting position is held in a related contract on another exchange. *See also Standard Portfolio Analysis of Risk (SPAN).*

N

Nakadachi: *See Saitori.*

Naked Option: An option writing (sale) position collateralized by cash or securities other than those on which the option is written. The potential loss on a naked option position can be very large — in the case of a naked call on common stock, the possible loss is theoretically unlimited. *Also called an Uncovered Option Position. See Covered Call Option, Option Hedge.*

The Profit /Loss Patterns of Naked Options

Naked Call

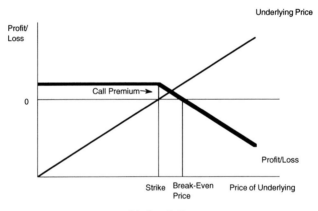

Naked Put

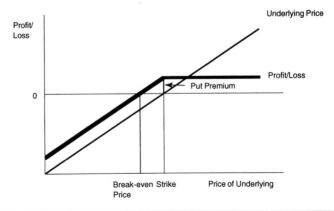

Natural Hedge: The shift of production facilities, working capital, or borrowing arrangements to an alternative currency area to offset undesirable cash flow exposures.

Near Month: The next futures or options contract due to expire.

Negative Carry: The net cost of carrying a position when the cost of funds is greater than the yield on the securities.

Negative Convexity: *See Convexity.*

Negative Pledge Agreement: A contract provision under which one party agrees *not* to do something that would have an adverse effect on the interests of the other party. *See also Covenant.*

Net Commission: In the United Kingdom, a net or principal trade with no commission payable.

Net Margin Requirement: The margin required after any option premium received by the investor is deducted from the stated option margin requirement.

Net Settlement: (1) A procedure for swap payment exchanges in which only one party makes a payment of the net amount due after subtracting the amount owed by the other party. (2) The difference payment from one swap counterparty to the other after their gross obligations to one another are netted against each other.

Net Trade: A principal (dealer) trade on which no commission is charged.

Net Yield: Dividend yield to a foreign investor after deducting a stock's withholding tax.

Netting Agreement: Contractual offset of payables against receivables to reduce credit exposure to a counterparty. Netting swap payments in bankruptcy, for example, reduces credit exposure to the net obligation of a counterparty. Netting in bankruptcy or insolvency may not be enforceable in all jurisdictions, but the United States federal bankruptcy code and the Financial Institutions Reform, Recovery, and Enforcement Act of 1989 (FIRREA) are designed to permit netting among United States–based counterparties.

Netting by Novation: Replacement of all agreements between two parties with a single agreement and a single net payment stream. Formal netting by novation is often a response to financial distress on the part of one counterparty. Also called by various other names, most including the word "netting."

Neutral Hedge: A combination of long and short positions in related securities or other instruments that is designed to earn the risk-free interest rate whether the underlying goes up or down slightly in price.

Neutral Hedge Ratio: The fraction of a point by which the price of an option contract is expected to change in response to a one-point change in the price of the underlying instrument. Mathematically, the first partial derivative of the option price with respect to the underlying price. If its neutral hedge ratio is 0.5, an option contract should change in price by about $.50 for each $1.00 change in the price of the underlying. This relationship is the primary basis of risk management with instruments containing option payoff patterns. Of course, higher derivatives such as gamma and other relationships also must be monitored and evaluated in an effective risk management program. *Also called Delta Factor and Elasticity* (2). *See also Delta/Gamma Hedge.*

New Issue Swap: Any of a variety of swap structures which converts an issuer's lowest relative borrowing cost structure to a structure that fits the issuer's liability management targets. For example, a AA-rated United States–based borrower might borrow at *relatively* lower cost in the fixed rate dollar market than in the floating rate sterling market. A lower-rated United Kingdom borrower might borrow at floating rates in sterling with only a small credit penalty. These borrowers could swap interest payments and/or currencies to their mutual advantage. A medium-term note offering from the AA-rated borrower might be sold with the express design of implementing such a swap.

Nikkei-linked Bond (NLB): An equity index-linked bond with the Nikkei-225 stock average as the underlying index.

No-Arbitrage Condition: A boundary condition on option and underlying price relationships which eliminates the possibility of risk-free arbitrage between and among puts, calls, and underlying instruments. *See also Put/Call Parity.*

No-Regrets Options: Lookback options. Because lookback calls are always struck at the lowest price during the life of the option, and lookback puts are struck at the highest price, an investor will have no regrets that he might have gotten a more favorable strike. Lookback options carry a higher premium than standard options, so the size of the premium might be a source of regret.

Nominal Quotation: *See Indicative Prices.*

Non-Par Swap: Any swap with one or both of the equivalent securities underlying the swap payments selling at a discount or premium to parity. *See, for example, Discount Swap, High Coupon Swap, Low Coupon Swap.*

Non-Standard Options: *See Exotic Options.*

Non-Sticky Jump (NSJ) Bond: A collateralized mortgage obligation whose principal paydown is changed by the occurrence of one or more "triggering" event(s). Each time the trigger condition is met, the bond changes to its new priority for receiving principal, and it reverts to its old priority for each payment date that the trigger condition is not met.

Nonsystematic Risk: An element of price risk which can be largely eliminated by diversification within an asset class. *See also Systematic Risk, Diversification.*

Normal Density: The integral under the normal distribution function between two points or between one point and infinity.

The Normal Density Between 20 and 21

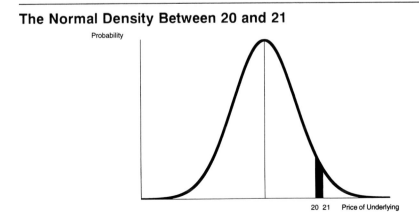

Normal Distribution: A probability distribution which describes the behavior of many natural and man-made phenomena. The normal distribution is particularly useful because it can be described with a relatively simple equation and analyzed to reveal detailed characteristics of segments of the distribution. For example, about 2/3 of total observations fall within 1 standard deviation on either side of the mean of a normal distribution. About 95 percent of observations fall within 2 standard deviations, and 99 percent fall within 3 standard deviations of the mean. If a population distribution is not normal, a sample standard deviation will not have these distribution characteristics which are often used to estimate the confidence an investigator can have that an observation falls inside or outside the population described by the distribution. *See also Lognormal Distribution, Confidence Intervals, Standard Deviation.*

Normal Price of an Option: The option price predicted by an econometric model or any similar technique used to estimate typical stock price-option price relationships. The normal price is an estimate based on the assumption that relationships that existed in a prior period are still meaningful. Normal price is a prediction of what an option price will be, not necessarily what it should be if fairly valued relative to likely payoffs at expiration. In contrast to a market neutral hedged position taken at fair value, a position taken at normal price does not necessarily offer an investor the expectation of earning the risk-free rate if the neutral hedged position is maintained (without frictional costs) through expiration. *See Fair Value of an Option.*

Note Over Bond (NOB) Spread: A yield curve spread created by selling the 10-year United States Treasury note futures contract and buying the 30-year bond contract or the reverse. Alternately, an equivalent position can be created in the cash/repo market. An investor expecting a steepening yield curve would purchase the note contract and sell the bond contract in some proportion. An investor expecting inversion of a flat yield curve would buy the bond contract and sell the note contract.

Notional Bond: A standardized bond with hypothetical terms (coupon and maturity) that is the basis for a bond futures contract. Each market has its own standard terms and conversion factors for adjusting the terms of actual bonds to the notional standard.

Notional Principal Amount: The nominal value used to calculate swap payments and on which many other risk management contract payments are based. In an interest rate swap, each period's rates will be multiplied by the notional principal amount to determine the dollar amount of each counterparty's payment.

Notional Principal Contract: Any swap, forward rate agreement, cap, floor, or similar instrument whose value is based on a nominal face amount that is not itself an obligation of one party to the other.

Notionnel: (French) (1) Notional or standardized. (2) The French government bond contract traded on the Marché à Terme International de France (MATIF).

Novation: Replacing one or a series of contracts with a new contract, often with a third party replacing one of the original parties. Novation may be used to cancel agreements which have already been offset with other agreements. It is usually reserved for situations where any risk associated with the creation of a new agreement is offset by the release of capital or credit lines tied up in an unnecessarily complex structure. *See also Netting by Novation.*

O

Obligations Assimilables du Trésor (OATs):   French government bonds underlying the principal French bond futures and options contracts.

Off Balance Sheet (OBS) Instrument: A notional principal contract that changes an economic unit's risk structure without appearing as an asset or liability on a traditional balance sheet. The size and impact of these instruments in the aggregate is usually summarized in a footnote to financial statements. Swaps, forward rate agreements, and various currency contracts are common OBS instruments.

Off-Exchange Option Contracts: Unlisted options designed to meet specific commercial or investment needs. *Also called Over-The-Counter Options.*

Off-Exchange Task Force (OETF):   A group of Commodity Futures Trading Commission officials who monitor hybrid instruments and other over-the-counter (OTC) risk management contracts.

Off-Market Coupon Swap: An interest rate or other swap contract with a fixed rate payment materially different from current coupon rates on bonds or notes of similar term. Ordinarily, this swap will have a net present value that requires the counterparties to exchange an extra payment at the beginning or end of the swap tenor. *See High Coupon Swap, Low Coupon Swap, Discount Swap.*

Offer Price: The price at which a trader or market maker is willing to sell a security.

Offset: (1) A closing transaction in an exchange market which cancels or eliminates an option or futures position. (2) A position with identical but opposite price or rate responses which cancels some or all of the market risk of an open position but not necessarily the position's credit or settlement risk.

Offsetting Swap: A swap which exactly counters the interest rate or other market risk of a pre-existing swap but does not cancel the earlier swap. This structure does not eliminate all risk of the earlier position.

Offsetting Transaction: A trade that creates a new position to offset the market risk characteristics of an old one or, if the instruments in the new position are fungible with those in the old, cancels or closes out the old position. *See also Fungibility.*

Oil Price Derivatives: Virtually any risk management structure available on common stocks, bonds, or indexes is available with oil as the primary underlying.

Omega Ω: (1) Currency risk associated with translating the value of a currency option position in a different currency. (2) Third derivative of the option price with respect to the price of the underlying.

One-Off Transaction: (1) An unusual customized contract designed especially to meet a specific requirement, unlikely to be useful in other risk management situations. (2) A transaction between two parties who do not usually trade with one another.

One Touch Option: *See Touch Option.*

Open Interest: The number of listed option contracts of a class or series or the number of identical futures contracts outstanding at a particular time. Open-interest figures are available on each listed contract and are often a better indicator than trading volume of public interest in a contract.

Open Outcry: A method of trading that brings representatives of buyers and sellers together to shout bids and offers aloud. Open outcry provides a high degree of assurance that all contemporary bids and offers have an opportunity to be heard and matched with the most attractive offers and bids from investors on the other side of the market.

Opening Purchase Transaction: A transaction in which an investor becomes the holder or buyer of an option or futures contract.

Opening Rotation: *See Rotation.*

Opening Sale Transaction: A transaction in which an investor becomes the writer or seller of an option or futures contract.

Opportunity Loss or Cost: The value of a lost chance or a potential profit that was not realized because a course of action was taken that did not permit the investor to obtain that profit. The actual or expected cost of following one course of action measured relative to the most attractive alternative. Opportunity loss will not be reflected in an accounting statement. An example of an opportunity loss might be the $20 per share profit forgone by a covered call writer who sells a call with a $45 strike price for $5, only to see the underlying stock jump to $70 in response to a take-over bid.

Opportunity Value: *See Volatility Value.*

Optimization of a Portfolio: Use of a linear or quadratic model to structure a portfolio to maximize or minimize yield, long-term rate sensitivity, etc., or to increase or reduce exposure to certain industries, market sectors, or macroeconomic factors, subject to prespecified constraints.

Option: A stipulated privilege of buying or selling a stated property, security, or commodity at a given price (strike price) within a specified time (for an American-style option, at any time prior to or on the expiration date). A securities option is a negotiable contract in which the seller (writer), for a certain sum of money called the *option premium,* gives the buyer the right to demand within a specified time the purchase (call) or sale (put) by the option seller of a specified number of bonds, currency units, index units, or shares of stock, at a fixed price or rate, called the *strike price* or *rate.* Many options are settled for cash equal to the difference between spot value and the aggregate strike price rather than by delivery of the underlying. In the United States and many other countries, stock options are written for units of 100 shares. Other units of underlying coverage are standard in other option markets. Options are ordinarily issued for periods of less than one year, but longer term options are increasingly common. *See Call Option, Combination Option, Commodity Option, Expiration Date, Premium, Put Option, Strike, Terms of Option Contract.*

Option-adjusted Duration: A modified duration calculation which incorporates the expected duration-shortening effect of an issuer's embedded call provision.

Option-adjusted Spread: An alternate way to calculate the call-adjusted yield of callable bonds by calculating the noncallable bond equivalent spread versus the Treasury yield curve. *See also Call-adjusted Yield, Option-adjusted Yield.*

Option-adjusted Yield: The expected yield to maturity of a bond or note after adjusting for the probability-weighted impact of an embedded option, usually an issuer's call provision.

Option Business: *See Premium Business.*

Option Buyer: The investor who buys options to increase leverage, hedge the risks in a portfolio of assets or liabilities, or attain other investment objectives.

Option on a Cap: *See Caption.*

Option Contract: In over-the-counter options, a contract document sets forth the provisions of the option. The terms of a listed option are stated in clearing corporation documents. The buyer's evidence of ownership of an exchange-traded option is his confirmation slip from the executing broker. *See also Option.*

Option-dated Forward: A forward foreign exchange contract with an option to select the date of exchange.

Option to Double: *See Double Option (2), Sinking Fund.*

Option on a Floor: *See Floortion.*

Option Hedge: A partially or fully price-hedged position in which the investor sells more than one risk offsetting option against each corresponding underlying unit. The net effect of this position is to maximize the option seller's profit when the underlying sells at the strike price at expiration. The rate of return at expiration declines if the shares sell either above or below the strike price. The writer loses money only if the stock rises or falls beyond a break-even point at expiration. *See also Reverse Option Hedge, Naked Option.* See figures on next page.

Option on an Option: *See Compound Option.*

Option Portfolio: Any portfolio that includes long option positions or collateralized short option positions.

Option Premium: (1) In the United States, the amount of money an option buyer pays for a conventional put or call or the quoted price of a listed option. (2) The amount by which the price of an option exceeds its intrinsic

Buy One Unit of Underlying

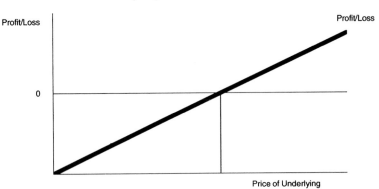

Sell Two Calls

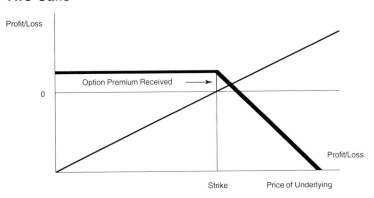

Two to One Option Hedge Profit/Loss Pattern

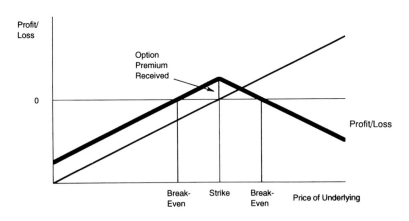

value. For example, if an option to buy XYZ Corporation at $100 is selling at $9 and the stock is selling at $103, the premium is said to be $6. To avoid confusion between (1) and (2), the term "option price" or "premium" is used to designate the market price of an option, and the term "premium over intrinsic value" is used to designate the amount by which the stock price must *rise* before the expiration date for the option buyer to break even, neglecting commissions. Premium over intrinsic value is also called time value, volatility value, or opportunity value with differing degrees of accuracy and usefulness. *See also Premium, Time Value.*

Option Replication: (1) A technique to create an option-like payoff pattern through a series of transactions in the underlying or in related futures contracts as in dynamic hedging and traditional portfolio insurance. (2) Creating a long-term option out of a sequence of baskets of short-term options. As the price of the underlying moves, there may be a need to trade the replicating options dynamically, but long-term option replication with short-term options will generally require fewer portfolio adjustments than option replication with the underlying or with related futures contracts.

Option on a Swap: *See Swaption.*

Option Writer: An investor who sells options collateralized by a portfolio of securities or other performance bonds.

Optioned Stock: The underlying stock which is the subject of a stock option contract.

Options Clearing Corporation: The guarantor of listed security option contracts in the United States. It is owned proportionately by each of the exchanges trading listed security option contracts. Similar organizations act as contract guarantors in most other option and futures markets. *See Clearing Corporation.*

Options Disclosure Document: Boilerplate warning distributed to prospective users of United States securities options. A triumph of form over substance.

Options Exchange: A securities or futures exchange authorized to trade listed options.

Order Flow: The customer purchase and sale inquiries coming to a dealer. A large dealer may be able to offer more competitive terms on a larger fraction of the orders he sees because heavy order flow helps him judge the state of the market and increases the probability he will find the other side of a transaction without incurring large hedging costs.

Out of the Money: Refers to an option that has no intrinsic value because the current underlying price is below the strike price of a call or above the strike price of a put. For example, a put at $100 when stock is selling at $105 is said to be 5 points out of the money. *See At the Money, In the Money.*

Out Option: An option with an expiration price as well as an expiration time. The option contract expires or pays off (depending on specific contract terms) if the underlying trades at or through the outstrike price. In the case of a down-and-out call, for example, the option expires immediately if the underlying touches the outstrike before the stated expiration date.

Outperformance Option: A call option with a payoff based on the amount by which one of two underlying instruments or indexes outperforms the other. *Also called Margrabe Option, Multi-Index Option, Relative Performance Option. See also Cross-Currency Option. Compare to Alternative Option.*

Outright Forward Currency Transaction: An isolated forward currency trade which is not part of a swap. *See also Forward Outright Rate.*

Outstrike: The price at which a down-and-out or up-and-out call or down-and-out or up-and-out put expires or pays off if the price of the underlying touches or trades through it under circumstances meeting the requirements of the contract. Generically, outstrike is used to refer to any price at which the terms of a nonstandard option change.

Over-and-Out Put: *See Up-and-Out Put.*

Over The Counter (OTC): A security or other instrument that is not traded on an organized exchange or a market that is not part of an organized exchange. OTC instruments can be created with any provisions allowed by law and acceptable to counterparties. OTC markets and instruments are less closely regulated in some ways than exchange markets and instruments.

Over-The-Top Option: An up-and-out option.

Overcollateralization: The requirement or provision of asset backing that exceeds the value of an obligation.

Overlay Risk Management: An approach to asset risk management which turns over most of the assets of a portfolio to managers selected for their unique skill in particular markets, and assigns an overlay manager responsibility for partial or full asset allocation and/or currency risk management. The overlay manager typically uses options, futures, swaps, and other derivative risk management instruments rather than cash markets to reduce execution costs.

Overlay Strategies: Any of a number of techniques to add risk management of currency or asset allocation on top of the activities of traditional portfolio managers. Call option overwriting, asset allocation and currency overlays are probably the most common overlay strategies. *See also Overlay Risk Management.*

Overnight Delivery Risk: The risk incurred when one side of a trade settles the day before the other side. This overnight delay exposes one of the counterparties to the risk that the other side will fail to meet its obligations.

Overwriting: Most frequently, the sale of stock index or common stock call options against a fixed common stock portfolio with the expectation that the options, on average, will expire worthless or be repurchased at a profit. Call overwriting strategies are frequently complex and may involve repurchasing unprofitable options and selling a larger number of options at a higher strike price in an attempt to turn losses into profits. Investor experience with overwriting strategies has been uneven. In general, overwriting adds modestly to returns in most periods with an occasional dramatic opportunity loss in a bull market. Theory predicts that overwriting will reduce variance rather than enhance return, contrary to the statements of many overwriting advocates. Consequently, overwriters should not expect to improve their long-term risk-adjusted returns. *See also Dynamic Overwriting.*

P

Package Trade: A portfolio trade.

Packaged Equity Trust Securities (PETS): *See Short-Term Equity Participation Units (STEP Units).*

Par: The face value or nominal value of a security. Used more frequently for bonds and other fixed income securities than for stocks.

Parallel Loans: An early form of swap in which a party in country A made a loan denominated in currency A to a party in country B. The party in country B, in turn, made a loan in currency B to the party in country A. This parallel loan structure has largely been abandoned in favor of swaps with netting agreements which expose the parties to substantially less credit risk.

Parallel Shift: A movement of each point on a yield curve up or down by the same amount. Many duration-matching and control strategies assume that any yield curve shifts will be parallel.

Pari Passu: Two securities or obligations that have equal rights to payment are said to rank pari passu.

Parity: (1) The condition in which an option sells at its intrinsic value. The maximum of 0 or spot minus strike for a call and the maximum of 0 or strike minus spot for a put. (2) The condition in which a bond sells at its nominal or face value.

Parity Graph: A representation of the value of a financial instrument when any premium from the insurance value of an option or the basis of a forward or futures contract has been eliminated by the passage of time — a valuation at expiration or in exercise.

Partial Lookback Warrants: A warrant which provides a time window of, say, 30 to 90 days, during which the strike price is set or reset at the most favorable level during that period. After that period, the option is an ordinary American-style option. Because the lookback characteristic covers a limited time, the partial lookback option will sell for a price intermediate between a traditional option and a full lookback option. A call warrant of this general type is occasionally called an anti-crash warrant because the reset allows the holder to obtain a lower strike if a crash occurs during the lookback period. *See also Reset Option or Warrant, Step-Down Warrant.*

Participating Account: A separate account at a financial institution used as a synthetic guaranteed investment contract (GIC). A participating account is not subject to claims from the institution's general creditors. *See also Bank Investment Contract (BIC), Guaranteed Investment Contract (GIC), Synthetic Guaranteed Investment Contract.*

Participating Cap: A partial cap that reduces but does not eliminate exposure to an upward price or rate move. The cap covers a smaller notional amount than the value of the underlying, giving the parties to the cap a participation structure when they average the capped and the uncapped positions.

Participating Capped Floating Rate Note: Behaves like a mixture or an average of an ordinary floating rate note and a capped floating rate note. *See also Floating Rate Note (FRN) and Capped Floating Rate Note.*

Participating Forward Contract: A contingent forward contract in which the buyer accepts a floor price below the current forward market in return for a fixed-percentage participation in any favorable difference between the spot at expiration and the floor rate. Although used most frequently in currency markets, the participation structure is also used in equity and debt structures. The diagram illustrates a floor price below spot, but the floor could be above spot (but still below the forward price), particularly with a dividend or interest payment on the underlying and a low participation rate. Other things equal, the lower the floor, the higher the participation rate. *See also Participating Interest Rate Agreement (diagram).*

An Illustration of a Participating Forward Contract

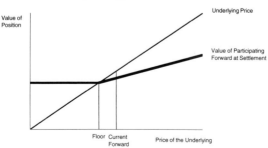

Participating Interest Rate Agreement (PIRA): An off-exchange contract designed to meet an investor's or borrower's need to reduce exposure to adverse interest rate changes while continuing fractional participation in interest rate changes. Similar in structure to a participating forward contract. The borrower's side of the participating interest rate agreement is illustrated in contrast to the investor's side of the participating forward agreement.

A Participating Interest Rate Agreement that Caps a Borrower's Cost of Funds and Provides Participation in Any Rate Decline

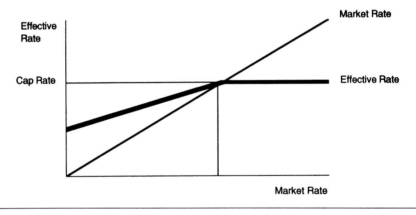

Participating Option: Any option that changes the rate of participation in a price or rate movement beyond the strike. The term is usually applied only to options that give some participation but not 100 percent participation in a price or rate movement.

Participating Range Forward: A variant of the risk reversal, range forward, or forward rate bracket structure with some participation in movement of the underlying below the lower strike or above the upper strike. *Also called Forward Plus.*

Participating Swap: An interest rate swap with a participating interest rate agreement modifying the floating rate payments.

Participation: An option-like structure which typically provides a floor return combined with reduced exposure to a favorable return on the underlying or a ceiling return combined with reduced exposure to an unfavorable return. The reduction in exposure to favorable events usually pays for the protection of the floor or cap. Intuitively, the most useful way to view a participation is as a combination or an average of an option and a forward or as an average of an option and cash. *See, for example, Participating Forward Contract (diagram), Participating Interest Rate Agreement (diagram).*

Participation Certificate: (1) A security issued by a corporation with a payoff pattern similar to an equity-linked note. (2) A security issued to create an additional class of equity shares with a different dividend rate or reduced restrictions on share transfer.

Partly Paid Bonds: Debt instruments issued in the United Kingdom with part of the price paid at issuance and the balance paid in one or several installments. Interest is ordinarily paid only on the principal paid in.

Pass-through Securities: Securitized mortgages or other debt contracts with interest and principal paid to the investor by the servicing intermediary shortly after payments are received from the borrowers. *See also Securitization.*

Passing the Book: All major financial intermediaries have equity, fixed income, and currency trading organizations operating in a number of time zones. Currencies and, to a lesser extent, fixed income and equity positions are traded in a 24-hour market. Control of the intermediary's risk positions passes from one time zone to another in a procedure known as passing the book.

Passive Management: Most commonly, indexation of a portfolio, giving up the opportunity for superior performance within an asset class in return for protection from inferior performance. *See also Passive Manager.*

Passive Manager: An asset manager who invests assets in index portfolios or unmanaged baskets of securities and other instruments without attempting to select individual securities. Some passive managers who made little or no effort to outperform an index in the past, now try to improve upon index returns with derivatives and return enhancement strategies, blurring the line between passive and active managers.

Path-dependent Option: Whereas the value of a traditional option depends only on the price of the underlying on the day of exercise or expiration, the value of a path-dependent option depends partly or exclusively on the price pattern the underlying follows in reaching exercise or expiration. Asian (average price or rate) options, look-back options, and barrier options are all examples of path-dependent options. If early exercise could be appropriate for an American option under certain circumstances, that option is also path dependent in a sense.

Pay-In-Kind (PIK) Securities: Bonds, notes, or preferred stocks with interest or dividends paid in securities rather than cash. The securities used to pay the interest or dividends are usually identical to the underlying securities, but occasionally they have different terms. Issuance of PIKs ordinarily suggests that the issuer has cash flow problems, but a PIK structure can be selected primarily to relieve an investor of reinvestment risk. A PIK bond with redemption in cash at maturity is the functional equivalent of a zero coupon bond.

Pay Later Option: Ordinarily, this name refers to a contingent premium option rather than a deferred premium option, but contract terms should be checked. *See also Contingent Premium Option, Deferred Premium Option.*

Pay-through Securities: *See Pass-through Securities.*

Payback Period: *See Break-Even Time.*

Payer's Swaption: A swap option giving the holder the right to pay a fixed rate and receive a floating rate in an interest rate swap. Broadly analogous to a put on a fixed rate instrument. *See also Swaption.*

Payment Netting: When partially offsetting swap payments are due on the same date, the party owing the most will send a difference check. *See also Netting Agreement.*

Payoff: The value of an option at expiration.

Payoff Pattern: A graph of an option's value at expiration over a range of underlying prices.

Pension Benefit Guaranty Corporation (PBGC): The United States government agency that collects insurance premiums from sponsors of defined benefit pension plans and assumes the assets and most of the liabilities of failed plans.

Pension Livrée: A financing and securities lending technique used in French markets comparable in structure to a repurchase agreement. *See also Réméré.*

PERCS: *See Preference Equity Redemption Cumulative Stock (PERCS).*

Performance Bond: (1) A name preferred by some futures exchanges for what is more popularly called margin. (2) Any surety for performance used to collateralize a financial contract.

Performance Index Paper (PIP): A commercial paper variation on the currency coupon swap. The rate on the paper is denominated and paid in a base currency but the rate rises or falls depending on the exchange rate with an alternate currency.

Performance Plus Shares: Synthetic common stock or stock index instruments issued by a financial intermediary which promises the buyer the total return from the underlying security or index plus an additional return based on a dividend withholding tax credit, a stock loan premium, or some other element of return which the intermediary can obtain more easily than the buyer of these special shares.

Periodic Reset Swap: A swap with a floating rate payment based on the average rate on the reference index rate rather than the rate on one day.

Perpendicular Spread: *See Vertical Bear Spread and Vertical Bull Spread.*

Perpetual Floating Rate Note: A floating rate note with no fixed maturity. The rate reset mechanism may include a procedure under which the investor could force redemption if the floating rate were no longer attractive. For symmetry, the notes would ordinarily be callable under certain conditions.

Perpetual Warrant: A warrant granting the right to buy shares of common stock at a fixed price with no expiration date. A perpetual warrant will only be exercised if the stock's dividend rate is high enough and safe enough to entice the warrant holder to exercise and claim the dividend stream.

Physical Commodities: Agricultural and industrial products which may underlie commodity futures contracts as distinguished from financial instruments which may underlie financial futures contracts.

Pick-up: A gain in yield from the sale of one security and the purchase of another. Used primarily in the bond market. *See Swap (2).*

Pin Risk: The market value risk of an at-the-money option shortly before expiration. A small move in the underlying can have a highly leveraged impact on the value of the option.

Pips: Basis points. The term is used primarily in currency markets. *Also called Points or Ticks.*

Pit: A location on the floor of an exchange where trading in a particular instrument or type of instrument occurs. Pits usually have physical features such as tiers of steps, screens, and electronic equipment to facilitate trading and communication.

Pit Broker: *See Local.*

Plain Vanilla: A reference to a standard financial instrument or risk management structure with few or no bells and whistles.

Planned Amortization Class (PAC) Bond: A collateralized mortgage obligation that pays principal based upon a predetermined schedule, derived by amortizing the collateral at two different prepayment speeds. These two speeds are the endpoints for the "structuring PAC range." The PAC II range must be tighter than the PAC I range. PAC III's are defined as classes with a structuring range narrower than the structuring range of the PAC II's, and so forth.

Playing the Yield Curve: With a normal yield curve, funding a long-term asset with short-term liabilities.

Points: (1) Digits added to or subtracted from the fourth decimal place to convert a spot exchange rate to a forward rate or to reflect the trading basis in a currency market. *See Pips.* (2) Multiples of the minimum price fluctuation or tick in any market.

Poison Put: (1) A provision of a bond or note which makes the instrument puttable to the issuer following a change of control or a restructuring which reduces the credit quality of the issue. (2) A right distributed to common stock holders which makes some or all of their stock puttable to an acquirer at a very high price in the event of a takeover.

Pollution Futures: A proposed futures contract that would create a listed market in United States–based utilities' rights to emit sulphur dioxide.

Pop-Up Option: An up-and-in option.

Portfolio Approach to Risk Management: Rather than focus on the specific risk characteristics of each position or obligation, an asset or liability manager using a portfolio approach will analyze and aggregate risks by type and try to achieve an overall balance of risk and return. *See also Global Hedge.*

Portfolio Income Notes (PINs): *See Equity-linked Notes.*

Portfolio Insurance: Any of several techniques used to change a portfolio's market exposure systematically in reaction to prior market movements with the objective of avoiding large losses and securing as much participation as possible in any favorable market move. The most popular forms of portfolio insurance have attempted to create synthetic options with portfolio trades in the cash or futures markets. *See also Dynamic Hedging, Constant Proportion Portfolio Insurance.*

Portfolio Optimization: *See Optimization of a Portfolio.*

Portfolio Trade: The purchase or sale of a basket of stocks. By New York Stock Exchange definition, a portfolio trade (or program trade) includes more than 15 different stocks with a total value of $1,000,000 or more entered as a coordinated transaction. Portfolio trades may be undertaken to increase or reduce market exposure in a portfolio or as one side of an EFP or index arbitrage trade. *See Exchange for Physicals, Index Arbitrage, Portfolio Insurance, Program Trading.*

Position Limits: Exchange rules mandated by the SEC that restrict the size of option positions that can be taken by a single investor or a group of investors acting in concert. Generally, CFTC-regulated financial futures options have no meaningful position restrictions. These ill-considered regulations forced portfolio insurers to undertake dynamic hedging of stock positions in the stock index futures markets rather than in the option markets. The contribution of position limits to concern over the impact of portfolio insurance trades on the stock market was largely responsible for the magnitude of the October 1987 market break.

Position Trading: An approach to trading and market making in which a trader typically holds meaningful positions for a period of time rather than attempting to trade out of a position by the end of the day to avoid carrying it overnight.

Positive Carry: The net gain from carrying a position when the cost of funds is less than the yield on the securities held.

Power Bond: A variant of the reverse floating rate note with the interest rate set equal to the value of

$$\text{coupon} = \sqrt{(fixed\ rate)^2 - (floating\ rate)^2}$$

See also Reverse Floating Rate Note.

Preference Equity Redemption Cumulative Stock (PERCS): A limited term, limited participation convertible preferred stock with an enhanced dividend. PERCS shares are convertible at maturity into one share of the underlying common stock if the common stock is selling below the PERCS strike price and into a fractional share equal in value to the PERCS strike value if the common is selling above the strike. After three years, the PERCS shares are converted to common automatically on these terms, and the dividend drops back to the regular common stock dividend. PERCS were the most successful financial product of 1991, because they provided a relatively high current yield in a declining yield environment. As the illustration indicates, the PERCS structure is essentially a covered call structure. *See also Americus Trust, Equity Yield Enhancement Securities (EYES).*

A Comparison of PERCS and Common Stock Values

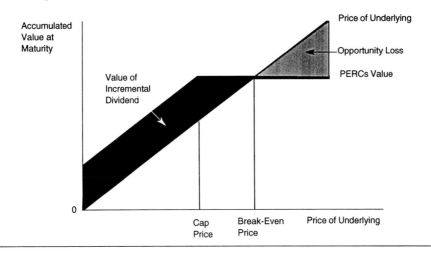

Premium: (1) In the United States, the amount of money an option buyer pays or an option writer receives for a conventional put or call or the price of a listed option. (2) The amount by which the price of an option exceeds its intrinsic value. For example, if an option to buy XYZ Corporation at $100 is selling at $9 and the stock is selling at $103, the premium is often said to be $6. To avoid confusion between (1) and (2), the term "option price" or "premium" is used to designate the market price of an option, and the term "premium over intrinsic value" is used to designate the amount by which the underlying price must move beyond the strike price (for out-of-the-money options) or the current price (for at- or in-the-money options) before expiration for the option buyer to break even, neglecting commissions. (3) In warrant markets based on the traditions of the United Kingdom, premium is the amount by which the value of an investor's position would *decrease* if the option or warrant were exercised immediately. *See also Gearing, Leverage.* (4) In convertible bond markets, the amount by which the value of a position would decrease if the conversion occurred immediately. (5) The amount by which a coupon bearing debt instrument sells over par because its coupon provides an above market yield. (6) The quality or credit yield differential which an issuer must pay above the rate on a government bond with a comparable maturity. (7) The amount by which the price on a futures contract exceeds the price of another contract or the underlying cash instrument. *See also Basis.* See figures on next page.

Premium Bond: A bond selling above par because its coupon is higher than current market levels.

Premium Business: In Switzerland, the functional equivalent of a call option contract in the form of a cancellable forward agreement which gives the buyer the right to buy the shares on the due date or to withdraw from the contract. *Also called Option Business. See also Abandonment.*

Premium Currency: A currency in which interest rates are lower than rates in the reference (domestic) currency. For many years, the yen and the Deutsche mark were premium currencies with respect to many other world currencies. Interest rates in yen and D-marks were low relative to rates denominated in other currencies. Interest rates and exchange rates are kept in equilibrium by an arbitrage mechanism, but it may be useful to think of premium currencies as belonging to countries with relatively low expected inflation rates. *See also Interest Rate Parity, Discount Currency.*

Premium Free Option: A zero cost option such as a zero cost collar where the premium is "paid" with the premium from the sale of another option.

Premium/Gearing Ratio: Premium (3), (United Kingdom definition) divided by gearing. Often used in the United Kingdom warrant market as a rough indication of the attractiveness of a warrant. Unfortunately, many of the major determinants of warrant value such as volatility, interest rates, dividend yields, and even the extent to which the warrant is in or out of the money are ignored or seriously distorted by this calculation. In the diagram, the relationship between the premium (3) line and the gearing line when the warrant is in the money hints that the premium/gearing ratio is

U.S. Option Terminology: Premium as Price of Option

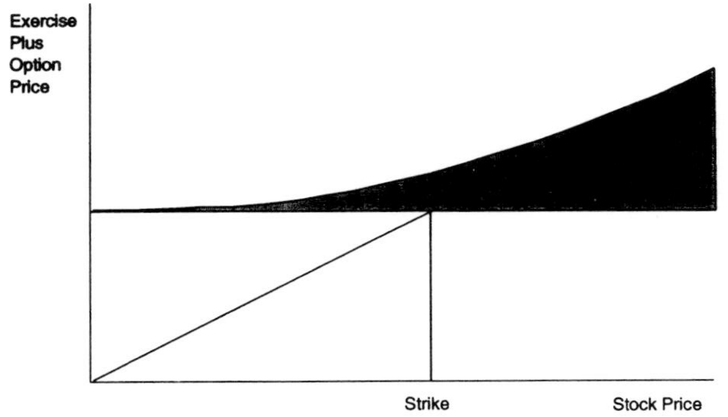

Exercise
Plus
Option
Price

Strike

Stock Price

U.S. Option Terminology: Premium Over Intrinsic Value

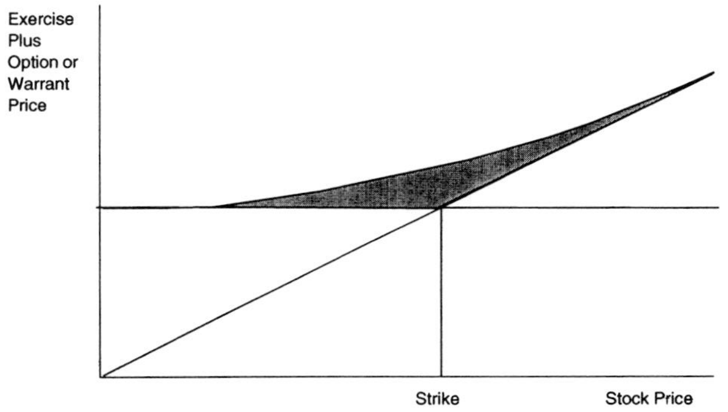

Exercise
Plus
Option or
Warrant
Price

Strike

Stock Price

U.K./Japanese Warrant Terminology: Premium as Loss on Exercise

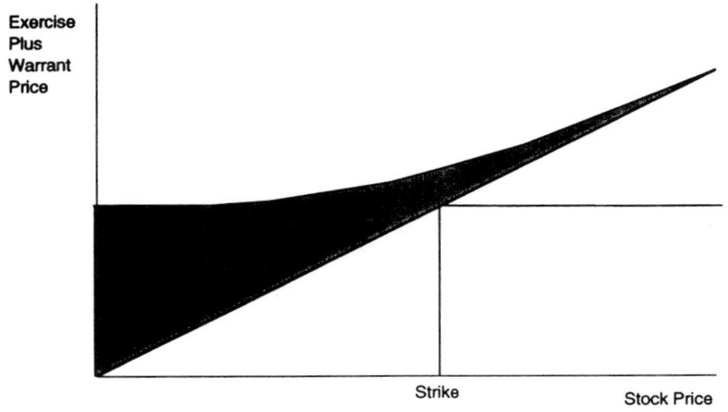

Exercise
Plus
Warrant
Price

Strike

Stock Price

Convertible Bond Terminology: Premium as Loss on Conversion

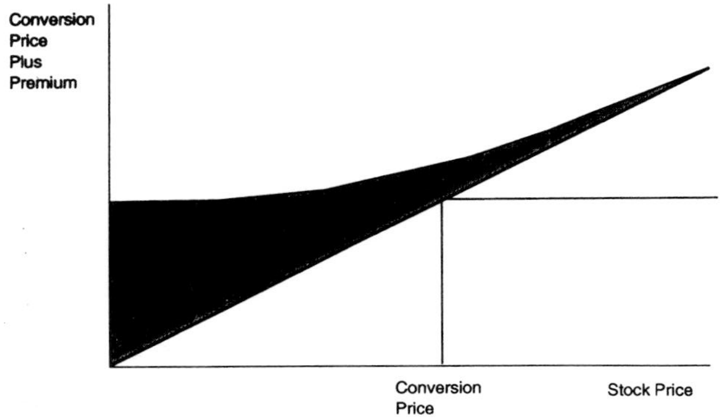

Conversion
Price
Plus
Premium

Conversion
Price

Stock Price

very sensitive to the life of the warrant and the level of interest rates. *See also Gearing, Effective Gearing.*

Warrant Price, Premium, and Gearing for a Four-Year Warrant

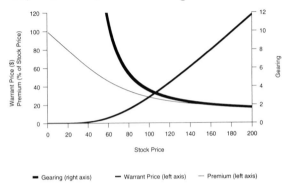

Premium Income: A frequently used term for the proceeds from the sale of an option contract. The term inappropriately refers to the reward side of the transaction with no mention of the possible opportunity loss associated with fulfillment of the option obligation.

Premium Put Convertible Bond: In addition to the traditional features of a convertible bond, this instrument has an embedded put that permits the investor to redeem it at a premium over parity at some point(s) over the life of the bond.

Premium Swap: *See High-Coupon Swap.*

Prepaid Swap: An annuity-like transaction in which the present value of future payments on one side of a swap is paid up front and the other (variable) side payments are paid on a traditional swap schedule. The functional equivalent of a variable rate loan.

Prepayment: A payment of principal prior to the scheduled payment date.

Prepayment Option: (1) A mortgagee's right to prepay a mortgage, often subject to a fee or penalty. The prepayment option may be exercised if the building is sold or if interest rates decline and the mortgage can be refinanced at a lower rate. (2) The embedded call option that allows a bond issuer to retire or refinance a bond prior to its nominal maturity. *See also Callable Securities, Embedded Options, Mortgage Prepayment Caps, Refi Rate.*

Prepayment Risk: The opportunity cost associated with early principal repayment of high yield debt instruments. Common examples include prepayment of mortgage debt and call of high coupon bonds. *See also Reinvestment Risk.*

Present Value: The current value of a future cash flow or series of cash flows discounted at an appropriate interest rate or rates.

Price Limits: A system of fixed or variable constraints on price changes in a single trading session. The rules of each exchange should be checked to determine how that exchange handles trading when the price goes limit up or limit down. Variable limits may expand price limits during volatile market periods.

Price Risk: Exposure to loss as a result of a change in the price of a commodity or a financial instrument. Price or market risk is the most common risk addressed with risk management instruments.

Primary Market: The market in which issuers sell securities to investors, either directly or through financial intermediaries.

PRIME: An acronym for **P**rescribed **R**ight to **I**ncome and **M**aximum **E**quity. PRIMEs, the income component of an Americus Trust Unit, were the equivalent of a five-year covered-call writer's position at issuance. *See Americus Trust.*

Value of Americus Trust PRIME Termination Claim

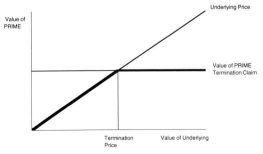

Principal: (1) Par or face value of a debt instrument or preferred stock. (2) The value of funds invested, the base for a return on investment calculation.

Principal Exchange Rate-Linked Securities (PERLS): A variation on a dual currency bond which pays both coupon and principal in the base currency, but the variable principal payment is set according to a redemption formula which links it to movements in currency exchange rates between the issue date and maturity. PERLS' principal payments increase as the foreign currency appreciates relative to the base currency and decrease as the foreign currency declines. Reverse PERLS' principal payments increase as the base currency appreciates relative to the foreign currency and decrease as the base currency depreciates. *See also Dual Currency Bond, Indexed Currency Option Notes (ICONS).*

Principal Only Obligation (PO): A special purpose CMO tranche created from a mortgage pool, POs pay holders only from the principal payments made by mortgagees. The value of an early payment PO can increase if interest rates fall and mortgagees exercise their prepayment options at a faster than anticipated rate. Conversely, if rates rise, principal payments may be much slower than anticipated and the value of early payment POs will decline. Various PO tranches will have different characteristics in different environments. *See also Collateralized Mortgage Obligation (CMO), Interest Only Obligation (IO), Planned Amortization Class (PAC), Tranche.*

Principal Relationship: In contrast to an agency or broker relationship, a principal or dealer relationship is a relationship of counterparties to a trade. The dealer who buys securities from or sells them to a customer for the dealer's account acts as a principal.

Principal Risk: The risk of losing some of the nominal or face amount or some of the purchase cost of an investment.

Privileges: An archaic name for options. Still used occasionally in the United Kingdom.

Pro Rata Strip (PRS) Bond: A collateralized mortgage obligation that pays principal in a fixed proportion to the aggregate collateral paydowns.

Profit-Sharing Option: *See Participating Option.*

Program Trading: (1) Originally, trading an entire portfolio in a single coordinated transaction, the term has come to encompass (2) index options and futures arbitrage trading designed to take advantage of temporary pricing discrepancies between index futures and/or option contracts and the underlying stocks and (3) portfolio insurance. The more specific alternative terms (1) portfolio trading, (2) index arbitrage and (3) portfolio insurance are more descriptive and leave the overused term "program trading" to politicians and polemicists.

Projected Benefit Obligation (PBO): The estimated total pension liability of a defined benefit plan sponsor. *See also Accumulated Benefit Obligation.*

Protected Equity Notes (PENs): *See Equity-linked Notes.*

Protected Equity Participations (PEPs): Principal guaranteed equity-linked notes with upside participation in an individual stock or a basket of stocks and with no cap on return. Identical in structure to a protected index participation (PIP). *See also Equity-linked Notes, Protected Index Participations (PIPS).*

Protected Index Participations (PIPs): Principal guaranteed equity index-linked notes with upside index participation but with no cap on return. The instrument's rate of participation in the upside movement of the index varies with the dividend rate on the stocks in the index, interest rates, market volatility, yield on the note (if any), and life of the PIP. *See Equity-linked Notes.*

Protective Put: A combination of a long put contract and a long position in the underlying. The combination is the risk equivalent of a long call with the same strike price — with some differences in the timing and desirability of early exercise if the put is American-style. A protective put sets a downside limit at expiration equal to the strike less the put premium. See figures on next page.

Prudent Expert Rule of ERISA: The Employee Retirement Income Security Act (ERISA) applies a revised and restated version of the prudent man rule to pension and profit sharing portfolios. ERISA requires that a fiduciary manage a portfolio "with the care, skill, prudence, and diligence, under the circumstances then prevailing, that a prudent man acting in a like capacity and familiar with such matters would use in the conduct of an

Payout Pattern of a Protective Put at Expiration

Long Underlying

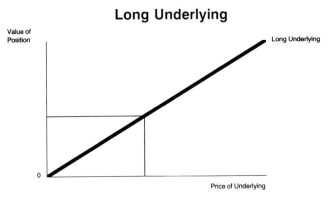

Plus   Long Put

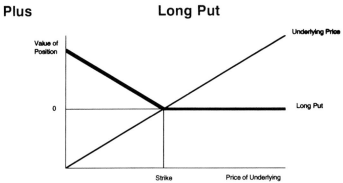

Equals   Protective Put

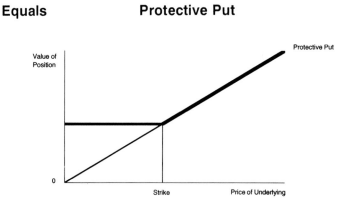

enterprise of a like character and with like aims." This statement differs from the classic prudent man rule in that familiarity with such matters suggests a higher standard than simple prudence — hence the name, prudent expert rule. Other provisions of the law and United States Department of Labor regulations suggest a portfolio approach under which a position imprudent in isolation may be acceptable in a portfolio context. *See also Employee Retirement Income Security Act (ERISA), Prudent Man Rule.*

Prudent Man Rule: A standard of prudence in investment policy that emphasizes how prudent men invest for "income and safety of principal with a view to the permanent disposition of their funds." The prudent man rule focuses on each investment. A good portfolio performance does not excuse a single bad decision. *See also Prudent Expert Rule of ERISA.*

Public Securities Association (PSA): An industry organization best known by risk managers for its standardized mortgage-backed securities prepayment rate assumptions.

Purchasing Power Parity (PPP): The principle that, in the long run, currency exchange rates will adjust so that the cost of similar goods and services will tend to be the same in all markets and in all currencies. To preserve purchasing power parity, exchange rate movements will tend to reflect relative inflation rates. Unlike interest rate parity, which is enforced by financial arbitrage, purchasing power parity is a long-term influence enforced, in the long run, by goods and goods price arbitrage. *See also Interest Rate Parity.*

Purgatory and Hell Bond: A heaven and hell bond with a cap on the redemption proceeds.

Put Bonds: *See Early Redemption (Put) Options.*

Put and Call Brokers and Dealers Association (PCBDA): The principal self-regulatory organization for the conventional (unlisted) stock option market in the United States. Today it exists largely on paper with only two active members. The PCBDA has no role in OTC transactions in index or basket options or in any non-equity options. With most actively traded stocks claimed by at least one option exchange, conventional stock option volume is negligible in the United States.

Put/Call Parity: A boundary condition which, subject to transaction costs in the marketplace and the possibility of early exercise, holds relative put and call price relationships within a narrow range. For European options, put/call parity in advance of expiration will be subject to the liquidity of the market for the options and the underlying. For American options, a violation of put/call parity is often an indication that early exercise is appropriate.

Put/Call Ratio: The number of puts traded in a market divided by the number of calls traded. Although this ratio is often used as an indication of market sentiment, the necessity for maintenance of approximate put/call parity and the interchangeability of long calls and protective puts for many investors make the put/call ratio's usefulness as a market indicator highly doubtful.

Put Guarantee Letter: A collateralization mechanism to assure performance by the seller of a put option. A bank will issue a guarantee that it holds and is prepared to deliver segregated cash equivalent to the aggregate strike price of the put.

Put Option: The right but not the obligation to sell an underlying at a particular price (strike price) on or before the expiration date of the contract. Alternatively, a short forward position with an upside insurance policy. *See also Option.*

Put Spread: A spread consisting of a long position and a short position in puts on the same underlying. Virtually any call spread structure has an analogous put spread, but put spreads are not commonly used in markets where early exercise is frequent. *See specific types of spreads.*

Put Warrant: A security which, in contrast to a conventional warrant, gives the holder the right to sell the underlying or to receive a cash payment that increases as the value of the underlying declines. Put warrants, like their call warrant counterparts, generally have an initial term of more than one year.

Puttable Bonds: *See Puttable Notes, Early Redemption (Put) Options.*

Puttable Extendable Notes: At the end of each interest period, the issuer may redeem these notes at par or attempt to extend the maturity on terms that he believes the note holder will accept. The note holder can put the notes back to the issuer if the new rate is unacceptable. Holders may have one or more additional put options during the initial interest period. *Compare with Lender's Option-Borrower's Option.*

Puttable Notes: A traditional bond or note with an embedded put which permits the bond holder to sell the notes back to the issuer, usually at par. This put gives the holder some protection from loss of principal due to higher interest rates or credit deterioration of the issuer. *See Early Redemption (Put) Options.*

Puttable Stock: A unit consisting of common stock and a put giving the buyer of the unit the right to put the stock back to the issuing corporation. In addition, the put feature usually gives the holder the right to obtain more shares at no additional cost if the market price of the shares falls below a stated level, as of a predetermined date or dates. This combination of provisions provides a floor value for each unit holder's position. If the market value of the stock rises above the stated floor value on the valuation date(s), the put has no value. If the market value of the position falls below the floor, the issuer is obligated to issue additional common shares or repurchase the stock. Variations on this basic structure include limitations on the number of shares to be issued, restrictions on the ability of the issuing corporation to make the unit purchaser whole through the issuance of additional shares or by cash payments, or by debt or preferred stock issuance. Puttable stock units enable investors to participate fully in the upside potential of a company with reduced downside risk. Although the structures are very different, the payoff pattern of a puttable stock issue is very similar to that of a convertible bond.

Puttable Swaps: Swap contracts which are cancellable or terminable at the option of one or both of the counterparties. A puttable swap permits the fixed rate payer to terminate the contract when interest rates decline to a specified level, or when a bond on which the fixed rate payment is based is called. *See also Callable Swap.*

Puttable Warrant: *See Redeemable Warrant.*

Pyramiding: Although the term is often used loosely, pyramiding typically refers to the practice of using the excess margin or "buying power" generated by a successful speculative operation to increase the commitment to that operation. In options, an example might be the naked option writer who writes more options as a favorable move in the price of the underlying frees up margin. A buyer might sell a profitable in-the-money position and invest the proceeds in a larger number of at-the-money options. Pyramiding is probably more common in futures than options trading, because margin requirements are often lower.

Q

Qualified Covered Call: Covered call writers have a limited exemption from the loss-deferral provision of the United States tax code's straddle rule if they follow complex qualified covered call guidelines in selling one or a sequence of calls against a stock position.

Qualified Institutional Buyers (QIBs): Investors or investment managers who meet SEC requirements to purchase 144a offerings for their own accounts or for clients.

Qualified Professional Asset Manager (QPAM): An investment advisor, registered with the Securities and Exchange Commission, who represents United States pension plans in certain private placement transactions.

Quality Spread: The difference between the interest rate paid for funds of a given maturity by a sovereign issuer and the rate required of a less creditworthy borrower.

Quality Spread Differential: The difference in quality spreads at two different maturities. Typically, the quality spread and, hence, the quality spread differential will widen as the term of financing moves farther out on the yield curve. Lenders are more comfortable with their ability to evaluate and accept credit risks in the very short term than over a longer period. The quality spread differential is a consideration in the pricing of interest rate swaps.

Quantity Adjusting Options (QUANTOS): (1) A fixed exchange rate foreign equity option in which the face amount of the currency coverage expands or contracts to cover changes in the foreign currency value of a designated underlying security or package of securities. Quantos are used to adjust the investor's base currency protection on an underlying position which varies in value in the nonbase currency. The most common example is a cross-border, equity-linked instrument with currency protection on the value of the foreign equity position in the domestic currency. *Compare with Equity-linked Foreign Exchange Option.* (2) An option on a percentage change in a currency pair ratio applied to a face amount denominated in a third (base) currency. Double and triple currency QUANTOS combine or offset percentage changes in two or three currency pair ratios, none involving the base currency. The similarity of the equity and currency

QUANTOs lies in the difficulty of estimating or hedging the value of the exchange into the base currency.

Quarterly Index Expirations (QIXs): Proposed index option contracts with expirations on the last business day of each calendar quarter.

Quasi-American Option: *See Bermuda Option, Japanese Option.*

R

Rainbow Option: *See Outperformance Option.*

Range Forward Contract: A contingent forward contract used primarily in currency markets. The investor can take advantage of favorable price moves to the upper end of the contract range while remaining protected against moves below the lower end of the contract range. Within the range, the contract settles at the spot rate in effect at maturity. The range is usually chosen so that the customer pays no option premium. As the diagram illustrates, the payoff pattern is identical to an interest rate collar or a risk reversal in fixed income and equity markets respectively. *See also Risk Reversal.*

An Exchange Rate Range Forward Contract—Rate Pattern at Settlement

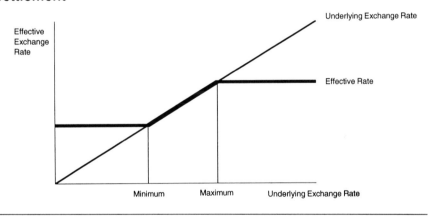

Range Warrant: (1) A multitranche structure which allocates a fixed return on the premium pool collected to range tranches on the basis of the price of the underlying at expiration. One tranche might get the return if the underlying price falls between 0 and 100. The second might get the return if the underlying falls between 101 and 200, and so on. Unsuccessful tranches get a rebate of their premium with a zero return. (2) *See Trading Range Warrant.*

Ranking: A credit quality hierarchy within a corporation's debt structure. Subject to specific features of isolated instruments, the following terms designate a typical hierarchy from highest to lowest quality: secured, senior, subordinated, junior subordinated.

Ratchet Option: *See Ladder Option or Note, Cliquet Option.*

Rate Differential Swap: An interest rate or other swap with one of the payment rates or returns denominated in a currency different than the currency used to state the notional principal amount. Both rates are calculated against the base currency. *Also called Cross Index Basis (CRIB) Swap, Cross Rate Swap, Currency Protected Swap, Diff Swap, Differential Swap, Interest Rate Index Swap, LIBOR Differential Swap.*

Rate Fixing Date: Varies with market custom, but in the United States the swap rate fixing date is usually two business days prior to the first date the new rates are effective in a swap or other periodic reset agreement. *Also called Reset Date and Roll Date.*

Rating: *See Table of Debt Ratings in the Appendix.*

Rating Sensitive Notes: *See Credit Sensitive Note.*

Ratio Forward: *See Participating Forward Contract.*

Ratio Spread: An option spread in which the number of contracts purchased and the number of contracts sold are not equal. *Also Called a Variable Spread.*

One of Many Possible Ratio Spread Payoff Patterns at Expiration

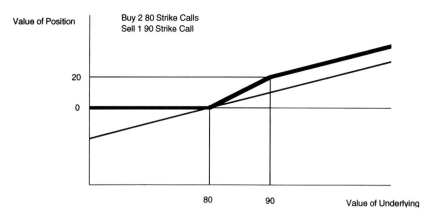

Ratio Write: *See Option Hedge.*

Ratio Writer: A call option writer who sells more options than he holds units of the underlying. *See Option Hedge.*

Ready Market: An active market. Dealers' spreads will be relatively narrow and the prices quoted by different dealers will be nearly identical.

Real Estate Investment Trust (REIT): A vehicle for the securitization of real property and loans on real property.

Real Estate Mortgage Investment Conduit (REMIC): A collateralized mortgage obligation (CMO) issued after January 1, 1987, under legislation designed to eliminate certain tax and regulatory problems which limited issuer and investor participation in multiple series (tranche) CMOs. *See also Collateralized Mortgage Obligation (CMO) and Tranche.*

Real Interest Rate: The nominal interest rate less the rate of price inflation. *Also called Real Rate of Return and Real Yield.*

Real Yield Security: Typically, a floating rate note with a coupon reset quarterly to the greater of the increase in the consumer price index plus a predetermined real yield spread or, if the consumer price index should be flat or decline, to the level of the real yield spread.

Realized Yield: The return actually earned on an investment in a security over a period of time, including the return on reinvested interest or dividend payments.

Rebalancing: Periodic revisions to a portfolio necessitated by the effect of the passage of time on asset and liability duration, changes in the constitution of an index, or portfolio cash flows.

Rebate: A sum repaid to an option buyer if an in option is not activated or an out option is terminated because the underlying hits the outstrike. Rebates provide a payoff pattern intermediate between a traditional option structure where the position has a minimum value of zero and a debt-based structure where the minimum value at expiration might be the value of the initial investment. A structure calling for a rebate may facilitate a dealer's hedging activity.

Receivable Pay-through Securities: Instruments which give an investor an undivided interest in a pool of securitized receivables.

Receiver's Swaption: A swaption giving the holder the right to pay a floating rate and receive a fixed rate. Broadly analogous to a call on a fixed rate instrument in terms of its value under different interest rate scenarios.

Reconstitution: Combining stripped coupon and principal cash flows to create a traditional coupon security.

Reconversion: Most commonly, the process of changing a synthetic call back into a put, typically by selling a position in the underlying. *Also called a Reversal or Reverse Conversion.*

Redeemable Warrant: A warrant with a cash redemption value as an alternative to traditional exercise *Also called a Puttable Warrant.*

Reduced Cost Option: Generically, any option with a reduced premium resulting from the sale of another option or acceptance of a less favorable strike or participation rate.

Reference Index: An index underlying and determining some component of the value or the payoff of a risk management instrument.

Reference Index Rate: The interest rate serving as the reference index for a risk management instrument. Frequently, a floating rate such as LIBOR.

Refi Rate: The refinancing rate of a pool of mortgages. A high refi rate reduces the value of a high rate mortgage pool as mortgagees refinance their debt at lower rates and repay their old mortgages, liquidating the pool.

Refunding: Issuance of new debt instruments to replace called or matured debt.

Registered Options Principal (ROP): An employee of a brokerage firm who has passed a test on exchange and SEC rules for handling customer option accounts. A senior registered option principal (SROP) must approve new option accounts, and a compliance registered option principal (CROP) is responsible for the brokerage firm's option compliance program.

Registered Representative (RR):   The formal name for a salesperson licensed to sell securities to the public in the United States.

Registered Shares: *See Restricted Shares.*

Regular Settlement: The standard settlement period for a securities transaction. In the United States, the settlement convention ranges from next day for government securities, futures, and options to five business days for common stocks. Other markets have a variety of settlement conventions. Customized risk management instruments tend to settle in line with the convention in their underlying markets.

Regulatory Arbitrage: A financial contract or a series of transactions undertaken, entirely or in part, because the transaction(s) enable(s) one or both of the counterparties to accomplish a financial or operating objective which is unavailable to them directly because of regulatory obstacles. Recent regulatory arbitrage with customized equity-linked derivative structures has enabled United States–based investors to take positions linked to foreign equity indexes when they could not make direct investments in exchange-traded stock index futures contracts.

Regulatory Spread: The difference in yield as a result of differences in registration requirements and fees that a borrower will encounter in the traditional bond or medium-term note market in the United States relative to the yield in the Eurobond market. Changes in domestic registration procedures have narrowed the regulatory spread substantially since Eurobond trading began.

Reinvestment Rate: The interest rate or yield at which any cash flow from coupon or principal payments can be reinvested.

Reinvestment Risk: A type of interest rate risk that stems from an asset manager's inability to reinvest interest coupons and principal repayments at the same high rates the funds earned before he received the cash payments. Zero coupon bonds defer all reinvestment risk until they mature.

Relationship Trade: *See Basis Trade.*

Relative Performance Option: *See Outperformance Option.*

Remarketed Preferred Stock: Perpetual preferred stock with a dividend rate that resets at the end of each dividend period to a level determined by a remarketing agent, subject to certain maximums relative to commercial paper rates. Dividend periods and payments may be variable even within a single issue to meet issuer and investor needs. Similar to other adjustable rate preferred structures except for the rate reset and redistribution mechanism. *See also Auction Rate Preferred Stock.*

Remarketed Reset Notes: Floating rate notes with an interest rate reset to a rate determined by a remarketing agent, typically a bank or investment bank, which determines what rate will cause the notes to sell at par. If the issuer disagrees with the remarketing agent, the coupon is determined by a formula. Note holders have a put to protect them from a below market coupon.

Réméré: A collateralized financing technique incorporating transfer of ownership of the collateral as in a repurchase agreement or *pension livrée* with the distinction that the borrower has an option, not an obligation, to repurchase the collateral. *See also Repurchase Agreement, Pension Livrée.*

Replicating Portfolios: Combinations of stock, cash, and borrowing that reproduce the return pattern of an option or option-based instrument and form the basis for portfolio insurance and other dynamic hedging strategies or synthetic structures. *See Option Replication.*

Repo Rate: The financing rate for government securities sold against repurchase agreements. A repurchase agreement is essentially a loan collateralized by a government securities position with the collateral fully controlled by the lender.

Reporting Level: Positions in exchange-traded futures and options must be reported to the exchange when they exceed a mandated reporting level.

Repurchase Agreement (Repo), (RP): A financing arrangement used primarily in the government securities markets whereby a dealer or other holder of government securities sells the securities to a lender and agrees to repurchase them at an agreed future date at an agreed price which will provide the lender with an extremely low risk return. Repos are popular because they can virtually eliminate credit problems. The repo market is enlarged and enhanced by its use in Federal Reserve Board open market operations in the United States. Repos operate slightly differently in other markets. *See also Dollar Roll, Gensaki Rate, Pension Livrée, Réméré, Reverse Repurchase Agreement.*

Reset Date: (1) The date a swap's periodic payment terms are established. Usually the date is the same as the payment date or two days earlier, depending on local conventions or the agreement of the couterparties. *Also called Reset Date and Roll Date.* (2) The date on which the strike of a reset or similar option or warrant is determined or modified. *See Reset Option or Warrant.*

Reset Frequency: The period between reset dates on a swap. Common intervals are three months, six months, and one year.

Reset Note: Any of several varieties of floating rate note (FRN).

Reset Option or Warrant: Typically, a stock or equity index call option or warrant whose strike price may be reset to a lower strike or a put whose strike price may be reset to a higher strike at some point during the life of the instrument if the option is out of the money on the reset date. There may be a limit to the magnitude of the strike price adjustment and the reset may be triggered by a specific price on the underlying rather than set on a specific reset date. *See Anti-Crash Warrant, Partial Lookback Warrants, Step-Down Warrant. Also called Strike Reset Option or Warrant.*

Reset Swap: An interest rate swap with the floating rate payment based on the reference index rate at the end of the period rather than the rate at the start of the period. A floating rate receiver will prefer a reset swap when a rising yield curve (rising forward rate curve) implies higher rates in the future. *Also called Arrears Swap, Back End Set Swap, In-Arrears Swap.*

Residual Unhedged Risk: Risk remaining after the implementation of a hedging position.

Restricted Shares: Shares which may not be freely transferred in the marketplace because host country law forbids their ownership by foreign investors, prevents their transfer without the approval of the issuer, or restricts their marketability as a matter of investor protection. Restricted or, as they are sometimes called, registered shares are common in Finland, Switzerland, and in some emerging markets. Sales restrictions based on investor protection legislation are a regulatory issue principally in the United States.

Retractable Swap: A swap with an embedded option giving one party, usually the fixed rate payer, the right to cancel the swap under certain conditions. The conditions may be as general as a decline in interest rates or as specific as an issuer's call of the instrument used to generate the fixed rate payments. *See also Callable Swap, Puttable Swap.*

Return to Hedged Portfolio (RHP): *See Implied Repo Rate.*

Reversal: (1) The termination of a swap through cancellation of the original agreement or, less frequently, initiation of an offsetting or mirror swap to offset the original swap. (2) *See Reconversion, Reverse Conversion.* (3) Buying a call to lock in a profit on a short outright forward currency position.

Reverse Conversion: A financing and risk management technique based on put/call parity and an investor's ability to obtain interest on the use of proceeds from a short sale. In a typical transaction, a brokerage firm sells stock short, buys a call, and sells a put (short actual, long synthetic). Depending on borrowing costs for the stock sold short and the relative pricing of puts and calls, a better than money market return might be obtained at very low risk. If the options are American-style, there is some risk that the stock will decline sharply and the short put will be exercised after the long out-of-the-money call has lost nearly all of its value.

Reverse Dual Currency Bond: A bond which pays coupons in a non-base currency (typically the currency of the issuer) and pays principal in the base currency (the currency of the investor). *See Dual Currency Bonds, Indexed Currency Options Notes (ICONs) and Principal Exchange Rate-Linked Securities (PERLS).*

Reverse Floating Rate Note: A popular floating rate note structure in which the rate paid increases as market floating rates decline. In a typical case, the rate paid on the note is set by doubling the swap rate (fixed rate) in effect at the time the contract is signed, and subtracting the floating reference index rate for each payment period. If floating rates fall, the result of this calculation will be a higher return on the reverse floating rate note. If floating rates rise, the payment on the reverse floating rate note will decline. *Also called a Bull Floater and a Bull Floating Rate Note. See also Leveraged Reverse Floating Rate Notes. Compare with Bear Floater (diagram).*

Anatomy of a Five-Year Reverse Floating Rate Note

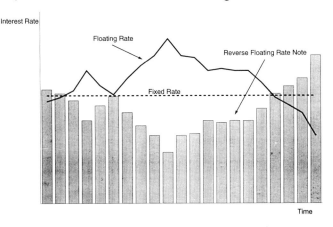

Reverse Floating Rate Swap: A swap structure with a reverse floating rate note payment from one counterparty.

Reverse Interest Rate Collar: A combination of an interest rate collar and a reverse floating rate note, the reverse interest rate collar provides an interest cost or yield that decreases as rates rise and increases as market rates fall — within a range. This structure might appeal to a liability manager who has too much floating rate exposure or to an asset manager who is constrained as to allowable portfolio duration but who expects rates to decline. *See also Reverse Risk Reversal (diagram).*

Reverse Option Hedge: A hedged position in which the investor owns more than one call option for each unit of the underlying he is short. This position becomes profitable as the market price moves away from the strike price of the options *in either direction. See also Option Hedge.*

Sell One Unit of Underlying Short

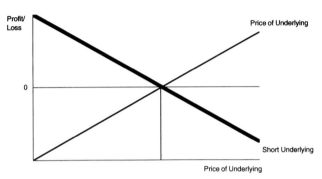

Buy Two Calls

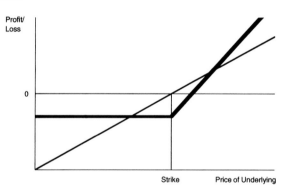

Two to One Reverse Option Hedge Profit/Loss Pattern at Expiration

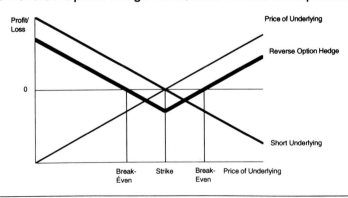

Reverse Principal Exchange Rate-Linked Securities (Reverse PERLS): See Principal Exchange Rate-Linked Securities (PERLS).

Reverse Range Forward: *See Reverse Risk Reversal (diagram).*

Reverse Repurchase Agreement: An overnight or similar term cash equivalent investment collateralized by transfer of ownership in a Treasury security. The investor side of a repurchase agreement.

Reverse Risk Reversal: Typically, a combination of a short out-of-the-money put, a long out-of-the-money call, and a short futures or cash market position. This combination is the mirror image of the traditional range forward or risk reversal structure *(see diagram).* This structure is generally used when a simple short swap or futures transaction with unlimited exposure to extreme market movements does not meet risk control objectives. As the diagram illustrates, the value of the investor's position will increase if the value of the underlying declines and will fall if the value of the underlying increases—with a limit on the downside—in the case of a market advance—and on the upside—in the case of a market decline.

Payoff Pattern of a Reverse Risk Reversal

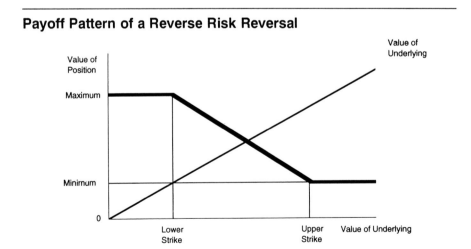

Reverse Swap: A swap agreement with identical terms and opposite counterparties to an existing swap. A reverse swap eliminates net obligations under the original swap but will be used only if tax or accounting reasons make simple cancellation of the original swap unattractive to one of the counterparties.

Reverse Zero Coupon Swap: The zero coupon payment is made upfront, and interest rate and principal payments are paid by the counterparty over time. Like a zero coupon swap, this is the functional equivalent of a loan. *See also Zero Coupon Swap.*

Reversible Swap: A combination of an interest rate swap and a swaption on twice the notional principal of that swap. The swaption will permit one of the counterparties to reverse the swap, e.g., switch from paying fixed to receiving fixed.

Reversion: Removal of assets from an overfunded defined benefit pension plan by the plan sponsor. Increasing tax and regulatory obstacles have made reversion uncommon.

Rho ρ: The dollar change in an option price in response to a percentage point change in the risk-free interest rate.

Right: An in-the-money option, usually with a very short life, distributed to a firm's shareholders and giving them the opportunity to purchase a new issue of securities below current market prices. Rights may be sold or exercised or, on rare occasions, allowed to expire. Because rights are in the money at issuance, expiration is more often a result of error or inattention than of the rights having lost all value.

Risk: Exposure to change. In popular usage, adverse change is appropriately emphasized. Annualized standard deviation of return is the generic measurement of risk in most markets, but both asset and liability managers increasingly add other statistical measures such as skewness and kurtosis to a risk profile or, even better, look directly at the probability distribution of risks and the maximum cost of adverse developments. *See Kurtosis, Skewness, Standard Deviation, Volatility, and specific types or causes of risk.*

Risk-adjusted Return: A modified (usually reduced) return which allows for the cost or value of a specific risk exposure or for aggregate risk exposures.

Risk Arbitrage: *See Arbitrage.*

Risk Averse: Having a tendency or inclination to avoid risk unless compensated with a greater than proportional increase in expected return.

Risk Controlled Arbitrage: A complex risk management strategy practiced by some savings institutions. The bank buys mortgages financed with short-term borrowings and swaps the mortgage cash flows to reduce various components of interest rate and prepayment risk.

Risk-Free Rate: Modern portfolio theory postulates the existence of at least one risky asset and one risk-free asset, usually taken to be Treasury bills or comparable short-term sovereign debt. The risk-free rate is the rate of return on the risk-free asset. This risk-free rate is lower than the expected return on the risky asset, because any issuer will have to offer a risk-averse investor the expectation of a higher return to induce him to abandon the risk-free asset for an investment with uncertain returns or, say, credit risk.

Risk Management: The application of financial analysis and diverse financial instruments to the control and, typically, the reduction of selected types of risk.

Risk Management Advisors (RMAs): Financial applications engineers analogous to technically-trained customer engineers in high technology industries. RMAs work with sales and trading personnel and customers to develop cost-effective solutions to risk management problems.

Risk Premium: The difference between the expected total return from a risky investment and the risk-free rate.

Risk Reversal: A contract or pair of contracts which in combination provide a payoff pattern in an equity instrument similar to the interest rate collar or range forward contract in fixed income and currency markets respectively. The term "risk reversal" is also used to describe the comparable interest rate and currency market positions. In the most common structure, the investor buys a put which provides downside protection and pays for the put with the sale of a call, which caps upside return. Although there is no necessary connection between the premium paid for the put and the premium received for the call, most users elect a zero premium risk reversal rather than pay or receive a net premium. Some users fail to appreciate that they may be called upon to make payments on the short option. These payments may be covered by failure to participate in the price movement of the underlying in some structures. *Also called a Collar, Fence, Fence Spread, Cylinder, Spread Conversion, Conversion Spread, Forward Rate Bracket, Range Forward, Tunnel Option, and Cap and Floor.*

Payoff Pattern of a Risk Reversal

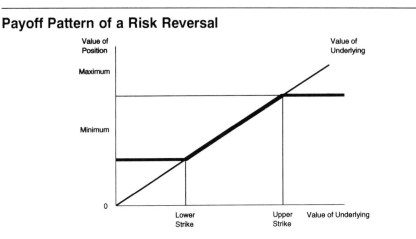

Risk Transfer: The use of a security or contract to change the pattern of cash flows in a portfolio of assets or liabilities.

Rocket Scientist: The popular press's designation for the creators of risk management products and services and for the managers of risk management programs. Frequently used as a pejorative.

Roll Date: *See Reset Date, Rate Fixing Date.*

Roll Down: To close an option position and replace it with a new position with a lower strike price.

Roll Forward: To close an option or futures position and replace it with a new position with a more distant expiration date.

Roll Over Risk: Exposure to actual or opportunity loss from mispricing of an option or futures contract at the time an old position must be closed and a new position opened.

Roll Up: To close an option position and replace it with a new position with a higher strike price.

Rollercoaster Swap: An interest rate swap with a notional principal amount that fluctuates periodically, usually to accommodate the seasonal or other periodic financing requirements of a counterparty.

Rolling Down the Yield Curve: *See Playing the Yield Curve.*

Rolling Hedge: Using the relatively high liquidity in exchange-traded futures and option contracts to maintain a continuous (relatively short-term) risk offsetting position by closing contracts as they approach maturity and opening more distant positions.

Rolling Over: (1) The process by which an investor closes an option or futures contract with a near term expiration and opens a contract on the same side of the market (long or short) with a more distant expiration. (2) More generally, substituting a position with a different expiration date and/or a different strike price for a previously established position. The process is called *rolling up* when substituting an option with a higher strike price, *rolling down* when substituting an option with a lower strike price, and *rolling forward* when substituting an option or futures contract with a more distant expiration.

Rotation: In some markets, notably, most listed stock and index option markets, market makers go through an opening rotation in which all of the option series in a particular underlying are opened in turn using a call auction procedure. A similar reopening rotation is followed if trading is interrupted due to a major development during the course of a trading day. A closing rotation is followed to determine appropriate closing prices, particularly on inactive issues.

Round Trip: A purchase followed by a sale or a sale followed by a purchase of a cash instrument or a derivative security. After a round trip, an investor or issuer's risk position should be unchanged except for the effect of any profit or loss from the round trip.

Round Turn: An opening trade in a futures market followed by a closing trade. Futures commissions are usually charged on a round turn rather than on a single transaction.

Rule 144a: An SEC rule issued in 1990 that modified a two-year holding period requirement on privately placed securities by permitting large institutions to trade these positions among themselves.

S

Safe Harbor: A set of conditions issued by a regulatory body describing the circumstances under which an activity may be conducted without regulatory risk or interference.

Safe Return Certificate: An equity-linked note with a guaranteed return of principal. *See Equity-linked Notes.*

Saitori: Special members of the Tokyo Stock Exchange who match buy and sell orders in stock, futures, and options markets. In contrast to specialists in some United States markets and market makers in most world equity markets, Saitori do not take positions for their own account. They do assume responsibility for maintaining orderly and — to the extent possible — continuous markets. A trade which will have an adverse affect on market stability will often be delayed by the Saitori to see if an order on the other side of the market will arrive. Individuals filling a similar role on the Osaka stock exchange are called Nakadachi members.

Same Day Settlement: *See Cash Settlement (3).*

Sandwich Spread: *See Butterfly Spread, Alligator Spread.*

Scalping: A technique used by floor traders who buy at the bid and sell at the offer — taking out a small spread and attempting to avoid holding a position overnight. *Compare with Position Trading.*

Scheduled (SCH) Bond: A collateralized mortgage obligation that pays principal based upon a schedule, but does not fit the definition of a planned amortization class (PAC) bond or a targeted amortization class (TAC) bond.

SCORE: An acronym for Special Claim On Residual Equity and the equivalent of a five-year warrant at issuance. The warrant-like component of an Americus Trust Unit. *See also Americus Trust, PRIME.*

Value of Americus Trust SCORE Termination Claim

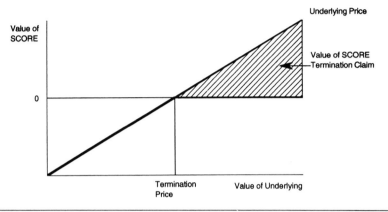

Seagull: A long at- or near-the-money call financed by the sale of an out-of-the-money call and an out-of-the-money put. A very high cost bird.

Payoff Pattern of a Seagull

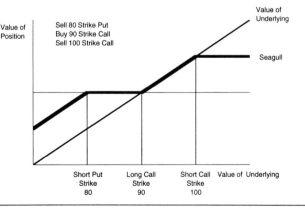

Seasonal Swap: A variable notional principal swap designed to accommodate the financing or currency needs of a seasonal business.

Secondary Currency Option: An option contract or an equity or debt instrument with a payoff in a different currency than the underlying's trading currency. *See, for example, Guaranteed Exchange Rate Warrant.*

Secondary Market: In contrast to the primary market in which new security issues are sold to investors, the secondary market is the traditional exchange or over-the-counter market in which previously issued securities are bought and sold by individual and institutional holders with brokers and dealers as intermediaries.

Secondary Warrants: A warrant with another warrant or a warrant fund as the underlying. A kind of compound warrant.

Securities and Exchange Commission (SEC):   The regulatory agency charged with regulation of securities and securities options markets in the United States.

Securities and Investment Board (SIB):   The regulatory body charged with regulation of securities and derivatives markets in the United Kingdom.

Securities Lending: A carefully collateralized process of loaning portfolio positions to custodians, dealers, and short sellers who must make physical delivery of fungible positions. Securities lending can reduce custody costs or enhance annual returns by a full percentage point or more in some markets at some times. Improvements in securities settlement procedures and systems to facilitate securities lending may reduce lending premiums.

Securitization: The process of converting assets which would normally serve as collateral for a bank loan into securities which are more liquid and can be traded at a lower cost than the underlying assets. The largest category of securitized assets is real estate mortgage loans which serve as collateral for mortgaged-backed securities. Auto loans and credit card obligations are also securitized.

Securitized Options: Packaged stock or stock index options combined with another security such as a note. *See Equity-linked Notes.*

Self-Regulatory Organizations (SROs):   Securities exchanges and the National Association of Securities Dealers (NASD) are responsible for front line regulation of securities markets in the United States. Roughly similar organizations fill similar roles in the United Kingdom, Japan, and other markets.

Sensitivity: A measurement, description, or graph of the relationship between or among two or more of the variables determining option value or option value derivatives.

Separately Traded Registered Interest and Principal Securities: *See Strips.*

Sequential Pay (SEQ) Bond: A collateralized mortgage obligation that starts to pay principal when classes with an earlier priority have paid to zero. The SEQ bond receives uninterrupted payment of principal until paid to zero balance. An SEQ may share principal paydown on a pro rata basis with another class.

Series of Options: All listed option contracts of the same class having the same exercise price and expiration date, e.g., all General Motors July $40 calls.

Set-Off: In case of default, the right of the non-defaulting party to reduce its debt to the defaulting party by the amount owed it. Rights of set-off, to the extent they exist in a specific situation, are a function of law in the appropriate jurisdiction, the nature of the respective obligations, and the agreement between the parties.

Settlement: (1) The process by which a trade is entered onto the books and records of all the parties to the transaction including brokers or dealers, a clearing house, and any other financial institution with a stake in the trade. (2) Completion of any required payment between two parties to discharge an obligation.

Settlement Date: The date on which the exchange of cash, securities, and paperwork involved in a transaction is completed.

Settlement Price: (1) A price, typically the exact or approximate closing price, on which any maintenance or variation margin payment or cash exercise settlement is based. (2) The final delivery price used to evaluate contracts held to maturity.

Settlement Risk: Related to credit risk but not identical, settlement risk is the risk that an expected settlement payment on an obligation will not be made on time. A common example involves bilateral obligations in which one party makes a required settlement payment and the counterparty does not. Settlement risk provides an important motivation to develop netting arrangements and other safeguards.

Severability: The right to separate a hybrid instrument into components such as a bond and a warrant. In the United States, certain customized instruments may not be severable without jeopardizing their regulatory exemption. Ironically, as a hybrid instrument, they may still be taxed as if they were separate instruments.

Shad-Johnson Agreement: An accord reached by the chairmen of the SEC and the CFTC to divide jurisdiction over options and futures on financial instruments in the United States. This agreement was ratified by legislation in 1982.

Shared Currency Option Under Tender (SCOUT):   A contingent currency forward contract bought jointly by bidders on a large contract which will subject the winner to exchange rate exposure. The successful bidder gets an option to acquire the needed foreign exchange protection on affordable terms.

Short: (1) A position whereby an investor incurs rights and obligations that mirror the risk-return characteristics of another investor's asset position and, consequently, change in value in opposite directions to the asset position. (2) An investment position which will benefit from a decline in price. (3) An investor whose position will benefit from a decline in the market. *See also Short Sale.*

Short Against the Box: A short sale of securities when an identical long position is owned in the account but will not be delivered against the sale until a later date. In the United States, selling short against the box is used to eliminate price risk while deferring taxes on profits.

Short the Basis: A hedged position consisting of a long futures or forward contract and a short cash or actual. The opposite position would be long the basis. *See also Basis.*

Short Hedge: A risk offsetting position which protects an investor or liability manager against a price decline.

Short Position: (1) A position that appreciates in value when the underlying market price decreases. Examples include selling a stock short, selling a future, buying a put, or selling a call. (2) The position of the stock or futures short seller or of the writer or seller of an option contract. Note the anomalous position of the short put which benefits from an increase in the price of the underlying.

Short Sale: The sale of a security or other financial instrument not previously owned by the seller in the expectation that it will be possible to repurchase that instrument at a lower price some time in the future. The term short sale is ordinarily applied only to the sale of securities, but an equivalent synthetic short position can be attained through the sale of an uncovered call option and the purchase of a put or by selling a forward or a future.

Short-Short Rule: A provision of the tax code that disqualifies a mutual fund from income pass-through treatment as a regulated investment company if more than 30 percent of its gross income before deduction of losses is from gains on positions held less than 3 months. The purpose of this rule is to discourage active trading by mutual funds. Also called the 30 percent rule. *See also Full Investment Note (FIN).*

Short Tendering: The practice of tendering more shares in response to a tender offer than an investor owns outright and has not covered with short in-the-money call positions. Most short tendering has been illegal in the United States since 1985.

Short-Term Appreciation and Investment Return Trust (STAIR):   A synthetic PERCS-type structure consisting of long positions in Treasury securities and short in-the-money puts on a portfolio. STAIRs have a payout pattern equivalent to PERCS and short-term equity participation units (STEP Units). *See also Preference Equity Redemption Cumulative Stock (PERCS) (diagram).*

Short-Term Equity Participation Units (STEP Units):   A synthetic PERCs structure using a portfolio or index (for legal reasons) rather than a single stock. The basic structure features a higher yield than the underlying instrument(s) and full participation in the value of the underlying up to a capped price. The proceeds from the sale of a cap (call) is invested in an annuity to pay the higher dividend yield. A minor tax feature defers tax on the incremental yield until maturity, typically three years. At expiration of the trust, large unit holders can elect to receive stock; otherwise, shares will be sold and proceeds distributed. Unlike PERCS, these synthetics raise no new capital for issuers. *See also Preference Equity Redemption Cumulative Stock (PERCS).*

A Comparison of STEP Units and Common Stock Values

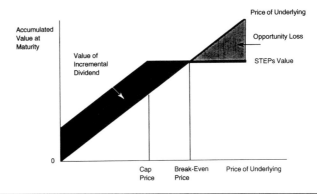

Shortfall Constraint: An approach to risk management that places primary emphasis on the undesirability of an asset shortfall, i.e., of having more liabilities than assets when the liabilities come due. This approach is beginning to supplant the traditional emphasis on standard deviation as the measure of risk for many pension plan sponsors.

Sigma σ: The standard deviation or volatility of the instrument underlying an option. *See Standard Deviation.*

Simulation: A technique used to illustrate what might have happened if a particular investment program had been followed during a past period or in a hypothetical random price or yield environment. Simulations may be useful at times, but they are often based on subtly unrealistic assumptions, particularly when options are involved.

Single Issue Options: Low strike price options traded in Finland to provide investors with most features of stock ownership when actual ownership of registered shares cannot be transferred. *See also Low Exercise Price Options (LEPOS).*

Single Point Adjustable Rate Stock (SPARS):   A floating rate preferred with a dividend reset every 49 days at a specified relationship to high grade commercial paper. *See Adjustable Rate Preferred Stock.*

Sinking Fund: A provision of a bond indenture which commits an issuer to call bonds prior to maturity or to purchase them in the open market. Option theory has been applied to evaluate a sinking fund provision to determine how best to meet the sinking fund obligation when the issuer has some flexibility.

Skewness: A measure of the non-symmetry of a distribution. Symmetrical distributions have a skewness value of zero. A distribution with negative skewness has more observations in the left tail (left of the peak or mode), and a distribution with positive skewness has more observations in the right tail.

Smithsonian Agreement: A currency exchange rate plan that replaced the fixed exchange rates and gold convertibility of the dollar under Bretton Woods with a major currency realignment and broader intervention ranges. A prelude to the subsequent floating exchange rate mechanism.

Sovereign Risk: *See Country Risk.*

Special Drawing Rights (SDRs):   A supplementary reserve currency created under the aegis of the International Monetary Fund. The primary purpose of SDRs was to help dampen exchange rate fluctuations in a floating rate environment. They have been used sparingly.

Special Expiration Price Option: *See Barrier Options, Down-and-Out Call, Out Option, Up-and-Out Put.*

Special Quotation (SQ):   The special opening settlement price that determines the value of a Japanese stock index futures or options contract at expiration.

Specialist: A floor member of an exchange who accepts primary responsibility for making a fair and orderly market in a security at all times the exchange is open for business. In general, a specialist will make a two-sided market and provide limited liquidity to other market participants.

Specific Risk: The unique risk attached to an individual security (usually a common stock) that is not caused by characteristics the security shares with the overall market or even its industry. *Also called Unsystematic Risk.*

Split-Fee Option: A compound option, usually a long call on a long put, used in mortgage markets to offset the risk of interest rate fluctuations between the time a mortgage commitment is made and the date the mortgages are delivered.

Split Cylinder or Split Risk Reversal: The classic risk reversal or collar structure with one modification: different expiration dates on the put and call/cap and floor.

Spot Market: The market for cash as opposed to future delivery.

Spot Month: The shortest available futures contract.

Spot Price: The current market price. For example, the current price of a stock on a stock exchange for normal delivery or of a cash commodity for prompt delivery.

Spot Start: A risk management contract whose effective life begins at the time the agreement is reached. *Contrast with Forward Start Agreement.*

Spot Versus Forward Delta Hedge: An adjustment in the size of a hedging position to allow for the effect of cost of carry on the forward price. The adjustment can be made on the delta of the position or on the forward price or rate. If the adjustment is made on the delta, the spot delta is multiplied by 1 + basis (with basis expressed as a rate or decimal fraction of the underlying) and the resulting forward delta is used to compute the size of the position to be taken in the forward or futures market.

Spraddle: A combination option similar to a straddle in which the put side and the call side have the same expiration date but different strike prices. The put strike price is below the call strike price, leaving a range of prices on the expiration date at which both options will expire worthless. *Often called a Strangle or a Surf and Turf. See also Spread (6).*

The Profit/Loss Pattern of a Short Spraddle

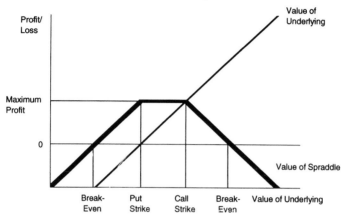

Spread: (1) The difference between the bid and the asked price in any market. (2) The difference between the yields or prices of two financial instruments. (3) The act of entering into a transaction designed to profit from a narrowing or widening of a price or yield spread. (4) For listed options: The purchase of one option and the sale of another option of the same type on the same security or index. The investor setting up the spread hopes to profit from a favorable change in the difference between the prices of the two options. If the number of options purchased is not equal to the number sold, the position may be called a ratio spread or a variable spread. (5) The difference between the price investors pay an underwriter for a new securities offering and the proceeds of the financing paid to the issuer. (6) In the old conventional stock option market (largely pre-1973): A straddle-like position in which the put side and the call side were struck at different prices. Typically, the put strike was below and the call strike was above the market price of the stock at the time the spread was established. In the listed-option market, this position is called a *Spraddle* or a *Strangle.*

Spread Conversion: *See Risk Reversal.*

Spread Hedge: An arbitrage or an operator's risk management position in a commodity complex. Examples include trades designed to lock in or profit from an expected change in the oil refiner's margin (the crack spread) or the soybean processor's margin (the crush spread).

Spread-Lock Agreement: (1) A contract to buy or issue a debt instrument at a pre-set spread to the yield on a specific bond or note at a specified future date. A forward contract on a yield spread. (2) A contract which guarantees an investor's cost of rolling futures contracts from one expiration to the next, relative to a calculated fair value basis. The cost of a futures roll spread-lock will be primarily a function of the liquidity of the market and the extent to which a rollover spread premium and/or discount is typically available.

Spread-Lock Option: (1) An option to enter into a spread-lock agreement on a yield spread. (2) An option to roll one or a sequence of futures contracts forward to more distant months at a fixed spread relative to the fair value basis.

Spread-Lock Swap: (1) An interest rate swap with an option to fix the floating rate payment at a fixed spread over a benchmark Treasury at some date or during some period in the future. (2) An interest rate swap with one payment stream referenced at a fixed spread over a benchmark rate.

Spread Option: An option to lock an interest rate spread into the terms of a financial instrument. The rates may be denominated in different currencies, and the spread option may be embedded in a note or bond.

Spread Position: *See Spread (3) or (4).*

Spread Put Bond: A bond puttable to the issuer or to an underwriter at a spread measured in basis points over the yield of a comparable maturity Treasury issue. The purpose behind a spread put provision is to protect the bond buyer from an adverse change in the issuer's credit rating.

Spread Warrant: *See International Spread Option, Warrant or Note, Spread Option.*

Spreadtion: *See Spread Option.*

Square Root Law: The principle that the variance of a Markov process increases proportionately to the square root of time.

Stack Hedge: A risk offsetting position using a sequence of risk offsetting contracts expiring on dates appropriate to the risk being hedged. Compared to a strip hedge, the stack hedge usually has more near-term contracts. *Sometimes called a Stack and Roll. See Strip Hedge.*

Staged Drawdown Swap: *See Accreting Principal Swap.*

Stamp Tax: A tax imposed on the issuance of new securities. *See also Transfer Tax.*

Standard Deviation (SD, σ): The square root of the mean of the squared deviations of members of a population from their mean. The most widely used measurement of variation about a mean and, for many purposes, a proxy for risk. The standard deviation of normally distributed random variables has many useful characteristics which, unfortunately, do not usually apply to distributions truncated or skewed by option payoff patterns. *See also Normal Distribution.*

$$\sigma = \sqrt{\frac{\sum\limits_{i=1}^{n} (x_i - \mu)^2}{n}}$$

σ = standard deviation of population
n = number of observations
μ = mean of population
x_i = value of each observation
Σ = summation sign

Note that the standard deviation for a sample is calculated by substituting $n - 1$ for n in the denominator.

Standard Option: A plain vanilla European- or American-style option with no bells or whistles to complicate its evaluation.

Standard & Poor's-500 Index Depository Receipts (**SPIDRs** — **pronounced** *spiders*): A warehouse receipt structure similar to the Toronto

Exchange's TIPs which provides the investor with an interest in the holdings of a trust designed to track the return of the S&P-500 index. SPIDRs are an inherently high cost structure planned by the American Stock Exchange as a replacement for their ill-fated but lower-cost index participations.

Standard & Poor's Index Notes (SPINs): A fixed coupon note with a below market yield and the principal payment linked to the value of the S&P-500 stock index. *See Equity-linked Notes.*

Standard Portfolio Analysis of Risk (SPAN): A margin calculation technique for a portfolio of futures and futures option positions. Originally developed for the Chicago Mercantile Exchange, it is now used by a growing number of futures and futures option markets as a mechanism for calculating margin requirements. *See also Mutual Offset.*

Standard Prepayment Assumptions: Standard monthly and annualized mortgage principal prepayment rates published by the Public Securities Association (PSA).

Standardization: A characteristic of exchange-traded derivative instruments and publicly traded corporate offerings which makes it possible for buyers and sellers to learn the pertinent characteristics of an instrument based on a few words of description or a security identification number or symbol.

Start Date: The date — spot or forward — when some feature of a risk management contract becomes effective or when interest payments or returns begin to be calculated.

STated Rate Auction Preferred Stock (STRAPS): A floating rate preferred with an initial fixed dividend period of several years. After the fixed dividend period, the issuer resets the rate every 49 days by Dutch auction. *See also Dutch Auction Interest and Dividend Resets.*

Step-Down Coupon Notes: A debt instrument with a high coupon in earlier payment periods and a lower coupon in later payment periods. This structure and a corresponding step-up coupon structure are usually motivated by regulatory or tax considerations.

Step-Down Swap: (1) An interest rate swap with a decrease in the fixed payment rate over the life of the swap. (2) A variety of amortizing swap with a small number of reductions in the notional principal amount.

Step-Down Warrant: A stock or equity index call warrant with a downward strike price reset during a limited period, at a specific future date, and/or as a consequence of a drop in the underlying to a predetermined level. Specific terms vary with the issue. *See also Anti-Crash Warrants, Partial Lookback Warrants, Reset Option or Warrant.*

Step-Lock Option or Note: *See Ladder Option or Note.*

Step-Up Capped Floating Rate Note: A capped floating rate note with a strike that increases annually.

Step-Up Coupon Notes: A debt instrument with a low initial coupon and a higher coupon in later payment periods. *See also Step-Down Coupon Notes.*

Step-Up Option or Warrant: A call option with one or more scheduled increases in the strike price. Most common in the common stock warrant market, these instruments are usually designed to be held to expiration barring a large increase in the dividend. Analytically, the value is rarely much greater than the value of a single strike option or warrant struck at the last (highest) strike.

Step-Up Swap: (1) An interest rate swap with an increase in the fixed rate at one or more dates over the life of the swap. (2) A variety of accreting swap with a small number of increases in the notional principal amount.

Sterling Transferable Accruing Government Securities (STAGS) :   Stripped United Kingdom gilts, comparable to STRIPS, Certificate of Accrual on Treasury Securities (CATS), and Treasury Investment Growth Receipts (TIGRs) in the United States.

Sticky Jump (SJ) Bond: A collateralized mortgage obligation whose principal paydown is changed by the occurrence of one or more "triggering" event(s). The first time the trigger condition is met, the bond changes to its new priority for receiving principal and remains in its new priority for the life of the bond.

Stillhalters: (Swiss) Covered calls.

Stochastic Process: A mathematical model tracking the occurrence, at each moment after the initial time, of a random phenomenon. Brownian motion, often used to describe security price changes, is a stochastic process. In finance, stochastic processes are a mechanism for describing future prices or rates based on a combination of spot rates or prices and a random variable. Developers of option models attempt to select the random variable-generating process that best matches the empirical pattern. A calculus of stochastic processes forms the basis of many option valuation models. *See also Brownian Motion, Martingale.*

Stock Equivalent: (1) A simple or complex option position that will change in value as if it were a position in the shares of the underlying stock as the price of the underlying stock changes. The option position has risk characteristics similar or identical to the number of shares it imitates. Note that an option position may or may not behave as a fixed stock equivalent position at all possible prices of the underlying. (2) The share equivalent of a single option position—approximately equal to the neutral hedge ratio of the spot price times the contract multiplier. *See also Synthetic Stock, Neutral Hedge Ratio.*

Stock Index Futures Contract: With one exception (the defunct Osaka Stock Futures 50), a cash-settled futures contract with a stock average or index as the underlying. These contracts have been among the most popular and useful futures contracts wherever they have been introduced.

Stock Index Growth Notes (SIGNs): *See Equity-linked Notes.*

Stock Lending: *See Securities Lending.*

Stock Loan Contracts: Exchange-traded contracts facilitating the lending of securities—traded on the OM in Sweden. *See also Securities Lending.*

Stock Options: Put and call options with an individual stock issue as the underlying. Traded on a number of exchanges worldwide and over the counter.

Stock-Over-Bond (SOB) Warrant: Outperformance warrant with a payoff based on the performance of a stock index less the return on a bond index. These instruments are issued on a variety of fixed income and equity indexes. *See also Bond-Over-Stock (BOS) Warrants.*

Stock Performance Exchange Linked Bonds (SPELBONDs): *See Standard & Poor's Index Notes (SPINS), Equity-linked Notes.*

Stoptions: *See Barrier Options.*

Straddle: A combination option consisting of one put and one call, both short or both long. Either option is exercisable or salable separately and the strike prices are identical.

The Profit/Loss Patterns of Short and Long Straddle Positions

Short Straddle

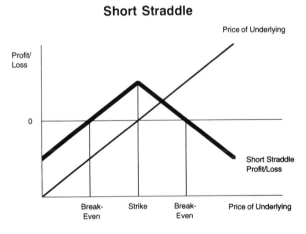

Long Straddle

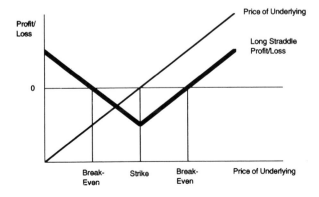

Straddle Rule: A United States tax provision enacted in 1986 that defers the realization of losses on transactions associated with other positions which reflect unrealized gains.

Strangle: A combination of a short put and a short call or a long put and a long call on the same underlying security, usually with the same expiration date and different strike prices. If both options are out of the money, the position is often called a surf and turf. If both options are in the money, an alternate name is mambo combo. *See Spraddle (diagram), Spread (6).*

Strap: A combination option consisting of two calls and one put, all short or all long.

Strategic Asset Allocation (SAA): A value or expected return-oriented portfolio management technique that, in contrast to portfolio insurance (or dynamic asset allocation), tends to increase exposure to a market when recent market performance has been poor and to reduce exposure when recent market performance has been good. *See Asset Allocation, Tactical Asset Allocation (TAA).*

Strategic Risks: Risk exposures that are part of an economic unit's natural environment and can have a significant effect on its revenues, earnings, market share, product offerings, etc. Strategic risks are usually the primary risk management focus.

Strike Level of a Swaption: A nominal fixed rate obligation underlying the subject swap contract.

Strike Premium: The premium paid for the second option in a compound option at the time the first option is exercised. *See also Compound Option.*

Strike Reset Option or Warrant: *See Reset Option or Warrant.*

Strike, Strike Price, Strike Interest Rate, or Strike Rate: The price or rate at which an option begins to have a settlement value at expiration. While the strike price or rate usually is set at the time the option contract originates, some strike prices are subject to adjustment under certain circumstances. *See Exotic Options, Adjusted Strike Price, Adjusted Exercise Price.*

Strip: (1) A sequence of options of the same type usually covering non-overlapping time periods. (2) A combination option consisting of two puts and one call, all short or all long. (3) A series of forward rate agreements. *Also called Tandem Options. See also Average Price or Rate Option.*

Strip Hedge: A risk offsetting position that uses a strip of risk management forward or option contracts expiring on dates appropriate to the risk being hedged. *See also Stack Hedge.*

Strippability: The combination of characteristics of a bond that makes it suitable for coupon stripping.

Stripped Mortgage-backed Securities: Any segment of the mortgage payment stream underlying a Collateralized Mortgage Obligation (CMO) or a Real Estate Mortgage Investment Conduit (REMIC) that has been divided into a series of tranches, usually based on the nominal coupons of the mortgages or the classification of payments as interest or principal. *See Collateralized Mortgage Obligation (CMO), Interest Only (IO) Obligation, Principal Only (PO) Obligation, and Real Estate Mortgage Investment Certificate (REMIC).*

Stripped Treasury Securities: *See Strips. Also called Certificate of Accrual on Treasury Securities (CATS) and Treasury Investment Growth Receipts (TIGRS).*

Stripping: The act of creating stripped Treasury securities from suitable bonds or notes.

STRIPS: An acronym for Separately Traded Registered Interest and Principal Securities. Zero coupon notes and bonds are created by trading note and bond coupon and principal payments stripped from Treasury securities. *Also called Certificate of Accrual on Treasury Securities (CATS) and Treasury Investment Growth Receipts (TIGRS).*

Structured Financial Transaction: (1) A security backed by financial assets such as loans or lower quality bonds or notes. The security may trade on a limited basis or be the subject of a public offering. *See Securitization.* (2) A combination of a conventional security and an embedded derivative. *See also Hybrid Security.*

Structured Product: An over-the-counter (OTC) financial instrument created specifically to meet the needs of one or a small number of investors. The instrument may consist of a warrant, an option, or a forward embedded in a note or any of a wide variety of debt, equity, and/or currency combinations.

Stub: (1) The highly leveraged common stock remaining after a leveraged buyout or other recapitalization. The stub's value is affected by the issuance of debt to replace much of the original common stock. The stub is difficult to evaluate except as an option on the firm. (2) An interim period at the beginning or end of a swap or other periodic reset risk management agreement which is of nonstandard length. For example, a two-month stub at the end of a quarterly reset swap. (3) The ex-warrant bond originally issued with a detachable warrant.

Style of Exercise: *See American Option, Bermuda Option, Deferred Payment American Option, European Option, Japanese Option, etc.*

Subordinated Obligations: Debt or preferred issues with claims on the cash flows and assets of an issuer that rank behind otherwise similar fixed obligations.

Suitability Rules: Principles required by the Securities and Exchange Commission and enforced by options exchanges that attempt to ensure that securities salespeople do not solicit option business from individuals who are unable to make informed decisions about risk. Individuals who may be qualified to engage in certain option transactions may not be encouraged to engage in other types or in numbers of transactions which may not be suitable given their capacity to accept risk, their net worth, and other aspects of their personal and financial situation.

Super-LYONS: *See Synthetic Zero Coupon Convertible Bond.*

SuperDOT (DOT): The New York Stock Exchange's name for its electronic order entry and reporting system. Although designed for small order entry, SuperDOT has played a major role in portfolio or basket trading. *See also Program Trading.*

Superfloater Swap: A fixed-for-floating rate swap with a reverse risk reversal on the floating rate payment. *See also Reverse Risk Reversal (diagram).*

Supershare Option: *See All-or-Nothing Option.* Not to be confused with any of the Supershare components.

Supershares: The risk management structures at the end of a complex series of trusts and funds sponsored by Leland O'Brien, Rubinstein Associates' Supershares Service Corporation. Supershares would come in a number of flavors that decompose the returns in an S&P-500 index fund and a money market fund into elements that resemble PRIMEs (covered calls), SCOREs (call warrants), and option spreads (risk reversals and reverse risk reversals).

Support (SUP) Bond: A collateralized mortgage obligation that receives principal payments after scheduled payments have been paid to some or all of the Planned Amortization Class (PAC), Targeted Amortization Class (TAC), and/or Scheduled (SCH) bonds for each payment date. *Also called Companion Collateralized Mortgage Obligation.*

Surf and Turf: *See Strangle.*

Swap: (1) A contractual agreement to exchange a stream of periodic payments with a counterparty. Swaps are available in and between all active financial markets. The traditional interest rate swap is an exchange of fixed interest payments for floating rate payments. A generic currency swap is an agreement to exchange one currency for another at a forward exchange rate. While an equity index swap might involve the exchange of one index return for another, a more common structure is the exchange of an equity index return for a floating interest rate. "Official" definitions of swaps and swap related terminology and standard swap provisions are provided in the International Swap Dealers Association publication, *Definitions.* (2) The practice of exchanging one bond for another to improve yield, change credit exposure, reflect an interest rate view, or register a tax loss. This type of swap is very different from an interest rate, currency, or index swap, but the term "swap" has been in use longer in this context. The different usages occasionally confuse new users of cash flow swaps.

A Basic Fixed-for-Floating Rate Swap

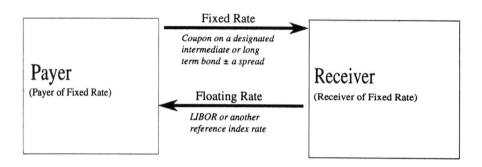

Swap Arranger: A third party who brings two swap counterparties together. The role of a swap arranger contrasts with the role of a market maker who will warehouse swaps, acting as a principal.

Swap Buyer: *See Fixed Rate Payer.*

Swap Curve: A yield curve illustrating the relationship of swap rates at various maturities. Based on the zero coupon yield curve.

Swap-driven Primary Issuance: It is often relatively cheaper for a United States–based borrower to use the US$ bond market, but the borrower's liability management objective may be to borrow D-marks and pay floating rates. The United States–based borrower may find it expedient to issue US$ bonds and swap with a relatively more efficient D-mark floating rate borrower. The choice of markets for the primary issuance is driven by the combination of swap opportunities and that market's relative cost to the borrower.

Swap Market Maker: A financial intermediary who runs an unmatched swap book and stands ready to quote terms for a variety of swaps which he hedges with offsetting swaps or with positions taken in other financial markets.

Swap Offset Agreement: A contract providing for a netting of payments between counterparties to an individual swap and for termination and netting of all swaps between two counterparties in the event of default on any swap. The purpose of a swap offset agreement is to reduce credit risk exposure.

Swap Option: *See Swaption.*

Swap Rate: (1) The market rate on the fixed rate side of a swap. At the time the swap is initiated, the swap rate will typically be the same as the fixed rate payment (adjusted for any negotiated premium or discount). As rates move, the swap rate may differ materially from the fixed rate exchanged under a specific swap agreement. (2) Forward points on a currency rate. Adjustments to the spot exchange rate to compensate for interest rate parity differences across the two currencies.

Swap Rate Differential: The difference between a bond or note yield and the default-free instrument swap rate for the same maturity.

Swap Rate Lock: An agreement which sets the absolute swap rate level for a swap with a future start date.

Swap Seller: *See Floating Rate Payer.*

Swap Spread: (1) The negotiated interest rate differential reflecting supply and demand and counterparty credit ratings which is added to or subtracted from the (fixed) swap rate. (2) The interest rate differential between the swap rate and the comparable government borrowing rate in the applicable currency. Adding (1) and (2) will give the spread between the rate on a specific swap and the comparable maturity default-free rate. The total swap spread will usually be expressed as a market maker's spread (bid/asked) over a specific United States Treasury rate.

Swap Spread Lock: An agreement which gives a would-be fixed rate payer (receiver) a guaranteed maximum (minimum) spread over a specific Treasury rate in a swap agreement starting on a fixed future date. *See Spread-Lock Swap.*

Swap de Taux d'Intérêt: (French) *See Interest Rate Swap.*

Swap Yield Curve: The term structure of swap rates in a specific currency. *See also Yield Curve.*

Swaps with Option Payoffs: The most common swap with an option payoff is a fixed-for-floating rate swap with the floating rate subject to a collar.

Swaps with Timing Mismatches: An uncommon type of swap in which one party is paying on a more frequent interval than the other so that opportunities for offsetting or netting flows are limited. This type of swap has inherently high credit/settlement risk.

Swaption: An option to enter into a swap contract. A payer's swaption is the right to be a fixed rate payer and a receiver's swaption is the right to be a fixed rate receiver. The strike of a swaption will be the nominal exchange called for under the swap agreement. *See Payer's Swaption, Receiver's Swaption.*

Yield Curve Shifts Down—Fixed Rate Receiver's Swaption is Exercised

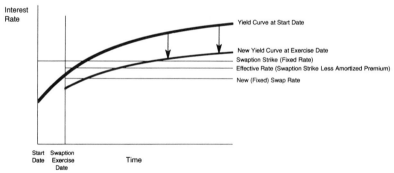

Yield Curve Rises—Fixed Rate Receiver's Swaption Expires

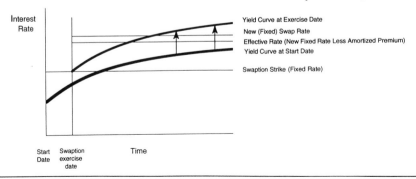

Sweetener: *See Kicker.*

Swiss Market Index Liierte Emission (SMILE): An equity index-linked note with a low coupon and a redemption payment linked to the Swiss Market Index.

Switch Option or Warrant: *See As-You-Like Warrant.*

Switchback Option or Warrant: A complex instrument combining a capped call and an up-and-in put or a floored put and a down-and-in call. To describe the former structure in more detail, the capped call would have an early exercise trigger which provides a maximum payoff to the holder when the underlying rises through the cap. Typically, the instrike of the put is identical to the cap/trigger price of the call, creating a standard put for the remaining life of the option.

Symmetric Distribution: A distribution without skewness—with each side symmetric about the mean and mode.

Symmetric Payoffs: A pattern of changes in value that moves continuously and proportionally up or down in response to price movements of an underlying security or other instrument. Traditional securities, futures, and forwards tend to have symmetric payoffs. Options and instruments with option components typically have asymmetric payoff patterns over some price ranges.

Synthetic Agreement for Foreign Exchange (SAFE): A type of forward currency exchange rate agreement designed to provide a currency hedge over a specific forward period. A notional principal agreement, like an FRA, a SAFE provides risk control usually linked but not attached to another position or transaction. A SAFE is equivalent to a forward period currency swap without a principal exchange.

Synthetic Asset: A package of risks and returns created by combining other instruments to approximate very closely the package of risks and returns available in a traditional security. A position that behaves like a put, call, or some other standard instrument but has been created using different positions or dynamic trading techniques. For example, portfolio insurers create synthetic puts, equity portfolio managers often create synthetic stock or synthetic calls, index arbitragers may create synthetic Treasury bills, and bond futures traders may create synthetic bonds.

Synthetic Bond: A combination of financial instruments or components designed to behave like long-term bonds. Examples might include money market instruments plus bond futures, a long bond call combined with a short bond put and a money market position, or any of a variety of other risk equivalent combinations.

Synthetic Call: Typically, a combination of a long put and a long position in the underlying.

Synthetic Convertible Debt: A debt and warrant package structured to resemble a traditional convertible debt issue. The components of the package may be separable, unlike traditional convertibles, or they may be in the form of an equity-linked note. *See also Hybrid Debt.*

Synthetic Equity: A derivative instrument with the essential risk/reward characteristics of a direct investment in a stock, a specific basket of stocks, or an appropriately weighted basket of stocks equivalent to a stock index.

Synthetic Forward: A combination of a long European call and a short European put with the same expiration date and strike price. This combination will provide the functional equivalent of a forward contract on the underlying.

Synthetic Guaranteed Investment Contract (Synthetic GIC): A guaranteed account secured by a pool of assets owned by the investor (to protect it from claims by the financial institution's general creditors) with a separate guarantee issued by the institution.

Synthetic Long: A combination of a long call and a short put plus a money market position. (The money market position is sometimes omitted from the definition.)

Synthetic Option: *See Option Replication.*

Synthetic Put: A combination of a long call and a short position in the underlying.

Synthetic Short: A combination of a long put and a short call plus a loan. (The loan is sometimes omitted from the definition.)

Synthetic Stock: Most commonly, a combination of a long call and a short put or a short call and a long put on the same stock with the same strike and expiration date. A separate cash adjustment may or may not be incorporated. Other ways of approximating the risk-reward characteristics of long or short stock positions with options are usually called stock equivalents.

Synthetic Zero Coupon Convertible Bond: A combination of a zero coupon note and a detachable warrant with an equal term to expiration. The notes are usable to exercise the warrants and the issuer may enjoy an advantage in interest deductibility over other issuers of zero coupon convertibles. *Also called Super-LYONS. See also Liquid Yield Option Note (LYON).*

Systematic Risk: Risk associated with the movement of a market or market segment as opposed to distinct elements of risk associated with a specific underlying security. *See also Diversification, Nonsystematic Risk.*

Systemic Risk: Risk associated with the general health or structure of the financial system. Almost invariably the result of the system's inability to handle large quantities of market, credit, or (most likely) settlement risk.

T

Tactical Asset Allocation (TAA): As usually described, TAA is indistinguishable from strategic asset allocation (SAA). Some practitioners of tactical asset allocation emphasize shorter-term adjustments, but there is no widely accepted distinction. *See Asset Allocation.*

Tail: (1) A reference to the ends of a probability distribution where the chances of an occurrence get relatively small. Some distributions, however, have fat tails, i.e., provide a relatively greater chance of a large price or rate movement and a smaller chance of a moderate movement. (2) The residual of a risk pool as in the tail of remaining obligations out of a series of long-term liabilities under an insurance policy. (3) The change in the number of futures contracts needed to hedge a position because of variation margin flows. (4) The number of excess futures contracts in a basis trade. (5) The difference between the average price and the lowest bid price in a Treasury auction.

Tail Hedging: Adjusting the number of futures contracts in a hedge position so that the present market exposure of the hedge offsets the underlying exposure. The need for tail hedging stems from the costs and benefits of interest expense or earnings associated with variation margin flows.

Tailored Swap: Any of a variety of changing notional principal swaps designed to meet the financing or currency needs of a business with seasonal, growing, or declining interest rate or currency risk management requirements. *See, for example, Accreting Principal Swap, Amortizing Swap, Seasonal Swap.*

Tandem Options: A sequence of options of the same type (call or put, cap or floor) usually covering non-overlapping time periods and often with variable strikes.

Targeted Amortization Class (TAC) Bond: A collateralized mortgage obligation that pays principal based upon a predetermined schedule, derived by amortizing the collateral at a single prepayment rate.

Tau T: The sensitivity of the value of an option to changes in the volatility variable. Usually expressed as the dollar change in the value or price of an option for a percentage point change in the standard deviation of the underlying. *Also known as Vega or, less frequently, Kappa,* tau was selected as the designation for this relationship by O'Connor purists who were unwilling to accept the name of a once and future pole star or an undersized Chevrolet as a substitute for a Greek letter.

Tax Arbitrage: The creation of risk management instruments or transactions which can be priced attractively to both counterparties because their joint tax bill is reduced.

Tax-exempt Swap: An interest rate swap with one or both of the payments based on municipal securities yields.

Tax Straddle: A reference to any of a large variety of low market risk tax reduction techniques. These techniques frequently use options and futures to create an advantageous tax position with deductions available early and income deferred. Alternately, nondeductible capital losses may be converted to ordinary losses which can be deducted against ordinary income. Opportunities for tax straddles were sharply reduced in the United States by the 1986 tax reform act.

Tender: (1) The notice from a futures contract seller to the clearing house that she intends to deliver securities or commodities in settlement of the contract. (2) Part of the process by which a company's shares change hands in a leveraged buyout or other recapitalization.

Tenor: The term or life of a contract or instrument.

Term to Maturity: The life of a financial instrument. The period until an instrument is to be exercised or converted into cash or an underlying position.

Term Structure of Interest Rates: The pattern of interest rates on default-free debt instruments with various terms to maturity, often illustrated graphically by a yield curve. The term structure determines the relationships between and among currency exchange rates and local market interest rates. It reflects the relationship between spot and forward interest rates. The term structure also sets relationships for arbitrage-free debt instrument option models. *See Yield Curve (diagram).*

Term Structure of Volatility: A curve, broadly analogous to a yield curve, which illustrates the relationship of yield or price volatility to maturity or duration.

Termination: Cancellation of a risk management agreement with settlement based on previously agreed terms.

Termination Claim: The exercise value of an Americus Trust PRIME or SCORE. With the exception of a small fee, the aggregate termination claims of the PRIMEs plus the aggregate termination claims of the SCOREs are equal in value to the underlying stocks deposited in the trust. *See diagrams for PRIME and SCORE.*

Termination Date: The effective date of termination of a swap or other agreement, often as a result of a default.

Termination Price: The strike price used to calculate Americus Trust termination claims.

Terms of an Option Contract: The terms of an option contract are defined by the conventions of the market in which the option is traded and the specifications of the contract. A securities option is defined by (1) exercise or strike price, (2) expiration date, (3) security on which the option is written, (4) dividend or interest adjustment, if any, (5) adjustment for splits and other capital changes, if any, and (6) quantity of the underlying security that makes up the unit of trading. Nonstandard or exotic options may have additional specifications.

Texas Hedge: A transaction that increases risk. Alternately, two or more related positions whose risk is additive rather than offsetting. An example might be buying calls to "hedge" a long position in the underlying.

Theoretical Value: The value of an option as determined by a specific option model based on the model's input parameters. Another name for fair value. The term is occasionally used disparagingly to suggest a lack of substance to option value calculations. Disparagement may be appropriate if the option evaluator's assumptions are unsound.

Theta θ: The sensitivity of an option's price to the passage of time with price of the underlying and implied volatility unchanged. A measurement of the "wasting asset" characteristic of an option, i.e., its rate of time decay.

Third Market: Off-exchange trading of NYSE or other exchange-listed stocks by institutions using a broker who is not a member of the NYSE as an intermediary.

Third Party Pledge System: A more flexible option collateralization technique than the escrow receipts used in early option trading to collateralize short option positions. The securities serving as collateral are pledged by a third party (usually a bank) for the benefit of the clearing corporation, the clearing member carrying the account, and the customer on the other side of the trade.

Third Party Warrants: *Another name for Covered Warrants.*

Tick: The minimum price fluctuation available in a marketplace — expressed in terms of points or fractions of a point of the price or rate.

Time Box: Offsetting synthetic stock positions with different expirations and, often, different strike prices. *See also Box Spread, Jellyroll.*

Time Decay: The loss in value of an option or an instrument with an embedded option as the expiration date approaches.

Time Hedge: Another name for an option hedge. The name comes from the tendency of this position to improve with time if the underlying security is not volatile. *See Option Hedge (diagram).*

Time Value: Commonly a reference to the difference between an option's price and its parity or intrinsic value. Unfortunately, the term is misleading because it fails to distinguish its two most important constituents: basis value and volatility value. A series of simple word equations should help clarify some of these relationships. Time value is in quotation marks in these equations to reflect its common but confusing usage.

$$\begin{aligned}
\text{option price} &= \text{intrinsic value} + \text{``time value''} \\
&= \text{parity} + \text{basis (1)} + \text{insurance} \\
\text{``time value''} &= \text{basis (1)} + \text{volatility value} \\
&= \text{basis (1)} + \text{insurance}
\end{aligned}$$

For out of the money options:

$$\text{``time value''} = \text{volatility value} = \text{opportunity value}$$

See also Premium.

Timing Option: A provision of some futures contracts that permits the short to make delivery at a time he chooses within the delivery month. Ordinarily the short must give notice of intention to deliver in advance.

Toronto Index Participations (TIPs): Warehouse receipt-based instruments designed to track the Toronto-35 index. Comparable in structure to the AMEX's proposed SPIDRs (Standard & Poor's-500 Index Depository Receipts).

Total Coverage Period: The life, from start date to final settlement determination, of a risk management instrument.

Total Return: Usually expressed as income plus any principal gain or minus any principal loss during a measurement period divided by principal (investment) and expressed as a percent.

Total Return Options: In contrast to most security options which pay off on a change in price, the payoff of these options includes (in the case of a call) or is reduced by (in the case of a put) any dividend or interest income attributed to the underlying during the life of the option.

Touch Option: Any of several variations of barrier options which become in, out, or explode in an early exercise trigger when the instrike, outstrike, or early exercise price is touched once, twice, or some other number of times or when the underlying trades at or through the barrier. One bizarre variation is a baseball option: three touches of the outstrike and you are out.

Tracking Error: An unplanned divergence between the price behavior of an underlying position or portfolio and the price behavior of a hedging position. Tracking error can create a windfall profit or loss. Usually expressed as a standard deviation percentage from the return of a benchmark portfolio or index.

Trading Limit: (1) The maximum number of futures contracts a trader may buy or sell in one trading session. (2) The maximum price change permitted in a trading session. *See Price Limits.*

Trading Range Warrant: An instrument which provides a relatively high return if the underlying sells within a specified trading range at expiration and a declining return if the underlying trades outside the trading range. As the diagram illustrates, the payoff pattern is much like that of a short straddle or strangle. *Compare with Range Warrant.*

Profit/Loss Pattern of a Trading Range Warrant

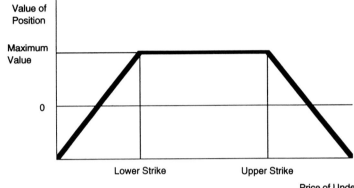

Tranche: One of a related series of security issues — each with different cash flows, strike prices, expiration dates, and/or return patterns — created to meet differing investor or issuer requirements or to carve up the returns from a set of underlying cash flows in a marketable way. Mortgage-backed securities and equity-linked notes are often created in tranches.

Transaction Cost: Cost associated with a trade including, at a minimum, any purchase or sale commission charged by the brokerage firm executing the trade and part of the spread between the bid and the asked prices. More sophisticated transaction cost measurement systems add the market impact of large trades and the opportunity cost of unexecuted trades.

Transaction Risk: Currency exchange rate risk for the period between the date a contract is signed and the date of payment. Can be hedged with a variety of currency instruments.

Transfer Tax: A tax levied on the seller or buyer of a security in a secondary market. Different from a stamp tax levied on new security issues. Ordinarily, exchange-traded and OTC options and other derivatives contracts are exempt from transfer taxes or are taxed at a lower rate.

Translation Risk: Currency exchange rate risk that affects the valuation of balance sheet assets and liabilities between financial reporting dates. Can be hedged with a variety of currency instruments.

Transparent Market: A trading system characterized by prompt availability of accurate price and volume information which gives participants comfort that the market is fair.

Treasury Eurodollar Spread (TED Spread): The yield differential between Treasury bill and Eurodollar futures contracts expiring at the same time. Because the Treasury rate is considered to be default-free while the Eurodollar rate reflects the credit standing of corporate borrowers, a wide spread suggests investors/lenders have a strong preference for safety.

Treasury Investment Growth Receipts (TIGRs): *See Treasury Receipts.*

Treasury Receipts (TRs): Stripped coupons and principal repayments from Treasury bonds and notes. Usually traded as zero coupon instruments.

Treasury STRIPS: *See Strips.*

Trigger Option: *See Barrier Options, Early Exercise Price Trigger.*

Triple Witching Hour: During a period in the mid-1980s, the triple congruence of stock option, index option, and index futures expirations at the stock market close on the 3rd Friday of March, June, September, and December led to brief flurries of extraordinary trading activity and, occasionally, extraordinary volatility. A series of changes in market structure and, more importantly, broader dissemination of information have largely diffused this phenomenon since late 1986.

Trust for Income Participation from Stocks (TIPS): A synthetic PERCS structure identical to STEPS and functionally equivalent to STAIRS. Renamed Package Equity Trust Securities (PETS) before issuance because of a name conflict with the Toronto Stock Exchange's index deposit receipt product. *See Preference Equity Redemption Cumulative Stock (PERCS) (diagram), Short-Term Appreciation and Investment Return Trust (STAIR), Short-Term Equity Participation Units (STEP Units).*

Tunnel Option: A set of collars with constant strike prices or rates covering nonoverlapping periods forward from the trade date.

Turbos: *See Long Bond Yield Decrease Warrants.*

Turnover: (1) In the United Kingdom, volume. (2) In a portfolio, usually calculated as (purchases + sales) / (beginning value + ending value). If a portfolio has an average turnover of 50 percent by this measure, approximately half the securities (in a portfolio with modest contributions and withdrawals) are replaced with new positions each year.

Type of Option: The classification of an option as a put, a call, or a combination option or specialized options such as caps, floors, and swaptions.

U

Ultra Vires Act: An act performed without any legal authority to act. An action beyond the scope of the powers of a corporation, state, province, or municipality.

Unbundled Stock Units (USUs):   A proposed division of common stock returns into three components: a 30-year bond with a yield equal to the stock's current dividend, a preferred issue that would pay dividends equal to any increase in the common stock dividend, and a 30-year warrant on the common. This proposed structure encountered investor disinterest and regulatory opposition.

Uncovered Writer: A call option writer who does not own or a put option writer who is not short the underlying instrument which is the subject of an option. *See Covered Writer, Naked Option (diagram).*

Underlying: The security, cash commodity, forward, futures contract, swap, or other contract or instrument which is the subject of a risk management contract.

Underlying Equivalent: *See Stock Equivalent.*

Underlying Tenor Period: The applicable term of the reference index rate. For example, LIBOR is quoted for one month, three month, and six month terms. The term chosen will have a significant effect on the magnitude of swap payments.

Unilateral Margin Agreement: A collateralization arrangement in which the least creditworthy of two counterparties is required to post initial and/or variation margin to assure performance on a contract.

Unit: (1) Often a derivative security will be combined with a conventional security at the time of initial issue to create a unit. This unit structure can be broken up and the derivative and conventional components traded separately. (2) The combination of a PRIME and a SCORE in an Americus Trust Unit.

Universal Hedge: An approach to currency risk management based on the capital asset pricing model developed by Fischer Black. Black argues that currency hedging is appropriate and that one "universal" hedging ratio applies to all investors. One difficulty in applying the technique is that the universal hedge ratio is sensitive to the assumptions used in compiling it.

Unmargined Spread: An option spread in which, for one or more of the following reasons, the short option is margined as a "naked" option rather than as part of a spread: (1) The long option expires before the short option. (2) The price relationships in certain vertical or diagonal spreads may be such that the margin requirements for a naked option are more favorable than those for spread margin treatment. (3) One or both of the options are unlisted.

Unmatched Swap: A swap agreement not linked to a specific asset or liability of either party. Examples would include swaps undertaken as part of a global or overall risk management strategy or as parts of a warehousing strategy by a swap dealer.

Unrelated Business Income Tax (UBIT):   A tax imposed on otherwise tax-exempt entities in the United States to prevent their noncharitable or noninvestment activities from enjoying a competitive advantage over taxpaying participants in similar businesses. Until 1992, there was some question of the applicability of this tax to swaps and other notional principal contracts. A recent Internal Revenue Service ruling has clarified the exemption of these contracts.

Unsystematic Risk: The risk associated with a particular company or a particular security as opposed to a market or asset class. *Also called Specific Risk.*

Unwinding Risk: The risk that reversing or closing out a risk management position will be difficult or costly.

Up-and-Away Option: *See Up-and-Out Call or Put.*

Up-Front Payment: A payment on the contract or trade date of a swap or other agreement to cover a fee or a dealer's spread or the current value of the right to pay or receive the fixed rate called for in the swap.

Up-and-In Option: *See Barrier Options.*

Up-and-Out Call: A call option spread that pays off early if an early exercise price trigger is tripped. An example would be exchange-traded CAPS. *See also Exploding Option.*

Up-and-Out Put: A put option that expires worthless (or provides a rebate of a portion of the option premium) if the market price of the underlying rises above a predetermined expiration price.

Up Tick Rule: In the United States, securities listed on a national securities exchange may not be sold short unless the last trade prior to the short sale at a different price was at a price lower than the price at which the short sale is executed.

Useable Security: A bond or, rarely, a preferred stock that may be valued at par and used as a substitute for cash in the exercise of a warrant.

Utility Theory: A set of principles behind every attempt at risk management. In general, utility theory holds that rational individuals attempt to maximize their expected utility. Subsidiary principles include risk aversion (risk is undesirable) and diminishing marginal utility (more is better than less, but more is worth progressively less per unit).

V

V-Rating: A formal grading of collateralized mortgage obligation (CMO) tranches according to their expected volatility.

Value of a Basis Point: A measure of a bond's price/yield relationship that specifies the dollar value of a basis point change in yield. Also called value of an "01."

Value Date: The date on which parties to a currency or swap transaction calculate and exchange payments to settle their respective obligations.

Vanishing Option: A down-and-out call, an up-and-out put, or any other option with an expiration price.

Variable Coupon Renewable Notes: Floating rate notes with a coupon set weekly at a fixed spread over the 91-day T-bill rate. Generally, these instruments are puttable to the issuer to protect holders against credit deterioration.

Variable Cumulative Preferred Stock: A floating rate preferred with an issuer option to select between a Dutch auction reset and a remarketing reset arrangement at the end of each dividend period. *See Adjustable Rate Preferred Stock.*

Variable Hedge: *See Option Hedge.*

Variable Rate Renewable Notes: Floating rate notes with a coupon rate set monthly at a fixed spread over the one-month commercial paper rate. Each quarter, the maturity automatically extends an additional quarter unless the investor elects to terminate the extension and put the notes back to the issuer.

Variable Redemption Bonds: Bonds with both fixed and variable components of principal redemption. The variable portion is linked to an index or rate. Examples include "heaven and hell" and other currency-linked bonds. *See Heaven and Hell Bond, Dual Currency Bond.*

Variable Spread: Partially offsetting long and short positions are taken in two options of the same type and class but with different strike prices and/or expiration dates. The number of contracts short will be different from the number of contracts long in a variable spread. *Also called a Ratio Spread.*

Variance: The mean of the squared deviations of each member of a population from the population mean. The square of the population standard deviation.

Variation Call: *See Variation Margin.*

Variation Margin: The cash transfer that takes place after each trading day in a futures market to mark long and short positions to the market. Unlike a forward contract which settles only when the contract matures, futures contracts are settled daily by the payment of variation margin from the party who has lost money that day to the party who has made money. If each point in the price of a contract is worth $1,000, and the futures price goes up by 1/2 point during a session, the short will pay the long $500 per contract in variation margin. Holders and sellers of futures options do not exchange variation margin under current margin procedures, but the ability to capture accumulated variation margin payments through exercise affects the value of an American-style futures option.

Vega: Dollar change in option price in response to a percentage point change in volatility when volatility is measured in percentage terms. *See Tau.*

Vertical Bear Spread: Regardless of whether two puts or two calls are used to create this option spread, the option purchased has a higher strike than the option sold. The number of contracts purchased equals the number sold, and both options expire on the same date.

Profit/Loss Pattern of a Vertical Bear Spread at Expiration

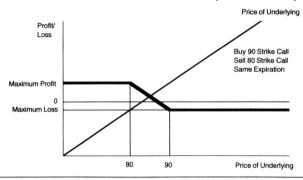

Vertical Bull Spread: Regardless of whether two puts or two calls are used to create this option spread, the option purchased has a lower strike than the option sold. The number of contracts purchased equals the number sold, and both options expire on the same date.

Profit/Loss Pattern of a Vertical Bull Spread at Expiration

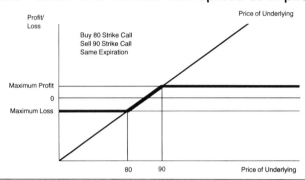

Vertical Cap: (1) The upper cap on a corridor interest rate cap structure or (2) the entire corridor structure.

Volatility: A statistical measure of the tendency of a market price or yield to vary over time. Volatility, usually measured by the variance or annualized standard deviation of the price, rate, or return, is said to be high if the price, yield, or return typically changes dramatically in a short period of time. Volatility is one of the most important elements in evaluating an option, because it is usually the only valuation variable not known with certainty in advance.

Volatility Auto-Regressive Integrated Moving Average (VARIMA): A mean reverting model for volatility estimation.

Volatility Option: A proposed option contract with a payoff linked to the level of volatility in a market.

Volatility Point (Vol Point): One percent of annualized standard deviation. Over-the-counter options often trade on the basis of bid/asked spreads expressed in vol points.

Volatility Risk: The risk that the holder or seller of a standard or embedded option incurs if actual volatility or the market's expectations for future volatility change. Other things equal, an option holder will benefit from an increase in actual or expected volatility and suffer from increased price or rate stability. An option seller will be hurt by an increase in volatility and helped by a decrease. Some compound barrier and average rate options can provide protection from various types of volatility risk.

Volatility Value: The entire value of an out-of-the-money option. With basis value added, the sum is the premium over intrinsic value for an in-the-money option. *Also called Insurance or Opportunity Value. See also Time Value.*

Volume: The number of shares, bonds, notes, or contracts traded in a market. Along with units outstanding and open interest, volume is one of the few measures available to an outside observer of the liquidity in a market.

W

Warehouse: The swaps market makers' practice of running a book of unmatched swaps, managing the book as a whole rather than as pairs of matched deals.

Warrant: An option to purchase or sell the underlying at a given price and time or at a series of prices and times outlined in the warrant agreement. A warrant differs from a put or call option in that it is ordinarily issued for a period in excess of one year. Warrants are issued alone or in connection with the sale of other securities, as part of a merger or recapitalization agreement, and, occasionally, to facilitate divestiture of the securities of another corporation. Ordinarily, exercise of a common stock warrant sold by the issuer of the underlying increases the number of shares of stock outstanding, whereas a call or a covered warrant is an option on shares already outstanding. Index warrants and many put warrants are cash settled. *See also Covered Warrant, Dilution.*

Warrant-driven Swap: A swap with an "attached" warrant allowing a counterparty affected by a bond warrant exercise to increase the size of the swap. This structure makes the impact/value of the warrant a factor in pricing the swap.

Weighted Average Coupon (WAC): The coupon of each position in a mortgage pool (or other debt instrument portfolio) weighted by the size of the position to compute an average coupon for the pool. Ordinarily, a detailed schedule of coupons will be more useful in predicting prepayment rates.

Weighted Average Life: The time-weighted average of expected principal repayments on a fixed income security. Used as a measure of portfolio tenor.

Weighted Average Maturity (WAM): The maturity of each position in a mortgage pool (or other debt instrument portfolio) is weighted by the dollar value of the position to compute an average maturity for the pool.

Weighted Average Rate Option: Similar to an average rate option except that the weighting of each daily, weekly, or monthly price or rate varies depending upon the agreement of the parties. The weighted average rate option may be used when the timing and magnitude of cash flows is known, but price or rate is uncertain. *See also Average Price or Rate Option.*

Weighted Collar: A collar or risk reversal with an imbalance between the quantities covered by the cap and the floor.

When-Issued Option: An option on the next Treasury bond or note to be issued with a specific maturity.

Whipsaw: A sharp price movement quickly followed by a sharp reversal.

Wiener Process: *See Brownian Motion.*

Wild Card: Provisions in several futures contracts whereby the investor who is short the contract can deliver any of a number of securities or commodities in settlement of the delivery obligation, can choose the instruments to be delivered at the last moment, and/or can deliver anytime within a prescribed period. The option to change the item delivered or the time of delivery enhances the flexibility of the short's position and occasionally exacerbates price volatility in the underlying near expiration.

Window Warrants: Warrants which can be exercised only during limited intervals in the life of a host bond.

Withholding Tax: Of pertinence to global risk management transactions, most governments impose a withholding tax ranging from 15 percent to 30 percent on some interest payments and nearly all dividends paid on securities owned by foreign investors. Reciprocal withholding tax treaties usually reduce the withholding tax within the major industrial countries to 15 percent.

Withholding Tax Agreement: One of a number of bilateral treaties which reduces nonresident dividend withholding taxes for stockholders in the signatory countries.

Work-Out Market: A market in which any quote a dealer may furnish is subject to his ability to find the other side of the trade. Frequently, these markets are thin and the dealer is not willing to commit his own capital except at a prohibitive markup. Prices quoted (or, more accurately, estimated) by different dealers may vary greatly in a work-out market. *See also Indicative Prices.*

Worst of Two Asset Option: *See Alternative Option.*

Writer: *See Option Writer.*

Y

Yield Curve: A graph illustrating the level of interest rates as a function of time — obtained by plotting the yields of all default-free coupon bonds in a given currency against maturity or, occasionally, duration. Yields on debt instruments of lower quality are expressed in terms of a spread relative to the default-free yield curve. In the diagrams below, a normal yield curve on the top features short-term yields lower than long-term yields. The inverted yield curve on the bottom illustrates short-term rates in excess of long-term rates and characterizes periods when the central bank is attempting to restrict growth in the money supply and, hence, the level of economic activity. Forward curves derived from each yield curve are also illustrated. *See also Forward Yield Curve, Zero Coupon Yield Curve.*

Normal Yield Curve and Forward Curve

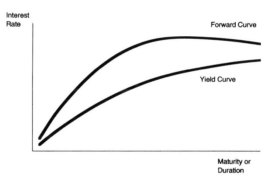

Inverted Yield Curve and Forward Curve

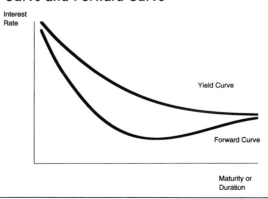

Yield Curve Flattening Warrants: An option with a payoff contingent on the yield spread between two debt instruments on opposite ends of the yield curve. For the maximum risk of a premium, the holder can participate in a narrowing of the yield spread relative to the strike spread. *See also Yield Curve Option.*

Yield Curve Note: *See Reverse Floating Rate Note.*

Yield Curve Option: An option on the spread between two rates at different maturities on a yield curve. Depending on the specific terms selected, the option will pay off on flattening or steepening of the yield curve. A yield curve option will cost less than separate put and call options on the representative issues used to construct the yield curve because the yield curve option pays off only on the change in the spread whereas one of a pair of separate options might be in the money as a result of a parallel shift in the yield curve. *See also Term Structure of Interest Rates.*

Yield Curve Swap: A swap with interest payments reflecting floating rates at two different points on the swap yield curve.

Yield Decrease Warrant: An interest rate warrant which increases in value as long bond yields decline and, conversely, declines in value when yields rise.

Yield Differential Warrant: Contract in which the payoff, if any, is a function of a yield differential in two markets, such as a short-term and a long-term rate in a particular country or a rate of the same maturity in two countries. *See, for example, BOATs.*

Yield Enhancement: Any of a variety of strategies used to increase the actual or apparent yield of a debt instrument. Frequently these strategies are based on continuous option selling programs which may increase apparent yields during most periods but can substantially reduce returns from time to time and in the long run. Occasionally yield enhancement strategies are based on arbitrage-type transactions where the probability of return enhancement is quite high during any period the position is in place.

Yield Spread Option or Warrant: *See Yield Differential Warrant.*

Yield to Worst: The yield to maturity under the least desirable of all possible bond repayment patterns under the assumption that market yields are unchanged. If market yields are higher than the coupon, the yield to worst would assume no prepayment. If market yields are below the coupon, yield to worst would assume prepayment at the earliest call date.

Yield-Enhanced Stock (YES):   A synthetic PERCS issue. *See Equity Yield Enhancement Securities (EYES), Preference Equity Redemption Cumulative Stock (PERCS) (diagram).*

You Choose Warrant: *See As-You-Like Warrant.*

Z

Z-bond: An accrual tranche of a collateralized mortgage obligation (CMO) — usually one of the last segments to be paid off in cash.

Zaitech: (Japanese) Financial engineering.

Zero Cost Collar: A risk reversal with equal premiums on the cap and floor. *See Risk Reversal.*

Zero Cost Hedge: *See Zero Cost Option, Risk Reversal.*

Zero Cost Option: A slightly misleading description of a situation in which the premium from an option sold pays the premium of an option purchased. *See Risk Reversal.*

Zero Coupon Bond: A debt instrument sold at a discount to its face value. The bond makes no payments until maturity, at which time it is redeemed at face value.

Zero Coupon Convertible Debt: Convertible bonds which are typically puttable to the issuer during the early years of their lives and are convertible into the issuer's common stock on terms calculated to provide a return somewhat less than the return on common stock with significantly reduced risk. In the United States, the issuer may be able to deduct an implied interest payment even if the instrument is converted and no interest is actually paid. *See Liquid Yield Option Note (LYON).*

Zero Coupon Currency Swap: A long-term currency forward exchange agreement (FXA) in the form of a swap agreement with a single cash exchange at maturity. *See also Forward Exchange Agreement (FXA).*

Zero Coupon Swap: An interest rate swap with the fixed rate side based on a zero coupon bond. With agreement of the counterparty, the swap agreement may call for a single fixed payment at maturity by the holder of the zero. The payments on the other side may follow typical swap interim payment schedules. Because of the payment mismatch, a zero coupon swap exposes one of the counterparties to significant credit risk and is the functional equivalent of a loan.

Zero Coupon Yield Curve: A graph of the term structure of default-free zero coupon rates. *See also Yield Curve, Forward Yield Curve, Implied Zero Coupon Swap Curve.*

Zero Premium Option: Any combination option or a combination of an option, a note, and a participation which provides an asymmetric return pattern characteristic of option payoffs without the explicit payment or receipt of a net premium by either party to the contract. Examples include zero premium collars and risk reversals and many equity-linked notes.

Zero Premium Risk Reversal: Reflecting the reluctance of many investors to pay a premium for an option, the premium taken from the sale of the call (cap) is designed to exactly match the cost of the put (floor) purchased. Typically, an investor will designate one strike price and expiration date, and the provider of the risk reversal will determine the other strike price. *Also called a No Cost Risk Reversal or Collar.*

Zero Strike Price Options: Options with an exercise price of zero, or very close to zero, traded on options exchanges in countries where there is a transfer tax, ownership restriction, or other obstacle to the transfer of securities, especially stock. Zero strike price options are frequently cash settled so that no transaction in the underlying occurs. The holder of the option has full participation in the underlying price, as if he held a long position in the stock, and the seller has full offsetting participation in the stock price, as if he had taken a short or short-against-the-box position. *See Low Exercise Price Options (LEPOS).*

APPENDIX

Common Currency Abbreviations and Symbols

Currency Name	County	Common Abrreviations/ Symbols	CME Symbol
Australian Dollar	Australia	A$, AUD	AD
Belgian Franc	Belgium	Bfr, BEF	
Canadian Dollar	Canada	C$, CAD	CD
Danish Krone	Denmark	DKr, DKK	
Deutsche Mark	Germany	DM, DEM	DM
Dutch Guilder	Netherlands	Dfl, NLG	
European Currency Unit	European Monetary System	ECU, XEU	
Finnish Markka	Finland	FIM	
French Franc	France	Ffr	FRF
Hong Kong Dollar	Hong Kong	HK$, HKD	
Italian Lira	Italy	ITL	
Luxembourg Franc	Luxembourg	Lfr, LUF	
New Zealand Dollar	New Zealand	NZ$, NZD	
Norwegian Krone	Norway	NKr, NKR	
Spanish Peseta	Spain	Pta, SPp, SPP, ESP	
Sterling	United Kingdom	£, GBP, STG	BP
Swedish Krona	Sweden	SKr, SEK	
Swiss Franc	Switzerland	Sfr, CHF, SWF	SF
U.S. Dollar	United States of America	Dollar, U.S.$, $, USD	
Yen	Japan	JPY, ¥	JY

Debt Ratings

Rating agencies usually have separate ratings for short-term instruments, but long-term ratings are the measure of credit quality emphasized by most risk managers.

Rating Agency						Description of Rating*
S&P	IBCA	Moody's	Duff & Phelps	Fitch	Thomson Bankwatch	
AAA	AAA	Aaa	AAA	AAA	AAA	Highest credit quality. The risk factors are negligible, being only slightly more than for risk-free U.S. Treasury debt.
AA	AA	Aa	AA	AA	AA	High credit quality. Protection factors are strong. Risk is modest but may vary slightly from time to time because of economic conditions.
A	A	A	A	A	A	Protection factors are average but adequate. However, risk factors are more variable and greater in periods of economic stress.
BBB	BBB	Baa	BBB	BBB	BBB	Below average protection factors but still considered sufficient for prudent investment. Considerable variability in risk during economic cycles.
BB	BB	Ba	BB	BB	BB	Below investment grade but deemed likely to meet obligations when due. Present or prospective financial protection factors fluctuate according to industry conditions or company fortunes. Overall quality may move up or down frequently within this category.
B	B	B	B	B	B	Below investment grade and possessing risk that obligations will not be met when due. Financial protection factors will fluctuate widely according to economic cycles, industry conditions and/or company fortunes. Potential exists for frequent changes in the rating within this category or into a higher or lower rating grade.

Debt Ratings (Continued)

Rating Agency						Description of Rating*
S&P	IBCA	Moody's	Duff & Phelps	Fitch	Thomson Bankwatch	
CCC CC C	CCC CC	Caa Ca C	CCC	CCC CC C	CCC CC	Well below investment grade securities. Considerable uncertainty exists as to timely payment of principal, interest, or preferred dividends. Protection factors are narrow and risk can be substantial with unfavorable economic/industry conditions, and/or with unfavorable company developments.
D	C		DD	DDD, DD, D	D	Defaulted debt obligations. Issuer failed to meet scheduled principal and/or interest payments.
+	+	1	+	+	+	Symbols used to provide more detailed gradation of quality.
		2				
-	-	3	-	-	-	
AA- CCC	AAA-C	Aa-B	AA-B	AA-C	AAA-D	Range of ratings for which quality graduations are provided.

*Duff and Phelps descriptions are used because they tend to be most concise. The rating agencies try to use similar definitions even if they do not always agree on an individual issuer's rating.

About the Publisher

PROBUS PUBLISHING COMPANY

Probus Publishing Company fills the informational needs of today's business professional by publishing authoritative, quality books on timely and relevant topics, including:

- Investing
- Futures/Options Trading
- Banking
- Finance
- Marketing and Sales
- Manufacturing and Project Management
- Personal Finance, Real Estate, Insurance and Estate Planning
- Entrepreneurship
- Management

Probus books are available at quantity discounts when purchased for business, educational or sales promotional use. For more information, please call the Director, Corporate/Institutional Sales at 1-800-PROBUS-1, or write:

Director, Corporate/Institutional Sales
Probus Publishing Company
1925 N. Clybourn Avenue
Chicago, Illinois 60614
FAX (312) 868-6250